Microsoft
Quick Reference

Que Quick Reference Series

Sue Plumley

Microsoft Office Quick Reference

Library of Congress Catalog No.: 94-66717

ISBN: 1-56529-880-2

97 96 95 94 4 3 2

Interpretation of the printing code: the rightmost double-digit number is the year of the book's printing; the rightmost single-digit number, the number of the book's printing. For example, a printing code of 94-1 shows that the first printing of the book occurred in 1994.

Publisher: David P. Ewing

Associate Publisher: Michael Miller

Publishing Director: Don Roche, Jr.

Managing Editor: Michael Cunningham

Marketing Manager: Greg Wiegand

Publishing Manager
Charles O. Stewart III

Acquisitions Editor
Thomas F. Godfrey III

Product Director
Lisa D. Wagner

Production Editor
Jeanne Terheide Lemen

Editor
Patrick Kanouse

Technical Editors
Gregory A. Dew
Bruce Wynn

Book Designer
Amy Peppler-Adams

Cover Designer
Dan Armstrong

Production Team
Cameron Booker, Angela Bannan, Karen Dodson, Aren Howell, Bob LaRoche, Elizabeth Lewis, G. Alan Palmore, Caroline Roop, Michael Thomas, Donna Winter, Lillian Yates

Indexer
Johnna VanHoose

Acquisitions Coordinator
Deborah Abshier

Editorial Assistant
Jill L. Stanley

Composed in *Stone* and *MCPdigital* by Que Corporation.

About the Author

Sue Plumley owns Humble Opinions, a consulting firm that offers training in popular software programs and system connectivity. In addition, Sue is the author of several Que books, including *Windows 3.1 SureSteps, Crystal Clear DOS,* and *Crystal Clear Word.* She is also a contributing author to *Using WordPerfect 6 for DOS, Using OS/2 2.1,* Special Edition, and *Using WordPerfect 6 for Windows.*

Acknowledgments

Que Corporation wishes to thank Jim Minatel for his special contribution to this project.

Table of Contents

Introduction 1

New Ways of Working 1

Conventions 3

Task Reference 5

Word 7

- Adding Text 8
- Alignment 9
- Annotations 9
- AutoCorrect 12
- AutoFormat 13
- AutoText (formerly Glossary) 16
- Bold 17
- Bookmarks 17
- Borders and Shading 18
- Bullets 19
- Captions 20
- Centering Text 21
- Change Case 21
- Clipboard 22
- Close 23
- Columns 23
- Compare Versions 24
- Copy 25
- Cross-reference 26
- Cut 27
- Date and Time 28
- Deleting 29
- Document Summary 29
- Drag-and-Drop 31
- Drawing 32
- Drop Caps 32
- Endnotes 33
- Envelopes 35
- Equation Editor 36

Exit 36
Find and Replace 36
Find File 41
Fonts 41
Footers 43
Footnotes 43
Formatting Characters 44
Formatting Paragraphs 46
Frames 51
Glossary 54
Go To 55
Grammar 56
Graphics 57
Hanging Indent 59
Headers and Footers 59
Help 61
Hyphenation 61
Indenting 62
Index 62
Insert File 64
Insert an OLE Object 65
Insert a Picture 65
Italic 65
Justify Text 65
Labels 65
Line Spacing 67
Link 67
Macros 68
Mail Merge 68
Margins 74
Move 76
Moving around in Word Documents 76
Numbered Lists 77
Numbering Lines 78
Numbering Pages 80
Open 81
Outlines 82
Page Breaks 84
Password Protection 86

Paste ... 89
Printing ... 89
Repeat ... 93
Revision Marks ... 94
Ruler ... 97
Save/Save As ... 99
Section Breaks ... 99
Section Layout ... 100
Select Text ... 102
Shading ... 103
Sort Text ... 103
Special Characters ... 104
Spelling ... 105
Starting Word for Windows ... 108
Styles ... 108
Summary Info ... 111
Table of Authorities ... 111
Table of Contents ... 113
Table of Figures ... 116
Tables ... 118
Tabs ... 120
Templates ... 121
Thesaurus ... 123
Toolbars ... 125
Underline ... 125
Undo ... 125
Views ... 125
Wizards ... 126
Word Count ... 128
WordArt ... 128
Zoom ... 128
Excel ... 131
Alignment ... 132
Auditing Worksheets ... 134
Bold ... 137
Borders ... 137
Calculating Worksheets ... 138
Centering ... 139
Charts ... 140

Closing Files 150
Color 150
Column Widths 152
Consolidation 153
Converting 155
Copying 155
Cross Tabulation 156
Currency 156
Database Management 156
Date Math 160
Decimal Places 161
Deleting 162
Drag and Drop 163
Drawing 163
Editing Groups of Worksheets 164
Entering Data 164
Exiting Excel 165
Filling a Range with Values 165
Finding and Replacing Data 166
Fonts 169
Formatting 172
Formulas 173
Fractions 174
Freeze Panes 175
Functions 176
Gridlines 177
Headers and Footers 178
Help 180
Hiding Data 180
In-Cell Editing 182
Inserting 182
Italic 183
Lines 184
Linking Dynamically 184
List 184
Macros 184
Margins 184
Menus 185
Moving Around the Worksheet 185

Moving Elements ... 186
Naming Cells and Ranges ... 188
Notes ... 189
Opening Files ... 191
Outlines ... 191
Page Breaks ... 192
Page Setup ... 192
Passwords ... 195
Percentages ... 195
Pivot Tables ... 196
Printing ... 199
Protecting Files ... 203
Records ... 206
Replace ... 206
Reports ... 206
Rounding ... 207
Row Heights ... 208
Saving Files ... 209
Search ... 209
Selecting ... 209
Shading Cells ... 211
Sorting ... 211
Spelling Checker ... 211
Split-Window ... 212
Starting Excel ... 212
Styles ... 212
Subtotals ... 213
Summing ... 215
Templates ... 215
Text Boxes ... 216
Toolbars ... 217
Underlining ... 217
Undo ... 217
Wizards ... 217
Worksheet Views ... 218
PowerPoint ... 221
Add Notes ... 222
Add Slide ... 222
Add Text ... 222

Align Objects 223
Align Text 225
Anchor Text 226
Annotate Slide Show 227
AutoContent Wizard 228
AutoLayout 230
AutoShapes 230
Borders 230
Builds and Transitions 231
Bullets 232
Chart 234
ClipArt Gallery 236
Close 238
Colors 238
Copy and Paste Text 242
Delete Objects 243
Delete Slides 244
Delete Text 244
Drag and Drop 245
Drawing 245
Editing Slides 249
Exiting PowerPoint 250
Fills and Patterns 250
Font 252
Font Size 253
Font Style 254
Finding and Replacing Text 255
Format Painter 255
Formatting Text 256
Grids and Guidelines 256
Handouts 257
Help 258
Layouts 258
Line Spacing 259
Line Styles 260
Masters 260
Moving Around in PowerPoint 260
Moving Text 261
New Presentation 261

Notes 264
Objects 264
Open 268
Organization Chart 268
Outlines 269
Patterns 270
Pick a Look Wizard 270
Pictures 271
Printing 271
Rehearse Presentation 272
Rulers 273
Run Slide Show 274
Save/Save As 275
Set Up Slides 275
Shading 276
Shadows 277
Slide Layouts 279
Slide Masters 279
Slide Setup 280
Slide Sorter 280
Speaker's Notes 282
Spelling 282
Starting PowerPoint 283
Table 283
Templates 283
Timings 284
Toolbars 284
Transitions 284
Undo 285
Views 285
Wizards 286
Word Art 286
Common Features 287
Closing Files 287
Cue Cards and Examples and Demos 288
Demos 290
Dialog Boxes 290
Examples and Demos 293
Exiting Applications 293

Find File 294
Help 299
Keyboard Shortcuts 303
Macros 304
Menus 304
Objects 306
Open 308
Printing 309
Save/Save As 310
Shortcut Menus 312
Starting Applications 313
Toolbars 314
ToolTips 317
Undo 318
Windows 318
Wizards 320
Integration 323
Chart 323
Clip Art 323
Clipboard 325
Closing Office 327
Copy 327
Customizing Microsoft Office 327
Customizing Applications 330
Cut 330
Drag and Drop 330
Drawing 331
E-mail 334
Embedding 334
Equation Editor 335
Exporting 336
Graphs (Microsoft Graph) 336
Importing and Exporting 339
Inserting a Picture 340
Installing Office 341
Linking Dynamically 343
Macros 344
Mail 346
Managing Files 354

Microsoft Office Manager 354
Object Linking and Embedding (OLE) 355
Opening Office 359
Organization Chart 359
Paste 359
Spelling Checker 359
Starting Office 361
Switching Between Applications 361
WordArt 362
Index 367

Introduction

Microsoft Office Quick Reference is a task-oriented guide to the most fundamental commands and features available in Word for Windows 6, PowerPoint 4, and Excel 5. This book presents reference material for specific procedures in each of the three Office applications. Additionally, *Microsoft Office Quick Reference* presents instructions common to the three programs and features that help you integrate the three applications.

Microsoft Office Quick Reference is not intended to replace comprehensive documentation. It presents condensed information about the features and commands of Office and its applications. For more detailed instructions, consult Que's *Using Microsoft Office* or *Microsoft Office QuickStart.*

New Ways of Working

Microsoft Office presents three applications that enable you to complete your work efficiently and effectively. Whether you want to create a memo describing the latest sales figures or a detailed report that includes spreadsheet data, charts, tables, and pictures, Microsoft Office contains all you need.

You can use Word for Windows 6, PowerPoint 4, and Excel 5 to create a variety of documents: letters, memos, reports, and other word processing documents; spreadsheets and graphs; and slide and overhead presentations. Additionally, you can add other Microsoft applications to the Office, such as Mail, Access, and Publisher.

When used separately, the power of each of these Microsoft applications provides an excellent beginning for any document. However, the added benefit of Microsoft Office helps you to easily bring the power of these applications together. Office enables you to apply your knowledge of one program to another program, quickly and easily switch between programs, share data between programs, and so much more.

One of the major advantages of the Microsoft Office applications is that in learning one application, you build a knowledge base that applies to the other Microsoft applications. When, for example, you learn to use Word, you become familiar with the toolbars, the commands in each menu, the rulers, the scroll bars, and many other screen elements. Additionally, you learn certain procedures, such as creating and running macros, customizing toolbars, inserting pictures and objects, and so on.

After you learn the basics of operating Word, you open the Excel application. Immediately you notice that the screen elements are familiar, many commands on the menus are similar, and many of the procedures are the same as they are in Word. The same assumption can be made about the PowerPoint program. Microsoft has based applications on the same or similar procedures and commands so you don't have to learn the characteristics of new programs; instead, you spend your valuable time producing the documents you need.

Another advantage of using Office is the Office Manager, or Office toolbar. The Office Manager displays icons, or buttons, that represent each of the programs in Office. With the click of a button, you can quickly open or switch to one of the other programs in the group. In addition to quickly switching between applications, you can customize the toolbar and the Office menu to contain items and commands that better suit your way of working.

Perhaps the most valuable advantage of using Office is sharing text and data between applications. Using the familiar cut, copy, and paste commands in conjunction with the Office Manager, you can quickly and effortlessly insert an Excel worksheet into a Word memo, or use a Word outline as a foundation for a PowerPoint Presentation.

Additionally, you can use the powerful Windows feature—OLE (Object Linking and Embedding)—to share information between the applications. Embed an Excel graph in your PowerPoint presentation so you can open the graph document for editing simply by double-clicking the object. Link an Excel worksheet to your Word report so that each time you edit the worksheet in Excel, it automatically updates in the Word report. Using OLE with the Office applications enables you to create documents using the most current information available, and without wasting your valuable time and energy.

Conventions

Microsoft Office Quick Reference is designed to guide you through performing tasks and procedures in the Office applications. This book assumes you know the Windows program and how to perform basic Windows procedures. If you need help using Windows, you can refer to other reference material, such as Que's *Windows 3.1 SureSteps.*

Within each task is a brief explanation of the task and step-by-step instructions for performing each task. Tasks are described in the same format, so you can quickly recognize and understand the procedures. In addition, many tasks include shortcuts, tips, notes, and detailed descriptions of dialog box options. Each procedure in the Task Reference presents instructions using specific conventions for clarity and facility. Following is a list of the conventions used in this book:

- Text you type and keys you press, such as underlined letters in application menus, appear in **boldface** type. To select a menu, command, or dialog box option using the keyboard, press and hold the Alt key while pressing the boldfaced letter or character.

- Two keys separated by a plus sign, such as Shift+F7, means to press and hold the first key, press the second key, then release both keys.

- Screen text and messages appear in a `special typeface`.
- Steps in each task present the procedure for accessing the menu and command (Choose the **F**ile **P**rint command). Additionally, shortcuts and notes present toolbar buttons and shortcut keys you can use as alternatives to the menu commands.

Task Reference

The Task Reference is divided into five sections: Word, Excel, PowerPoint, Common Features, and Integration. In each application section, you will find an alphabetical listing of features and commands; for example, if you want to print a document, go to the appropriate application and look under "Printing." The last two sections explain how to use common features of the three applications and how to integrate them.

Word

Microsoft Office includes the Microsoft Word word processor for creating documents of various types, including letters, memos, reports, and newsletters. Word includes many features and tools that make your work easier as well as more efficient. This section describes the use of those tools and features.

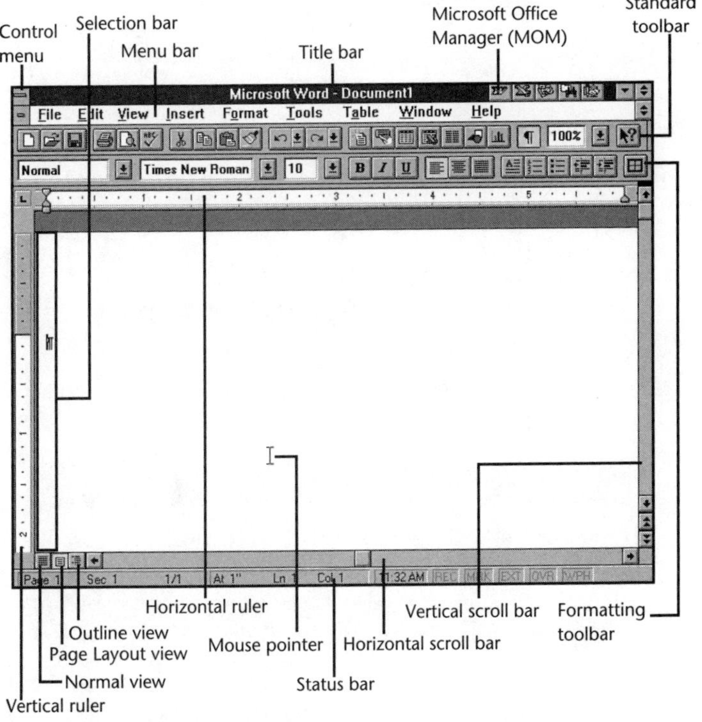

Adding Text

One of the reasons you use a word processor is so you can modify and add text to existing documents. Word makes it easy for you to add text to a document using either of two methods. If you want to add text, use the default *Insert* mode, in which you type the text and Word adjusts the existing text to accommodate the new. Use *Overtype* mode, on the other hand, to type new text over existing text, one character at a time.

Note

You also can add text to a document by pasting the text from another document or application.

To insert text

1. Position the insertion point; any text typed is added at the insertion point.

2. Type the new text. As you type, existing text moves to the right and wraps to the next line automatically.

To type over text

1. Position the insertion point at the beginning of the text you want to replace.

2. Press the Insert key; the OVR indicator on the Status bar displays when Overtype mode is active.

   Note

   You can, alternatively, double-click the OVR indicator when Overtype mode is off, to turn Overtype mode on. Additionally, double-clicking the indicator when Overtype mode is on turns the mode off again.

3. Enter the new text; Word replaces the old text—one character at a time—with the new text.

4. Press the Insert key when finished. You may need to press the Delete key to erase extra characters after entering the new text.

See also **Copy**, **Cut**, and **Paste**.

Alignment

See **Formatting Paragraphs**.

Annotations

Annotations are comments, or notes, added to a document without affecting the text in the document. Annotations appear in a special pane and can be shown or hidden from view.

Additionally, you can move quickly to an annotation without searching through individual lines of text. Annotations are represented by a reference mark that contains the initials of the person inserting the annotation, and the number of the annotation. You can also print annotations with a document or separately.

To insert an annotation

1. Select the text or position the insertion point at the end of the text on which you will comment.

> **Tip**
>
> Select the text before inserting the annotation so that same text appears highlighted when you view the annotation; that way there is no question about the text on which you are commenting.

2. Choose **I**nsert **A**nnotation. Word opens the annotation pane and inserts a reference mark in the document. The reference mark consists of initials and the number of the annotation (1, 2, 3, and so on).

Note

¶ The annotation reference mark is visible when the annotation pane is open or when the Show/Hide paragraph marks button is selected. The reference mark is formatted as hidden text, so it does not display otherwise.

3. In the annotation pane, type your comments or notes.

4. Choose **C**lose to close the annotation pane and return to the document. Alternatively, you can keep the annotation pane open to add more comments or edit the annotation; simply click the mouse in the document window. When you're ready to edit or add to an existing annotation, click the mouse in the annotation pane.

Shortcut

Press Alt+Ctrl+A to quickly insert an annotation reference mark and open the annotation pane.

To view an annotation

1. Choose the **V**iew **A**nnotations command. The Annotations pane appears. The annotations are listed, and the insertion point is positioned at the next annotation in the document.

2. In the F**r**om drop-down list box, choose the name of the reviewer whose annotations you want to view. The default is All Reviewers; alternatively, you can choose to view only the annotations of one reviewer. The name listed in the F**r**om list is the same as the name listed in the User Info tab of the **O**ptions dialog box (**T**ools menu).

3. You can edit or add text to any annotation. As you move the insertion point or scroll through the list, the

document window automatically moves to display the annotation mark in the document. Also, as you scroll through the document, the Annotations pane automatically scrolls to display the annotations for the portion of the document you are viewing. When finished, choose **C**lose to close the annotation pane.

> **Shortcut**
>
> You can double-click an annotation reference mark in the document text to view the annotation in the annotation pane. To view reference marks, click the Show/Hide paragraph marks button on the Standard toolbar.

To delete an annotation

1. If the annotations are not displayed, click the Show/Hide paragraph marks button from the Standard toolbar.
2. Select the annotation reference mark.
3. Press the Delete key.

To print annotations

1. Choose the **F**ile **P**rint command. The Print dialog box appears.
2. To print annotations only, choose the **P**rint What drop-down list and select Annotations.

   To print the document and annotations, choose **O**ptions. In the Include with Document area, choose **A**nnotations and choose OK.
3. Choose OK to print and close the Print dialog box.

See also **Go To**, **Printing**, as well as the Common Features section.

AutoCorrect

AutoCorrect is a Word feature that automatically corrects common typographical or spelling errors, as you type them. By default, Word's AutoCorrect feature contains some commonly misspelled words; you can, however, enter your own problem words to the AutoCorrect list. You can also add an AutoCorrect entry in the Spelling dialog box.

To create an AutoCorrect entry

1. Choose the **T**ools **A**utoCorrect command.
   The AutoCorrect dialog box appears.

2. In the R**e**place text box, enter a common spelling or typographical error or an abbreviation for a word or words you often use in your documents. The Replace text cannot contain any spaces.

3. In the **W**ith text box, enter the text as it should appear in the document.

4. Choose the **A**dd button to add the new entry to the list.

5. Choose OK to close the dialog box.

See also **Spelling**, **AutoText**.

To choose another AutoCorrect option

1. You can also choose any of the options listed at the top of the AutoCorrect dialog box:

Option	Description
Change 'Straight Quotes' to 'Smart **Q**uotes'marks	Change the straight quotes, or inch, to smart quotes, or typographical quotes (also called open and closed quotation marks)
Correct TWo INitial **C**apitals	Changes case of the second capital if you type two initial capital letters in a word

Option	Description
Capitalize First Letter **S**entences	Capitalizes the first letter of a sentence if you inadvertently enter a lowercase letter
Capitalize **N**ames of Days	Capitalizes the names of the days of the week automatically as you type

2. Those options with an X in the check box are activated; click the check box to add the X and activate the option. To deactivate an option, click the check box to remove the X.

Note

Word AutoCorrects as you type one of the Replace words (or one of the above options) followed by a space. To cancel an AutoCorrect action, press Ctrl+Z or click the Undo button.

AutoFormat

Word's AutoFormat feature automatically formats your document for you by applying styles—such as headings, bullets, and so on—to the unformatted text in the document. AutoFormat analyzes each paragraph and applies an appropriate style. After the formatting is complete, you can view the changes AutoFormat made and choose whether to accept, reject, or revise them.

By default, AutoFormat applies styles only to text that is formatted as Normal or Body Text. Any styles you have applied, such as the heading style, remain formatted in that style.

To format text automatically

1. Position the insertion point at the beginning of the document.

> **Note**
>
> You can also apply AutoFormat to a selection of text, as opposed to an entire document. Select the text before choosing the AutoFormat command.

2. Choose the F**o**rmat **A**utoFormat command. The AutoFormat dialog box appears.

3. Choose OK. Word automatically formats the document.

4. When the formatting is finished, Word displays another AutoFormat dialog box. Following are the options in that dialog box:

Option	Description
Accept	Accept all changes as made; you can modify any changes to the document by applying your own styles, if necessary.
Reject All	Cancel all of the changes made by AutoFormat and return the document to its original formatting.
Help	Get help on AutoFormat.
Review **C**hanges	Examine the document and choose whether to accept or reject individual modifications. Word enables you to view the changes using the Review AutoFormat Changes dialog box.

Option	Description
Style Gallery	Using the Style Gallery dialog box, choose a different template on which to base the document. Changes made by AutoFormat remain in place; however, such elements as fonts, font size, lines, and screens, change to suit the selected style.

To review and revise changes

1. In the AutoFormat dialog box, choose Review **C**hanges. The Review AutoFormat Changes dialog box appears.
2. Click the **F**ind button with the right arrow to move to the next change AutoFormat made in the document. Use the F**i**nd button with the left arrow to move to the previous change. Word selects the change in the document and then describes the change in the Description area of the dialog box.
3. To accept the change, click the Find button to move to the next modification.

   If you change your mind about the last change you accepted, choose **U**ndo Last to revert the change to its original state.

   To reject the change, click the **R**eject button in the dialog box.

Note

Select the Find Next After Reject option to reject a change and move to the next change.

4. Word displays, by default, the paragraph marks. Blue paragraph marks mean a style has been applied; red paragraph marks mean the paragraph mark has been deleted. Word also uses strike-through characters to indicate any spaces or text AutoFormat has deleted and the underline character to indicate added characters.

5. Choose Close to close the dialog box. Word returns to the AutoFormat dialog box. Choose an option to complete the formatting.

Shortcut

Click the AutoFormat button on the Standard toolbar.

AutoText (formerly Glossary)

You can create an AutoText entry that contains any text or graphics that you frequently use. For example, you can save your company's name, address, and phone number as an AutoText entry. Instead of typing the text over and over again, you simply insert the AutoText entry each time you need the text.

In addition to saving text and graphics in an AutoText entry, you can save the paragraph formatting as well. To save the paragraph formatting—such as alignment, indents, fonts, and so on—include the paragraph mark at the end of the text you are selecting.

To create an AutoText entry

1. Select the text you want to use as an AutoText entry.

2. Choose the **E**dit AutoTe**x**t command. The AutoText dialog box appears.

3. In the **N**ame text box, enter a short and easily recognizable name for the entry.

4. Choose the **A**dd button. The dialog box closes and the entry is created.

To insert an AutoText entry

1. Position the insertion point at the location you want to insert the text.

2. Choose the **E**dit AutoTe**x**t command. The AutoText dialog box appears.

3. Type the name of the entry in the **N**ame text box or choose the name from the list. Choose the **I**nsert button.

   Alternatively, type the name of the AutoText entry and press F3.

   Shortcut

   Type the AutoText name and then click the Insert AutoText button on the Standard toolbar to insert an AutoText entry.

See **AutoCorrect**.

Bold

See **Formatting Characters**.

Bookmarks

Use bookmarks to mark the location of text in your document. You can easily find text that is bookmarked or use the marked text to find a cross-reference or index entry.

To create a bookmark

1. Select the text or item you want to mark.

2. Choose **E**dit **B**ookmark. The Bookmark dialog box appears.

3. In the **B**ookmark Name text box, enter the name of the bookmark.

4. Choose the **A**dd button and the dialog box closes.

To view a bookmark

1. Choose the **T**ools **O**ptions command.
2. Choose the View tab.
3. In the Show area, choose Boo**k**marks.
4. Choose OK to close the dialog box. The bookmarks appear as gray brackets around the selected text or as a gray I-beam at the bookmark location.

See also **Go To**.

Borders and Shading

You can add various border styles to your documents to emphasize text and add pizzazz. You can choose from different line thicknesses and colors, and you can set the amount of space added between the border and the text.

Additionally, you can add shading or patterns to the document. Word's shading choices range from solid (100%) to 5%, and the pattern choices include diagonal, horizontal, vertical, and grid lines.

To add a border

1. Select the paragraph(s) of text around which you want to place the border.
2. Choose the F**o**rmat **B**orders and Shading command. The Paragraph Borders and Shading dialog box appears.
3. Choose the **B**orders tab.
4. In the Presets area, choose either the Bo**x** or Sh**a**dow option. Alternatively, click the border you want to apply in the Bo**r**der sample box.
5. In the **F**rom Text text box, enter the amount of space you want between the text and the border. The default is 1 point.

6. In the Line area, choose the St**y**le of line and the **C**olor of line.

7. Choose OK to insert the border and close the dialog box.

To add shading

1. Select the paragraph(s) of text around which you want to insert the border.

2. Choose the F**o**rmat **B**orders and Shading command. The Paragraph Borders and Shading dialog box appears.

3. Choose the **S**hading tab.

4. In the Fill area, choose Sha**d**ing or pattern.

5. Choose OK to close the dialog box and apply the shading.

Note

To remove a border or shading, choose the F**o**rmat **B**orders and Shading command. In the **B**orders tab, choose **N**one; in the **S**hading tab, choose **N**one.

Shortcut

You can apply both borders and shading using the Borders toolbar.

Bullets

You can add bullets to lists of items to emphasize each item and make them stand out in the text. Word enables you to add a variety of bullet styles quickly and easily.

You also can skip one or more lines of bulleted text, and then resume the bullets.

To add bullets

1. Select the text to which you want to add bullets or position the insertion point at the beginning of bullet text you are about to type.

2. Choose the F**o**rmat Bullets and **N**umbering command. The Bullets and Numbering dialog box appears.

3. Choose the **B**ulleted tab.

4. Select any of the six bullet styles.

Note

You also can choose the **M**odify button to change the bullet character and other options for formatting the bullet text.

5. Choose OK to insert the bullets into the text.

Shortcut

You can quickly begin or end a bulleted list by clicking the Bullet icon on the Formatting toolbar.

To skip a bullet

1. After you finish entering the bulleted text, select the line of text from which you want to remove the bullet.

2. Press the right mouse button to reveal the quick menu. Choose Skip Numbering to remove the bullet.

See also **Numbered Lists**.

Captions

You can add captions to pictures, graphs, tables, figures, and so on. Word labels and numbers the captions for you; all you have to do is enter the caption text.

To enter a caption

1. Select the table, equation, or other object to which you want to add the caption.

2. Choose the **I**nsert Cap**t**ion command. The Caption dialog box appears.

3. In the **L**abel drop-down list, choose the label you want for the caption. If you do not see the label you want, choose the **N**ew Label button to enter a label of your own. The New Label dialog box appears; enter the new label in the **L**abel text box. Choose OK to return to the Caption dialog box.

4. In **C**aption, enter the caption text.

5. In **P**osition, select the placement of the caption.

> **Note**
>
> You can change the numbering style of the caption by choosing the N**u**mbering button. The Caption Numbering dialog box appears from which you can choose a numbering format. Choose OK to return to the Caption dialog box.

6. Choose OK to close the dialog box.

Centering Text

See **Formatting Paragraphs**.

Change Case

Use the Change Case feature when you accidentally type in all caps, for example, and you want to change the text to lowercase or initial caps.

To change the case of text

1. Select the text to be changed.
2. Choose the Format Change Case command. The Change Case dialog box appears with the following options:

Option	Description
Sentence case	Capitalizes the first letter of the first word in the sentence
Lowercase	Changes selected text to all lowercase letters
Uppercase	Changes the selected text to all uppercase
Title Case	Capitalizes the first letter of each word
Toggle Case	Changes uppercase letters to lowercase and lowercase to uppercase.

3. Select an option and choose OK.

Shortcut

Select the text and press Shift+F3; each time you press Shift+F3, the case cycles through uppercase, lowercase, and sentence case.

Clipboard

The Clipboard is a Windows feature that is available to all Windows applications. The Clipboard acts as a temporary holding area for text and graphics. Any item you Cut or Copy is automatically stored on the Clipboard.

You can then Paste that item to a new location, document, or to another application. Additionally, you can paste the item again and again, for a copy remains on the Clipboard until you cut or copy another item. Only one item can remain on the Clipboard at any time.

See **Copy**, **Cut**, and **Paste**, as well as the Integration section.

Close

See the Common Features section.

Columns

You can divide a document into a number of columns so the text is organized and easier to read. Word enables you to set the number of columns for each section in your document, so that one section can have multiple numbers of columns.

To create columns

1. Choose the F**o**rmat **C**olumns command. The Columns dialog box appears.
2. In Presets, choose the number and type of columns you want.

   If you want a different number of columns, enter the number in the **N**umber of Columns text box.

   If you want different widths and spacing to the columns, enter the values, in inches, for the Column W**i**dth and **S**pacing in the Width and Spacing area.
3. If you want to add a line between the columns, choose the Line **B**etween option.

> **Note**
>
> You can only see the line between the columns in Page Layout or Print Preview.

4. Choose OK to close the dialog box.

Shortcut:

You can insert any number of columns, formatted with equal widths, by clicking the Columns button on the Standard toolbar, then dragging the pointer to the number of columns you want.

Note

You can break the text in a column by inserting a column break. When you insert a column break, the text after the break moves to the top of the next column. To insert a column break, position the insertion point and press Ctrl+Shift+Enter.

See also **Section Breaks**.

Compare Versions

You can compare two versions of the same document to see what changes have been made. The two documents must either have different filenames or be in different locations to use the Compare Versions feature.

To compare two versions of the same document

1. Open the edited version of the document.
2. Choose the **T**ools Re**v**isions command. The Revisions dialog box appears
3. Choose the **C**ompare Versions button. The Compare Versions dialog box appears.
4. In the Original File **N**ame text box, enter the name of the original document; alternatively, you can select the name from the list.

5. Choose OK. Word compares the documents and marks revisions in the edited document.

Note

The colors and methods of markings that Word uses is defined in the Options dialog box (**T**ools **O**ptions command, Revisions tab). You can change the marks and colors if you want. You can also access the Revisions table in the Options dialog box by choosing Options from the Revisions dialog box.

To remove revision marks

Choose the **E**dit **U**ndo command to remove revision markings. Alternatively, you can choose the Undo button from the Standard toolbar.

See also **Revision Marks**, as well as the Common Features section.

Copy

You can copy text, tables, pictures, graphs, and so on from one location to another, from one document to another, or from one application to another. When you copy an item, Word duplicates the item on the Clipboard, and then you paste the item to another location.

To copy an item

1. Select the text, picture, or other item you want to copy.
2. Choose the **E**dit **C**opy command. Word places a duplicate of the selected item on the Clipboard.

Shortcut

Click the Copy button on the Standard toolbar. You can also press Ctrl+C to copy a selected item.

See also **Clipboard, Cut**, **Paste**, **Drag and Drop**, as well as the Integration section.

Cross-reference

You can add cross-references to your documents to tell readers where related information is located in the same document. A sample cross-reference is "See page 42."

To create a cross-reference

1. Type the introductory text in the document, such as **For more information, see**. Type a space and leave the insertion point in position. The cross-reference appears at the insertion point in your document.

2. Choose the **I**nsert Cross-**r**eference command. The Cross-reference dialog box appears.

3. In Reference **T**ype, choose one of the following items for which to create a cross-reference: Heading, Bookmark, Footnote, Endnote, Figure/Table/Equation. If, for example, you have endnotes in your document and you want to cross-reference one of them, choose Endnote in the Reference **T**ype list.

4. Then, in the Insert **R**eference To list box, select the information to be inserted into the document, such as the page number, caption text, footnote number, and so on. The information choice displaying in this box depends on the choice you made in the Reference **T**ype box. If you chose to cross-reference an Endnote in step 3, you can choose either the Endnote Number or the Page Number in the Insert **R**eference To list box.

5. In the For **W**hich box, select the item to refer to. For example, if you select the Endnote option in the Reference **T**ype list, Word displays all Endnotes in the For **W**hich box. You choose the one endnote from the list that you want to cross-reference.

6. Choose the **I**nsert button. When finished, choose the Close button. The dialog box remains open. Add any additional information to the cross-reference or start a new cross-reference, if you want. You also can type in the document.

7. Word inserts the specified text at the insertion point.

Updating cross-references

1. Choose the **E**dit Select A**l**l command.

2. Press F9.

> **Tip**
>
> Position the insertion point within one cross-reference and press F9 to update only that cross-reference.

Cut

When you cut text or graphics from your document, you remove the item and place it on the Windows Clipboard, where it remains until another item is cut or copied. You can paste an item from the Clipboard as many times as you like.

To cut text or graphics

1. Select the text or graphics to be cut.

2. Choose the **E**dit Cu**t** command. Word places the selected item on the Clipboard; you can now paste the item to another location or document.

> **Shortcut**
>
> 
> Select the item to be cut and click the Cut button from the Standard toolbar.

See also **Clipboard, Paste**, **Copy**, **Drag-and-Drop**, as well as the Integration section.

Date and Time

Word enables you to insert the current date and time into a document in any of a variety of formats. Additionally, you can insert the date and time as a field, which enables you to automatically update the information at any time with the press of a shortcut key.

Note

Word uses the computer's clock for the time and date used in this command. If your computer's clock is wrong, you can correct it in the Windows Control Panel.

To insert the date and time

1. Position the insertion point at the location you want to insert the date and time.

2. Choose the **I**nsert Date and **T**ime command. The Date and Time dialog box appears.

3. In **A**vailable Formats, choose the format you want to use for the date and/or time.

   Note

   If you choose Insert as a field, you can update the date and time at any time by selecting the text and pressing F9.

4. Choose OK to close the dialog box and insert the date and time.

   Shortcut

   Position the insertion point and press Alt+Shift+D to insert the default format of the date as a field—for example, 3/30/94. Similarly, press Alt+Shift+T to insert the time as a field, like 9:50 PM.

Deleting

When you delete text or graphics, you erase that item. A deleted item is not stored on the Clipboard; however, you can often use the Undo list to reverse the deletion.

To delete text or graphics

1. Select the text or graphics.
2. Choose the **E**dit Cle**a**r command.

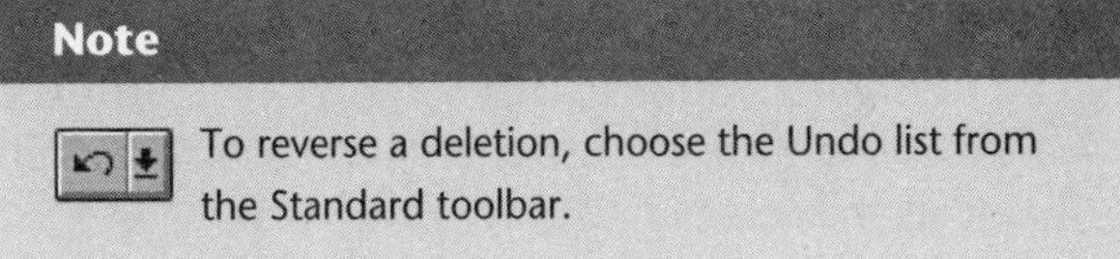

Note

To reverse a deletion, choose the Undo list from the Standard toolbar.

Shortcut

Select the text or item to be deleted and press the Delete or Backspace key.

See also **Select Text**.

Document Summary

Word provides the Summary Info feature to make it easier for you to find documents and information about your documents. The summary information includes such information as a title, the author, subject, and keywords about the document. Word also stores such information as the document's size, creation date, and the template on which it is based.

Note

When searching for a specific document using Find File, you can include information from the Document Summary to narrow your search.

By default, Word provides the Summary Info dialog box automatically when you save a document. You can also view and edit summary information and statistics for any active document.

To automatically hide/show Summary Info when saving

1. Choose **T**ools **O**ptions. The Options dialog box appears.
2. Choose the Save tab.
3. In Save Options, choose the Prompt for Summary **I**nfo option. An X in the option's check box means the option is active; a blank check box means the option is not active. Selecting the option once adds an X; selecting it a second time removes the X.
4. Choose OK to close the dialog box.

To view or edit Summary Info

1. Open the document for which you want to view the Summary Info.
2. Choose the **F**ile Summary **I**nfo command. The Summary Info dialog box appears.
3. Following are the text boxes you can use to enter information that will identify the document. It is not necessary to complete all information; complete only the information that will help identify the contents of the document file.

Option	Description
Title	The name of the document; if you do not enter a title, Word enters the first few words contained in the document as a title
Subject	Describe the document with a brief adjective

Option	Description
Author	Word inserts the name of the person on the User Info tab (**T**ools **O**ptions command); you can enter a different author's name.
Keywords	Add any names, topics, or other key words that help identify this specific document
Comments	Enter any notes or remarks about the document or its subject

4. Choose the Sta**t**istics button to view. The Document Statistics dialog box appears. Statistics include the file name, directory, template used for the document, save and create dates, file size, number of revisions, and the number of pages, words, characters, paragraphs, and so on. Choose Close when you are finished and Word returns to the Summary Info dialog box.

5. Choose OK to close the dialog box.

See also the Common Features section.

Drag-and-Drop

Use drag-and-drop editing to move or copy selected text within a document. Move, for example, a paragraph of text from the top to the bottom of the page.

To move items with drag-and-drop

1. Select the text or graphic to be moved.

2. Position the mouse pointer over the selection and drag the item to its new location. As you drag, the pointer changes to the drag-and-drop pointer and the selection is accompanied by a short vertical cursor. When that vertical cursor is in position, release the mouse button and the selection appears at the cursor's location.

To copy items with drag-and-drop

1. Select the text or graphics to be copied.

2. Point the mouse pointer at the selection, hold the Ctrl key, and drag the item to its new location. When it reaches its destination, release the mouse button and a copy of the selection appears at the new location.

See also **Select Text**, **Cut**, **Copy**, and **Paste**, as well as the Integration section.

Drawing

See the Integration section.

Drop Caps

Add a drop cap to the first paragraph of a chapter, for example, to attract attention and to decorate the page. A drop cap is inserted in place of the first letter of the first word in the first paragraph of body text.

To create a drop cap

1. Select the character to be formatted or position the insertion point in the paragraph that will contain the drop cap.

2. Choose the F**o**rmat **D**rop Cap command. The Drop Cap dialog box appears.

3. In the Position area, choose one of the following:

None	The default; no drop cap. This removes formatting.
Dropped	The enlarged character is positioned so the top of the character is even with the first line of text; the character carves out a space within the text.

In **M**argin	The character appears in the margin and the rest of the text lines up to the right of the drop cap. The first line of text is even with the top of the character.

4. If you choose either **D**ropped or In **M**argin, other choices in the dialog box become available, as follows:

Font	Choose the font you want the drop cap to be.
Lines to Drop	Sets the number of lines the drop cap extends down in the text.
Distance from Te**x**t	Sets the amount of space between the drop cap and the text.

5. Choose OK to close the dialog box.

Endnotes

Endnotes are credits or referrals you add at the end of a document. Word enables you to enter endnotes as you work or after you complete a document. Word automatically numbers endnotes for you, or you can choose your own numbers and numbering format.

To create an endnote

1. Position the insertion point in the text where you want to reference the endnote.
2. Choose the **I**nsert Foot**n**ote command. The Footnote and Endnote dialog box appears.
3. In the Insert area, choose **E**ndnote.

4. In the Numbering area, **A**utoNumber is the default choice. Beside the option is an example of how the numbers will appear.

   If you do not like the default numbering format, choose the **O**ptions button to display the Note Options dialog box and the All **E**ndnotes tab. In **N**umber Format, choose a different format and choose OK.

   Note

   As an alternative to numbering the endnotes, you can choose a **S**ymbol to use with the **C**ustom Mark option in the Numbering area. Choose a bullet, cross, or other symbol, if you want.

5. Choose OK to close the dialog box and insert the endnote. Word displays the superscript number or symbol at the insertion point, and moves the insertion point to either the endnote pane (Normal view) or the end of your document (Page Layout view).

6. Enter the text for the endnote.

7. If you are in Normal view, choose the **C**lose button when you are finished and Word inserts the text at the end of the document. In Page Layout view, simply reposition the insertion point and continue entering the text in your document.

   Note

   To delete an endnote, select the note reference mark in the text and press the Delete key. Word renumbers the remaining notes.

See also **Footnotes**.

Envelopes

Word makes it easy to create and print envelopes using the Envelope and Labels feature. If you have already set up a printer to work with Windows, Word uses the printer information to format the envelope; all you have to do is fill in the address.

To create an envelope

1. If you have a mailing address already entered in a document, select the address text. If you do not have an address to select, go to step 2.
2. Choose the **T**ools **E**nvelopes and Labels command. The Envelopes and Labels dialog box appears.
3. If it is not displayed, choose the **E**nvelopes tab.
4. In **D**elivery Address, the selected text appears. If you did not select text, enter the mailing address in this text box.
5. In **R**eturn Address, enter the appropriate address. If you prefer, you can choose O**m**it and not use a return address.

Note

The name appearing in the **R**eturn Address text box is that of the person and the company entered in the User Info tab (**T**ools **O**ptions command). You can delete the text, if you want, and enter a different name and address.

6. Choose any of the other options, as described in the following table:

Option	Description
Print	Prints the envelope directly to the printer

(continues)

Option	Description
Add to Document	Adds a section to the current document containing the envelope with the addresses on it; when you print the document, the envelope prints, as well
Cancel	Closes the dialog box and cancels all changes in the dialog box
Options	Offers options for envelope size and position and formatting of the addresses; also adds postal codes to the envelope
Help	Offers help on the dialog box options
Preview	Click the Preview area to quickly open the Envelope Options dialog box, **E**nvelope Options tab (the same as opens when you select the **O**ptions button)
Feed	Click the Feed area to quickly open the Envelope Options dialog box, **P**rinting Options tab, from which you can choose how your envelope feeds

Equation Editor

See the Integration section.

Exit

See the Common Features section.

Find and Replace

With Word's Find and Replace commands, you can search for specific text, such as a character, word, or phrase—even formatting and special characters (such as bold characters or tab characters). The Find command enables you to locate each occurrence of the specified text or formatting within your document. Additionally, the Replace command not only enables you to find specific text, but to substitute text or formatting for the found text.

To find text

1. Position the insertion point at the beginning of the document.

> **Note**
>
> You can, alternatively, choose the direction of the search after you open the Find dialog box. In the **S**earch area, choose All, Down, or Up.

2. Choose the **E**dit **F**ind command. The Find dialog box appears.
3. In the Fi**n**d What text box, enter the text for which you are searching.
4. In the **S**earch area, narrow the search by choosing any of the following options:

Option	Description
Match **C**ase	The search only locates matching text if the use of upper- and lowercase characters entered in the Fi**n**d What text box is matched exactly
Find **W**hole Words Only	The search matches only the whole word; for example, if you entered "the" in the Fi**n**d What text box and did not choose this option, the search would find words such as "them," "their," "therefore," and so on.

(continues)

Option	Description
Use Pattern **M**atching	Refers to special search operators used in the advanced search criteria; for example, using a search pattern of "t?e" locates any three-letter word beginning with t and ending with e.
Sounds **L**ike	Finds words that sound the same as the search text but are spelled differently, such as "hear" and "here."

5. Click the **F**ind Next button. Word advances the cursor to the next occurrence of the search text; the Find dialog box remains on-screen.

Tip

You can click the document window and edit text while the Find dialog box remains on-screen. When you are ready to resume a search, click in the Find dialog box.

6. Choose the **F**ind Next button to locate the next occurrence of the search text. When Word has found the last occurrence of the text, it displays a message box; choose OK to close the message box.

Note

The **R**eplace button in the Find dialog box opens the Replace dialog box. For more information, see "To replace text."

7. Choose Cancel when you are done.

Shortcut

To display the Find dialog box, press Ctrl+F.

To find formatting

1. In the Find dialog box (the **E**dit **F**ind command), choose the F**o**rmat button. A secondary menu appears.

> **Tip**
>
> You can apply the formatting to the search text by selecting the text; alternatively, you can use an empty Fi**n**d What text box to search for only formatting.

2. From the F**o**rmat menu, choose one of the following:

Option	Description
Font	Displays the Find Font dialog box: choose a font, font style, size, or other effect for which to search; choose OK to return to the Find dialog box
Paragraph	Displays the Find Paragraph dialog box: choose indentation, spacing, alignment, tab setting, and so on for which to search; choose OK to return to the Find dialog box
Language	Displays the Find Language dialog box: choose a language for which to search, such as Dutch, Italian, German, and so on
Style	Displays the Find Style dialog box: choose a style from the current template, such as Heading 1, Endnote Text, or Normal

> **Note**
>
> You also can choose from the Sp**e**cial list of characters for which to search, including tab characters, annotation marks, em dashes, and so on.

3. Choose **F**ind Next to locate the formatting or character. When Word finishes searching, it displays a message box; choose OK to close the message box.

4. Choose Cancel when finished.

To replace text

> **Tip**
>
> It is a good idea to save the document before beginning a Find and Replace operation, just in case you accidentally replace something you didn't mean to.

1. Position the insertion point at the beginning of the document.

> **Note**
>
> You can, alternatively, choose the direction of the search after you open the Find dialog box. In the **S**earch area, choose All, Down, or Up.

2. Choose the **E**dit R**e**place command. The Replace dialog box appears.

> **Tip**
>
> The Replace dialog box is similar to the Find dialog box. For a thorough explanation of the options and buttons, see the preceding section, "To find text."

3. In the Fi**n**d What text box, enter the text or formatting for which you are searching.

4. In the Re**p**lace With text box, enter the text or formatting you want to substitute.

5. You can choose any of the following options to continue the procedure:

Find Next	Searches for the next occurrence of the search text; you can then choose to **R**eplace the selection or skip it by choosing **F**ind Next
Replace	Substitutes the Re**p**lace With text for the found text
Replace **A**ll	Substitutes all instances of the search text with the replace text

6. Choose Cancel when you are finished.

> **Tip**
>
> If you want to limit a Find or Replace action to a portion of the document, select the text to be searched before beginning the action. Word searches the selected text and then asks if you want to search the rest of the document. Choose **N**o.

Find File

See the Common Features section.

Fonts

Word's versatile handling of fonts enables you to quickly change the typefaces, type styles, and type sizes of any text in your document. Using the Font dialog box, you can change the formatting of the selected text all at the same time.

Formatting fonts is one part of creating styles in Word. You can use styles to format text quicker, easier, and with more consistency.

See also **Styles**.

To change fonts

1. Select the text you want to change; or position the insertion point at the beginning of the text you are about to enter.

2. Choose the F**o**rmat **F**ont command. The Font dialog box appears.

3. Choose the Fo**n**t tab.

4. Change any of the following options of the font:

Option	Description
Font	Choose from available fonts, or typefaces; available fonts are those that are printer fonts and other fonts, such as TrueType, that are available with Windows and Windows' applications
F**o**nt Style	Choose from available formatting styles, such as bold, italic, and bold italic
Size	Available sizes depend on the type of printer you use; if you do not see the size you want, you may be able to type the size in the **S**ize text box, depending on your printer
Underline	Choose the type of underlining from the drop-down list
Color	Choose the color of the font
Effects	Choose from the six formatting styles listed in the Effects area
Preview	View the changes you have selected before accepting them

Note

The **D**efault button changes the formatting of the selected style—such as Normal, Heading 1, and so on—to match the changes made in the dialog box. Word displays a message box confirming your choice. Be careful when choosing this option; changing the default item affects all new documents based on that template.

5. Choose OK when you are finished to close the dialog box and accept the changes.

Shortcut

Use the Formatting toolbar to apply fonts, font sizes, and the bold, italic, or underline formatting.

Footers

See **Headers and Footers**.

Footnotes

Footnotes are credits or referrals you add at the bottom of each page in your document. Word enables you to enter footnotes as you work or after you complete a document. Word automatically numbers footnotes for you or you can choose your own numbers and numbering format.

To create a footnote

1. Position the insertion point in the text where you want to reference the footnote.

2. Choose the **I**nsert Foot**n**ote command. The Footnote and Endnote dialog box appears.

3. In the Insert area, **F**ootnote is the default selection.
4. In the Numbering area, **A**utoNumber is the default choice. Beside the option is an example of how the numbers will appear.

   If you do not like the default numbering format, choose the **O**ptions button to display the Note Options dialog box and the All **F**ootnotes tab. In **N**umber Format, choose a different format and choose OK.

   Note

   You can also choose a different location for the footnotes; you can choose Beneath Text instead of Bottom of Page.

5. Choose OK to close the dialog box and insert the footnote. Word displays the superscript number or symbol at the insertion point and moves the insertion point to either the footnote pane (Normal view) or the end of your document (Page Layout view).
6. Enter the text for the footnote.
7. If you are in Normal view, choose the **C**lose button when you are finished, and Word inserts the text. In Page Layout view, simply reposition the insertion point and continue entering the text in your document.

See also **Endnotes**.

Formatting Characters

You can assign various characteristics or formats to characters using the Format Font command, or by using shortcut commands or the Formatting toolbar. For information about using the Font dialog box, see **Fonts**. This section describes shortcuts for applying various character formatting.

To boldface text

1. Select the text you want to format as bold.
2. Click the Bold button on the Formatting toolbar.

   Alternatively, press Ctrl+B.

To italicize text

1. Select the text you want to format.
2. Click the Italic button on the Formatting toolbar.

   Alternatively, press Ctrl+I.

To underline text

1. Select the text you want to format.
2. Click the Underline button on the Formatting toolbar.

   Alternatively, press Ctrl+U.

To apply other character formats

Format	Key Combination
All Caps	Ctrl+Shift+A
Double underline	Ctrl+Shift+D
Hidden text	Ctrl+Shift+H
Small Caps	Ctrl+Shift+K
Subscript	Ctrl+= (equal sign)
Superscript	Ctrl+Shift+= (equal sign)
Word underline	Ctrl+Shift+W

See also **Fonts**.

Formatting Paragraphs

When formatting a paragraph of text in Word, you can modify many attributes of the text, including alignment, indentation, spacing, and so on. Word enables you to format the text to improve its appearance using the Format Paragraph command.

Formatting paragraphs is a part of creating styles in Word. You can use styles to format text quickly, easily, and with more consistency. For more information, see **Styles**.

Alignment

Word enables you to align, or arrange, the text in your document in any of four ways: left, right, center, or justified. Each alignment arranges the text in relation to the margins of the pages or any set left and right indents.

Button	Alignment	Description
	Left	Text with a flush left edge and a ragged right
	Right	Text with a flush right edge and a ragged left
	Center	Text aligned in the middle, so both the right and left edges are ragged
	Justified	Text with flush left and right edges

To align text

1. Position the insertion point in the text if aligning only one paragraph, or select several paragraphs or an entire document of text.

   Alternatively, position the insertion point at the beginning of where you will enter the text.

2. Choose the F**o**rmat **P**aragraph command. The Paragraph dialog box appears.
3. Choose the **I**ndents and Spacing tab.
4. Click the down arrow in the Ali**g**nment area and select one of the four alignments.
5. Choose OK.

> **Shortcut**
>
> You can quickly align text by selecting the text and clicking the align left, center, align right, or justify button on the Formatting toolbar.

Centering Text

Centering text vertically means to adjust the text on the page by adding space before the first paragraph and after the last paragraph, so that the text is centered vertically on the page. Word includes a vertical alignment option that automatically centers text between the top and bottom margins.

To center text vertically

1. Position the insertion point in the section to be centered.
2. Choose the **F**ile Page Set**u**p command. The Page Setup dialog box appears.
3. Choose the **L**ayout tab.
4. In **V**ertical Alignment, choose Center.
5. Choose OK to close the dialog box. Word vertically centers the text on the page.

> **Note**
>
> You can see the change in the vertical alignment only in Page Layout or Print Preview views.

See also **Section Layout**.

Indenting

Word enables you to indent paragraphs of text on the left and/or the right sides. Additionally, you can indent only the first line of text; you can indent it to the right or to the left (as in a hanging indent).

To indent text

1. Select the paragraphs to be indented, or position the insertion point.
2. Choose the F**o**rmat **P**aragraph command. The Paragraph dialog box appears.
3. Choose the **I**ndents and Spacing tab.
4. In the Indentation area, enter a value, in inches, for the **L**eft and/or **R**ight indents.

   You also can choose to create a first line or hanging indent by choosing **S**pecial, selecting the type of indent, and then entering the value for the indent in the B**y** text box.
5. Choose OK to close the dialog box.

> **Shortcut**
>
> Select the text and use the left, right, and first line indent markers on the ruler to create indents in your documents.

Hanging Indents

Use a hanging indent for bulleted text, numbered lists, or other special formatting, such as setting the dates off in a resume.

To set a hanging indent

1. Select the text or position the insertion point.
2. Choose the F**o**rmat **P**aragraph command. The Paragraph dialog box appears.
3. Choose the **I**ndents and Spacing tab.
4. In the Indentation area, choose **S**pecial and select Hanging.
5. The default measurement to indent is 1/2 inch. You can change the value by entering a new value in the B**y** text box.
6. Choose OK to close the dialog box. Word indents all lines *except* the first line in the paragraph by 1/2 inch, or whatever measurement you set.

Line Spacing

You can adjust the line spacing within a paragraph so the lines of text are close together or far apart. Similarly, you can add or remove spacing between paragraphs of text by setting the spacing before and after the selected text.

To set line spacing

1. Position the cursor, or select the paragraphs to be formatted.
2. Choose the F**o**rmat **P**aragraph command. The Paragraph dialog box appears.
3. Choose the **I**ndents and Spacing tab.

4. In the Spacing area, choose Li**n**e Spacing. Following are a list of the choices:

Option	Description
Single	Sets the spacing to the largest font in that line; so if the majority of the text is 12-point and only one character is 18-point, the spacing is set to allow enough room for the 18-point character (approximately 22-points of spacing)
1.5 Lines	Sets spacing one-and-a-half times single spacing for each line in the paragraph
Double	Sets spacing twice that of single spacing
At Least	The value you enter in the At text box is the minimum spacing set for the lines of text; if a larger character falls on a line set to At Least, Word accommodates the larger character by adding more spacing
Exactly	The value you enter in the At text box is the fixed line spacing set for the text; no adjustments are made for larger text
Multiple	Enter a value; the line spacing is multiplied by the value entered in the At text box. For example, set the line spacing at 3 and Word triple-spaces the selection

5. Choose OK to close the dialog box.

To set paragraph spacing

1. Select the text, or position the insertion point.

2. Choose the F**o**rmat **P**aragraph command. The Paragraph dialog box appears.

3. Choose the **I**ndents and Spacing tab.

4. In the Spacing area, enter a value, in points, in the **B**efore and/or Aft**e**r text boxes. The value added increases the spacing before and/or after the affected paragraphs.

5. Choose OK to close the dialog box.

See also **Styles**.

Frames

Use frames to hold text, pictures, graphs, tables, and other items. Frames enhance the document, and enable the objects in them to be moved around easily. You can format frames with various borders and shading. You also can size a frame and its contents.

To insert an empty frame

1. Change to Page Layout view or Print Preview. You cannot insert a frame in other views.

2. Choose the **I**nsert **F**rame command. The mouse pointer changes to a cross, with which you can draw a frame.

3. Drag the cross to create a frame, from the top left corner to the bottom right. If drawing around an object, drag the frame directly on top of the object. As you drag, a rectangular, dotted border appears to show the size of the frame you are creating.

4. Release the mouse button when the frame is the correct size. A screened border appears around the frame, indicating the size of the frame. To deselect the frame, click anywhere outside of the frame's border.

Note

When you draw an empty frame, a blinking cursor appears in the frame. You can enter text and format it as you would any text in Word.

To select a frame

1. Select the frame by positioning the mouse pointer directly on the frame's border. The pointer changes to a pointer plus a four-headed cross.

2. Click the mouse button. The frame appears with the screened border and eight selection handles, to indicate it is selected.

To move a frame

1. Select the frame.

2. Position the mouse pointer directly over the screened border and drag the frame to a new position.

To size a frame

1. Select the frame.

2. Position the pointer over one of the selection handles. The pointer changes to a double-headed arrow.

3. Drag the handle toward the center of the frame to reduce the frame, or away from the center to enlarge the frame. Release the mouse button.

Note

Hold the Shift key and use a corner selection handle to resize the frame proportionally; use a side, top, or bottom handle to resize in one direction only.

To format a frame

Tip

You can also add a border or shading to any frame by using the Border toolbar or the F**o**rmat **B**orders and Shading command. Alternatively, choose Borders and Shading from the Shortcut menu.

1. Select the frame.
2. Choose the F**o**rmat Fra**m**e command. The Frame dialog box appears.
3. Choose any of the options, as listed in the following table:

Area	Option	Description
Text Wrapping	**N**one	Text stops before the frame and resumes after
	Aro**u**nd	Text wraps on all sides of the frame, depending on the frame's positioning on the page
Size	**W**idth	Set the width of the frame by entering the measurement in the **A**t text box
	Hei**g**ht	Choose to set the height of the frame and enter the measurement in the **A**t text box
Horizontal	Po**s**ition	Enter a measurement to locate the frame in relation to the page, margin, or column
	Re**l**ative To	In conjunction with Po**s**ition, set the frame a specific distance from the Page, Margin, or Column
	Distance from Te**x**t	Enter a value to define the space between the frame and surrounding text

(continues)

Area	Option	Description
Vertical	Pos**i**tion	Enter a measurement to locate the frame in relation to the page, margin, or column
	R**e**lative To	In conjunction with Po**s**ition, set the frame a specific distance from the Page, Margin, or Column
	Distance **f**rom Text	Enter a value to define the space between the frame and surrounding text
	Move with Text	When you edit the text by adding or deleting text, the frame moves as the paragraph it is anchored to moves
	Loc**k** Anchor	Locks the anchor of the frame to the paragraph

Note

To remove a frame, you can click the **R**emove Frame button in the Frame dialog box; however, it is easier to select the frame in the document and press the Delete key.

4. Choose OK to close the dialog box.

Glossary

See **AutoText**.

Go To

Go To is a handy feature you can use to find a specific element in a document; it's especially useful in large documents. Go to a specific page, section, bookmark, annotation, or other element, quickly and effortlessly. You also can move between objects using Go To.

To go to a specific page

1. Choose the **E**dit **G**o To command. The Go To dialog box appears.
2. In Go to **W**hat, choose the element you want to move to.
3. In the **E**nter text box, type the page number, bookmark name, footnote number, or other identifier for the element you want to go to.
4. Choose either Nex**t** or **P**revious to go to the element. Word moves the insertion point to that element in the document, leaving the Go To dialog box displaying. You can click the document window and edit the text or continue to go to other elements in the document.

Tip

In the **E**nter text box, you can enter a plus or minus sign and a number, such as +6, to move forward (+) or back (-) that number of items. Enter the number and choose the Go **T**o button in the dialog box.

5. Choose Close when you are finished.

Shortcut

Double-click the Page area of the Status bar to display the Go To dialog box. Alternatively, press F5 to display the dialog box.

Grammar

Word's grammar checker examines your document for grammatical errors, style flaws, and misspelled words. Use the grammar checker to ensure your business and personal documents present an astute and favorable impression.

To check the grammar

1. Position the insertion point at the beginning of the document by pressing Ctrl+Home.
2. Choose the **T**ools **G**rammar command. The Grammar dialog box appears.

> **Note**
>
> If Word detects a spelling error before it detects a grammatical error, it will display the Spelling dialog box first.

3. The questionable sentence or phrase appears in the **S**entence text box of the Grammar dialog box. A recommendation for correcting the questionable sentence appears in the Su**g**gestions text box. You can edit the sentence in the **S**entence text box or choose from the following options in the Grammar dialog box:

> **Tip**
>
> You can click the document window and edit the document directly, if you want; the Grammar dialog box remains on-screen. Click the **S**tart button in the Grammar dialog box when you are ready to continue.

Option	Description
Ignore	Skip this instance
Next Sentence	Skip this instance and move to the next sentence

Option	Description
Change	Accept the Su**g**gestion Word offers or the changes you made in the **S**entence text box and change the sentence accordingly
Ignore **R**ule	Skips all instances of the specific rule
Cancel	Stops the grammar checking process
Explain	Displays a brief explanation of the grammar or style rule
Options	Displays the Options dialog box, in which you can choose style of writing, grammar rules, and so on
Undo **L**ast	Reverses the last correction

4. If you began checking the grammar at the beginning of the document, Word displays the Readability Statistics dialog box when it finishes checking the grammar. Choose OK to close the dialog box.

If you began checking the grammar in the middle of the document, Word displays a message box asking if you want to continue checking at the beginning. Choose **Y**es to continue, **N**o to stop checking the grammar.

Alternatively, you can choose Cancel at any time to stop the grammar checker.

Graphics

Word enables you to import a variety of graphics, or pictures, to your documents to illustrate the text and attract attention to the document. You can import various types of files to your document, including the following:

- Encapsulated PostScript (EPS)
- Tagged Image Format File (TIF)

- DrawPerfect (WPG)
- PC Paintbrush (PCX)
- Windows Bitmaps (BMP)
- Windows Metafile (WMF)
- Computer Graphics Metafile (CGM)
- HP Graphic Language (HGL)
- Micrografx Designer 3.0 (DRW)
- Lotus 1-2-3 Graphics (PIC)

Inserting a graphic

1. Position the insertion point at the location you want to insert the graphic; alternatively, create and select the frame.

2. Choose the **I**nsert **P**icture command. The Insert Picture dialog box appears.

3. Choose the file name from the File **N**ame list. Alternatively, you can choose List Files of **T**ype and choose a different file format. You can also change drives and directories to choose a file from a different location on disk.

Tip

Choose **P**review Picture if you want to view the graphic before accepting it.

4. Choose OK to insert the picture.

See also **Frames** and **WordArt**, as well as the Integration section.

Hanging Indent

See **Formatting Paragraphs**.

Headers and Footers

You can add headers and footers that repeat information on every page in a section or in an entire document. A header is an area specified in the top margin of the page and typically contains such information as the page number, chapter number, date, volume, issue number, or other similar information. A footer is located at the bottom of the page, in the margin, and typically contains information such as a page number, book title, author name, or other pertinent information.

When you add a header or a footer to a document, Word displays a header or footer pane plus a Header and Footer toolbar.

To create a header

1. On the page you want to start the header, change to Page Layout view. Alternatively, Word switches views for you when you choose the **H**eader and Footer command.
2. Choose the **V**iew **H**eader and Footer command. The Header pane appears, as does the Header and Footer toolbar.

> **Tip**
>
> Position the mouse pointer over each button on the Header and Footer toolbar to reveal the ToolTip box describing the function of each button.

3. Enter the header text in the Header pane. Word has preset tabs and margins according to the page setup of the document.

Note

If you want to add a page number, the date, or the time to the header text, use the corresponding button on the Header and Footer toolbar. By using the button, Word inserts a field that you can update at any time by selecting the field and pressing F9.

Tip

You also can select the header text, while in the header pane, and format the style, font, size, tab stops, and even add a graphic line or shading.

4. When you are finished with the header, click the **C**lose button on the Header and Footer toolbar. The header pane closes and Word inserts the header text. The text appears screened in Page Layout view; it does not appear at all in Normal or Outline view.

Tip

To edit the header text, double-click on the header on any page in the Page Layout or Print Preview views.

To create a footer

1. On the page you want to start the footer, change to Page Layout view. Alternatively, Word switches to the proper view for you when you choose the **H**eader and Footer command.

2. Choose the **V**iew **H**eader and Footer command. The Header pane appears, as does the Header and Footer toolbar.

3. On the Header and Footer toolbar, click the first button: Switch Between Header and Footer. Word moves to the bottom of the page and opens the Footer pane.

4. Enter the footer text and format it. Choose **C**lose on the Header and Footer toolbar when done. Word creates the footer text and closes the footer pane.

See also **Section Breaks**.

Help

See the Common Features section.

Hyphenation

Word includes a hyphenation feature that can automatically hyphenate your document. Use hyphenation whenever you use justified text in a document, because justification sometimes causes awkward word and letter spacing; hyphenation can correct most spacing problems. You may also want to hyphenate left-aligned text when the right edge is too ragged.

To hyphenate text

1. Position the insertion point at the beginning of the document by pressing Ctrl+Home.
2. Choose the **T**ools **H**yphenation command. The Hyphenation dialog box appears.
3. Choose **A**utomatically Hyphenate Document. This option automatically hyphenates the text as you type or after you are finished.

> **Tip**
>
> Make sure you hyphenate text in a document only after all writing and editing are complete. Otherwise, Word may constantly interrupt you while you type to confirm hyphenation, and that is extremely frustrating.

> **Note**
>
> Alternatively, you can choose the **M**anual button. Word moves the insertion point to the first word that needs a hyphen and displays the Manual Hyphenation dialog box. In the Hyphenate **A**t text box, Word displays the suggested hyphenation. Choose **Y**es if the hyphenation is right; or manually insert the hyphen in another area of the word in the Hyphenate **A**t text box.

4. Choose OK to close the dialog box. Word hyphenates the document and displays a message dialog box telling you the process is complete. Choose OK.

Indenting

See **Formatting Paragraphs**.

Index

The index is often the most valuable element in a document; many readers depend on the index to quickly and efficiently find topics they are interested in. Word enables you to mark index entries, create subentries, and choose whether to use one page or a range of pages for each entry.

After marking the index entries, you compile the index. Word enables you to select a preset format for the index and then the program sorts them, references the page numbers, and displays the index in a document.

To mark entries

1. Select the text to be marked or position the insertion point in the text.

2. Choose the **I**nsert Inde**x** and Tables command. The Index and Tables dialog box appears.

3. Choose the Inde**x** tab.

4. Choose the Mar**k** Entry button. The Mark Index Entry dialog box appears on the screen.

5. If you selected text before choosing to mark the index entry, the selected text appears in the Main **E**ntry dialog box. If you did not select text, type the index topic in the Main **E**ntry text box.

6. Enter a topic in the **S**ubentry text box, if you want.

> **Note**
>
> By default, the entry is marked to reference the current page in the index. You can use a page range by choosing Page **R**ange and entering the Bookmark name you used to mark the pages. See **Bookmarks** for more information.

7. In Page Number Format, choose either **B**old or **I**talic if you want to format the page number in the index.

8. Choose **M**ark. Word marks the entry and leaves the dialog box open. You can click the insertion point in the document window to position the insertion point in another topic. Then click the dialog box to activate it and continue to mark index entries.

9. When finished, choose Close.

> **Shortcut**
>
> To quickly display the Mark Index Entry dialog box, position the insertion point and press Alt+Shift+X.

To compile the index

1. Position the insertion point at the end of the document.

2. Choose the **I**nsert Inde**x** and Tables command. The Index and Tables dialog box appears.

3. Choose the Index tab.

4. In Type, choose one of the following:

Option	Description
Indented	Subentries are indented on the line below the main entry
Run-in	Subentries follow the main entry on the same line, in paragraph form

5. In Formats, choose any of the listed styles of indexes. View the different formats in the Preview box.

6. You can also choose from any of the following format options:

Option	Description
Right Align Page Numbers	Selected by default; if you deselect this option, the page numbers appear next to the entries
Columns	2 by default; you can choose more or less columns in which to format the index
Tab Leader	Separate the page number from the entry with your choice of a dotted, dashed, or line leader, or no leader at all

7. Choose OK to close the dialog box and compile the index. Word inserts a section break at the insertion point and places the index after the break.

Insert File

You can insert a text file into a document to combine two documents. The styles of both documents integrate so all styles are available in the new document. You can insert text files, other Word files, or text files you create with other software applications.

To insert a file

1. Position the insertion point at the location you want the inserted text file to appear.
2. Choose the **I**nsert Fi**l**e command. The File dialog box appears.
3. Choose the appropriate **D**irectory and Dri**v**e. You may change the file format in the List Files of **T**ype list.
4. In the File **N**ame list, choose the file you want to insert.
5. Choose OK to close the dialog box and insert the file into the document.

Insert an OLE Object

See the Integration section.

Insert a Picture

See the Integration section.

Italic

See **Formatting Characters**.

Justify Text

See **Formatting Paragraphs**.

Labels

Create mailing labels, file folder labels, diskette, video or audio tape labels, postcards, name tags, and more using Word's label feature. You can create and print a single label or a sheet of labels and save the labels in a document for use at any time.

Note

If you print a sheet of labels, all labels contain the same address, label, or other text. To create labels with different text on each label, see **Mail Merge**.

To create a label

1. Choose the **T**ools **E**nvelopes and Labels command. The Envelopes and Labels dialog box appears.
2. Choose the **L**abels tab.
3. In **A**ddress, enter the address or text you want to use for the label. If you selected text in the document, Word automatically inserts the selected text in the **A**ddress text box.

Tip

Choose Use **R**eturn Address if you want to print one label or a sheet of labels with the mailing address listed in the User Info tab of the Options dialog box. Alternatively, you can enter a return address in the text box.

4. In the Print area, choose to either print **F**ull Page of Same Label or to print a Si**n**gle Label. If you choose the single label, you can mark the label's position in the Ro**w** and **C**olumn text boxes.
5. In the Label area, click the mouse on the label to display the Label Options dialog box. In this box, choose options from the following:

Option	Description
Printer Information	Choose either a dot-matrix or laser printer
Tray	Choose the tray the label will load from

Option	Description
Label **P**roducts	Choose from the list of brand names; choose Other to list more brand names
Product **N**umber	Choose the number listed on the label box
Label Information	Displays details of the size and type of label you chose in Product **N**umber

Note

Click the Label Information area, or choose the **D**etails button, to view a dialog box containing information relating to the product number selected, in which you can customize the size of the label if you cannot find the exact label type in the Product **N**umber list. Choose OK when done.

6. Choose OK to close the dialog box and return to the Envelopes and Labels dialog box.

   If you chose Full Page of the Same Label in Step 4, you can choose New Document to create a document with the Label information you have entered. You can save this document to reprint the same labels at any time.

7. Choose **P**rint to print the labels.

Line Spacing

See **Formatting Paragraphs**.

Link

See the Integration section.

Macros

See the Integration section.

Mail Merge

You can create personalized form letters, address files from which to print envelopes and mailing labels, or membership directories, catalogs, and so on, using Word's mail merge feature. Additionally, you can create the mailing list in Word or use a list from another document, say from a database application, for example.

To create or open a mailing list

1. Choose the **T**ools Mail Me**r**ge command. The Mail Merge Helper dialog box appears.

2. Choose number 1, Main Document. Click the **C**reate button.

> **Note**
>
> You must choose a document type before you can create the data source or mailing list. After creating the mailing list, however, you can use it for any document type.

3. Choose the type of document you want to create. Word displays a message box asking if you want to use the current document or create a new one. Choose either **A**ctive Window or **N**ew Main Document.

4. In number 2, Data Source, click the **G**et Data button. From the drop-down list, choose from one of the following options:

Option	Description
Create Data Source	If you want to create the mailing list, or other data, in Word at this time, choose this option. If you choose this option, move to step 5

Option	Description
Open Data Source	Displays the Open Data Source dialog box from which you select the file containing the mailing list or other data. From this step, skip to the next section
Header Options	Displays the Header Options dialog box in which you choose to either create or open separate data and header sources

5. Choose **C**reate Data Source. The Create Data Source dialog box appears. In the list of Field **N**ames, choose any names you do not want to use in the data source, and select the **R**emove Field Name button. In the **F**ield Name text box, enter any new field names you want to add to the list and choose **A**dd Field Name.

6. When finished, choose OK to close the dialog box. The Save Data Source dialog box appears.

7. Enter a File **N**ame in the text box and press Enter to save the data source. Word displays a message box stating you can now add records to the data source or set up the main document.

8. To add records, choose Edit **D**ata Source. The Data Form dialog box appears listing text boxes for each field name you created. Enter the names, addresses, and other appropriate information in the text boxes for the first record.

9. Choose **A**dd New to add the record. Continue to add new data and records. Following are additional options for using the Data Form dialog box:

Option	**Description**
Delete	Removes the currently displaying record
Re**s**tore	Returns the current record to its original state if you edited it
Find	Displays the Find in Field dialog box you can use to search for specific information in the data source
View Source	Displays the data source information in table format so you can view multiple records at a time
Record	Type or select the number of the record you want to display

10. Choose OK when finished entering the data. Word closes the dialog box and displays the document to be used for the mail merge. Word also displays the Mail Merge toolbar.

To create a form letter

1. Choose the **T**ools Mail Me**r**ge command. The Mail Merge Helper dialog box appears.
2. Choose number 1, Main Document. Click the **C**reate button.
3. From the drop-down list, choose Form **L**etters. Word displays a message box; choose either **A**ctive Window or **N**ew Main Document.
4. Choose number 2, Data Source. Click the **G**et Data button and choose to either **C**reate Data Source or **O**pen Data Source. Word displays a message box.
5. Choose Edit **M**ain Document. Word displays the Merge toolbar and a document for the form letter.

6. Enter the text for the main document. When you are ready to enter the merge fields, position the insertion point and choose the Insert Merge Field button from the Merge toolbar. From the list of fields in the data source, choose the appropriate field to insert.

7. Continue to enter the text and insert merge fields until the letter is completed. Then save the letter.

To create envelopes

1. Choose the **T**ools Mail Me**r**ge command. The Mail Merge Helper dialog box appears.

2. Choose number 1, Main Document. Click the **C**reate button.

3. From the drop-down list, choose **E**nvelopes. Word displays a message box; choose either **A**ctive Window or **N**ew Main Document.

4. Choose number 2, Data Source. Click the **G**et Data button and choose to **C**reate Data Source or **O**pen Data Source. Word displays a message box.

5. Choose **S**et up Main Document. Word displays the Envelope Options dialog box.

6. Choose the Envelope **S**ize. You can also change the font for the addresses and the text position.

7. Choose OK when finished. Word displays the Envelope Address dialog box.

8. Position the insertion point and click the In**s**ert Merge Field button. From the drop-down list of merge fields, choose the fields to insert in the envelope address.

9. Choose OK when done to return to the Mail Merge Helper dialog box. Choose Close to close the dialog box and view the new document. Word displays the sample envelope with the merge fields entered. Save the document.

To create labels

1. Choose the Tools Mail Merge command. The Mail Merge Helper dialog box appears.
2. Choose number 1, Main Document. Click the Create button.
3. From the drop-down list, choose Mailing Labels. Word displays a message box. Choose either Active Window or New Main Document.
4. Choose number 2, Data Source. Click the Get Data button and choose to either Create Data Source or Open Data Source. Word displays a message box.
5. Choose Set up Main Document. Word displays the Label Options dialog box.
6. Choose the printer type—Dot Matrix or Laser—and select the Tray.
7. Choose the Label Products type and the Product Number of the labels you are using.
8. Choose OK to close the dialog box. Word displays the Create Labels dialog box.
9. Position the insertion point in the Sample Label text box. Select the Insert Merge Field button and choose the appropriate field name to be inserted.
10. Continue to enter field names, as well as spaces, commas, and other appropriate text and punctuation. Choose OK when finished and Word returns to the Mail Merge Helper.

To merge a document and data source

1. After creating the data source and the document to be used for the mail merge, Word returns to the Mail Merge Helper dialog box. If you created a form letter, you must first choose the Tools Mail Merge command.

2. In the Mail Merge Helper dialog box, choose number 3, Merge the Data with the Document. Choose **M**erge and the Merge dialog box appears.

3. In Me**r**ge To, choose to merge the data to a New Document or to the Printer. Alternatively, if you have Electronic Mail, you can merge the documents and send them to the mail addresses contained in the data source.

> **Tip**
>
> Merging to a new document can create a large, unwieldy document if you are using many names and addresses in the data source. Merging to the printer may be a better choice, especially if your computer doesn't have a lot of RAM.

4. In the Records to Be Merged area, choose either **A**ll or **F**rom and enter the record numbers you want to merge.

5. In the When Merging Records area, choose whether to print blank lines when data fields are empty.

6. Optionally, you can choose either or both of the following choices:

Check **E**rrors	Determines how Word reports any errors found in the data source or main document as the two are merged
Query Options	Determines the criteria you want to use when selecting or sorting records

7. Choose **M**erge when you are finished. Word merges the data source and the main document to the specified destination.

> **Tip**
>
> Use the Mail Merge toolbar to perform the merge, view the data source, and for other processes.

Margins

You can change the margins for a document or a section. The default margins are one inch for top and bottom and 1 1/4 inches for left and right. Word enables you to change margins in either of two ways: using the Page Setup dialog box or the ruler.

To change margins with the dialog box

1. Choose **F**ile Page Set**u**p. The Page Setup dialog box appears.

> **Tip**
>
> The insertion point can be located anywhere in the document or section to be changed. If you change one page's margins, all pages in the document or section also change.

2. Choose the **M**argins tab.
3. Enter or select values in the following text boxes to change margins and spacing:

Option	Description
Top	Defines the margin on the top of the page
Bottom	Defines the margin at the bottom of the page
Le**f**t	Defines the left margin
Ri**g**ht	Defines the right margin

Option	Description
Gutter	Defines extra space added to the margin for binding
From Edge	Defines the amount of space from the top edge of the page for the Header and from the bottom edge of the page for the Footer
Mirror margins	Mirrored margins are used when printing double-sided or facing pages. Outside margins are the left margin on a left page and the right margin on a right page, whereas Inside margins are the right margin on a left page and the left margin on a right page.

4. Choose OK to accept the changes and close the dialog box.

   You can view margin changes only in Page Layout or Print Preview views.

To change margins with the ruler

1. In Page Layout view, display the ruler if it is not already displaying, by choosing **V**iew **R**uler. In Print Preview, the ruler displays by default.

2. With the insertion point located anywhere in the document or section, position the mouse pointer between the gray and white border of the ruler until the pointer changes to a double-headed arrow.

Note

To change margins for multiple sections at the same time, select the sections to be changed.

Note

Use the horizontal ruler to change the left and right margins; use the vertical ruler to change the top and bottom margins.

3. Drag the double-headed arrow to the left or right; the margins change as you drag.

Tip

To display the margin measurements as you adjust them, hold down the left and right mouse buttons as you drag. Alternatively, you can hold down the Alt key as you drag.

Move

See **Cut** and **Paste**, as well as the Integration section.

Moving around in Word Documents

When editing text or modifying a document, you can use the mouse or the keyboard to move around the document window in Word. Additionally, you can move between documents and between applications; see the Integration section for more information.

To get around documents using the mouse

Aside from merely clicking the mouse at any location in the document, use the following to navigate the Word screen with the mouse:

To move	Click or drag
Up or down	Vertical scroll bar, arrows, and box
Left or right	Horizontal scroll bar, arrows, and box

To get around documents using the keyboard

Use the following keys and key combinations to navigate the Word screen:

To move	Press
One character left or right	Left or right arrow
One line up or down	Up or down arrow
One word left or right	Ctrl+left arrow, Ctrl+right arrow
One paragraph up or down	Ctrl+up arrow, Ctrl+down arrow
Beginning or end of the line	Home or End keys
Up or down one page	Alt+Ctrl+PageUp, Alt+Ctrl+PageDown
Up or Down one screen	PageUp or PageDown
Beginning or end of document	Ctrl+Home, Ctrl+End
Top or Bottom of the screen	Ctrl+PageUp or Ctrl+PageDown
Previous or Next Paragraph	Ctrl+up or down arrow
Previous or Next section	Alt+up or down arrow

See also **Go To**.

Numbered Lists

Word enables you to add numbers to lists of items; you can add a variety of numbering styles quickly and easily. You can also skip one or more lines of numbered text, and then resume the numbers.

To add numbers

1. Select the text that you want to number, or position the insertion point at the beginning of the numbered text you are about to type.

2. Choose the F**o**rmat Bullets and **N**umbering command. The Bullets and Numbering dialog box appears.
3. Choose the **N**umbered tab.
4. Select any of the six number styles.

> **Note**
>
> You also can choose the **M**odify button to change the numbering character and other formatting options.

5. Choose OK to insert the numbers into the text.

> **Shortcut**
>
>  You can quickly begin or end a numbered list by clicking the Numbering button on the Formatting toolbar.

To skip a number

1. After you finish entering the numbered text, select the line of text from which you want to remove the number.
2. Press the right mouse button to reveal the quick menu. Choose Skip Numbering to remove the number. The next numbered item resumes the numbering scheme.

> **Note**
>
> Choosing Skip Numbering removes only the number and not the style of the text. The text remains indented. You can resume numbering at any time while entering a list by clicking the Numbering button.

Numbering Lines

You can use Word's numbering feature to number lines in a document for reference or readability purposes. If you edit or move lines of text, Word automatically renumbers the lines for you.

To number lines of text

1. Position the insertion point at the location you want the line numbering to begin.

2. Choose **F**ile Page Set**u**p. The Page Setup dialog box appears.

3. Choose the **L**ayout tab.

4. Choose the Line **N**umbers button. The Line Numbers dialog box appears.

5. Choose Add **L**ine Numbering and the following options become available:

Option	**Description**
Start **A**t	Enter the starting number; the default is number 1
From **T**ext	Enter or select the distance between the right edge of the line numbers and the left edge of the line; the default is 1/4 inch for a single column and .13 inch for newspaper columns
Count **B**y	Enter or select increments; for example, display line numbers as 2, 4, 6, 8, and so on, enter 2
Numbering	Choose where to restart numbering: Restart Each **P**age, Restart Each **S**ection, or **C**ontinuous

6. Choose OK to close the dialog box and return to the Page Setup dialog box.

7. Choose OK to close the dialog box and return to the document.

To remove line numbers

1. Position the insertion point at the top of the page on which you want the line numbering to end.
2. Choose **F**ile Page Set**u**p. The Page Setup dialog box appears.
3. Choose the **L**ayout tab.
4. Choose the Line **N**umbers button. The Line Numbers dialog box appears.
5. Choose the Add **L**ine Numbering check box to deactivate the option. The X disappears from the check box.
6. Choose OK to close the dialog box and return to the Page Setup dialog box. Choose OK again to return to the document.

Numbering Pages

You can add page numbers to your documents and let Word enter the actual numbers for you. If you add or remove pages, Word adjusts the page numbers. Additionally, you can choose a position and an alignment for the page numbers and change the default formatting, as well.

To add page numbers

1. Choose the **I**nsert Page N**u**mbers command. The Page Numbers dialog box appears.
2. In **P**osition, choose where to place the page numbers: Bottom of Page (Footer) or Top of Page (Header).

> **Note**
>
> When you add page numbers, Word places the text in a header or footer pane. You can add text to your page numbers by opening the Header or Footer pane.

3. In **A**lignment, choose Left, Right, Center, Inside, or Outside.

> **Note**
>
> Inside and Outside are options generally associated with mirrored margins. See **Margins** for more information.

4. Choose whether to **S**how Number on First Page.

5. Choose OK to close the dialog box and add page numbers to the document.

To format page numbers

1. In the Page Numbers dialog box, choose the **F**ormat button.

2. Choose from the following options:

Option	Description
Number **F**ormat	Choose from such number formats as Roman numerals, letters, and so on
Include Chapter **N**umber	Choose the style of the chapter title and the type of character you want to use to separate the chapter number from the page number
Page Numbering	Choose whether to **C**ontinue from Previous Section (if your document has more than one section), or choose the starting number for the section

3. Choose OK to close the Page Number Format dialog box. Choose OK to close the Page Numbers dialog box. Word adds the page numbers.

See also **Headers and Footers**.

Open

See the Common Features section.

Outlines

Create an outline to organize the text in an existing document, or to help begin a new document. Word's outline feature offers a special outline view as well as an Outline toolbar that can help you quickly construct or arrange the text in your document.

To outline an existing document

1. Choose the **V**iew **O**utline command. Word displays the document in Outline view and adds the Outlining toolbar.

2. Select the text or position the insertion point at the location of the first level of outline text. Click the Promote button on the Outlining toolbar.

> **Tip**
>
> You also can assign levels using the Style box in the Formatting toolbar: Heading 1 is level one, Heading 2 is level two, and so on.

3. Select the text or position the insertion point on level two text. Click the promote button once and then click the demote button to change the text to Heading 2.

4. Continue to assign various levels to the text in the document.

Button	Description
	Promote
	Demote

Shortcut

Choose the Outline View button beside the horizontal scroll bar to change the view to Outline.

To expand or collapse an outline

1. Position the insertion point in the heading to be expanded.
2. Click the Expand button on the Outlining toolbar to show the next level of the outline. Click the Expand button again to show additional levels, including body text.
3. Click the Show Heading 1 button on the Outlining toolbar to show only level one text; click Show Heading 2 to show only levels one and two, and so on. Click the All button to show all levels of the outline, including body text.
4. Position the insertion point in the heading to be collapsed.
5. Click the Collapse button on the Outlining toolbar to collapse the outline, one level at a time.

Tip

You can quickly expand or collapse a heading completely by double-clicking the plus sign to the left of the heading.

Button	Description
+	Expand
1 2	Show Level 1 and Show Level 2
−	Collapse

To move or reposition text in an outline

1. Collapse the outline to the level of the text you want to move.

2. Position the mouse pointer on the plus or minus sign next to the heading you want to move. The mouse pointer changes to a four-headed arrow.

> **Tip**
>
> A plus sign next to a collapsed heading means that topic consists of text that is hidden; a minus sign means there is no text under that topic.

3. Drag the pointer, and the heading, to a new location. A dotted horizontal line and an arrow move with the pointer, indicating where the moved text will go.

> **Note**
>
> You can also move a heading, along with its subheadings and body text, by clicking the plus sign to select the heading (and subheadings and body text) and then clicking the MoveUp or MoveDown buttons on the toolbar.

Page Breaks

Word inserts soft page breaks when you enter enough text and/or graphics to fill a page. If you edit, add, or delete text, the soft page break moves up or down the page. You can, alternatively, insert your own page break, also called a hard page break, at any point in a document. When you edit text, however, a hard page break remains in place.

To insert a hard page break

1. Position the insertion point.

2. Choose the **I**nsert **B**reak command. The Break dialog box appears.

3. In the Insert area, choose **P**age Break (the default) and choose OK. Word inserts the page break.

Shortcut
Position the insertion point and press Ctrl+Enter.

To remove a page break

1. Position the insertion point on the dotted line created by the page break (Normal view).
2. Press the Delete key. The page break is erased.

To control page breaks

You can control how selected text reacts with a page break. Use these controls when you have a paragraph you do not want to split between pages, or when you want to keep two specific paragraphs together.

1. Position the insertion point where you want to control the page breaks.
2. Choose the F**o**rmat **P**aragraph command. The Paragraph dialog box appears.
3. Choose the Text **F**low tab.
4. In the Pagination area, the following options are available:

Option	Description
Widow/Orphan Control	Prevents Word from placing the last line of a paragraph at the top of a page by itself (widow) or the first line of a paragraph at the bottom of a page by itself (orphan)
Keep Lines Together	Prevents a page break within the designated paragraph

(continues)

Option	Description
Keep with Ne**x**t	Prevents a page break between the selected paragraph and the one that follows it
Page Breaks Before	Inserts a page break before the specified paragraph

5. Choose OK to close the Paragraph dialog box and return to the document.

Password Protection

You can assign a password to a document to prevent others from opening the document. The only people who can open a password-protected file are those who know the password. A password can consist of up to 15 characters; you can include numbers, letters, symbols, and spaces. Additionally, a password is case-sensitive—each time you enter the word, you must match the upper- and lowercase characters exactly.

To assign a password to a document

1. Choose the **F**ile Save **A**s command. Enter a name for the document.
2. Choose the **O**ptions button. The Options dialog box appears with the Save tab displaying.
3. In the File Sharing Options for Document area, do one of the following:

Option	Description
Protection Password	Enter a password; only those who know the password can open the document
Write Reservation Password	Enter a password; only those who know the password can open the document to make changes. Others can open the document as Read Only by choosing that option in the Password dialog box.

Option	Description
Read-Only Recommended	Recommends, but doesn't require, that others open the document as read-only

4. If you choose any of the password options, Word displays a Confirm Password dialog box, in which you re-enter the password and choose OK. Word returns to the Save As dialog box.

Tip

When you type the password, Word displays an asterisk (*) for each character for privacy.

Tip

A password-protected document cannot be opened if you do not have or cannot remember the exact password.

5. Choose OK to save the document.

Tip

You can choose an option that enables others to open and view the document, and add only Revisions, Annotations, or Forms. They won't be able to make other changes besides the changes you specify. Choose the **T**ools menu **P**rotect Document command. In the Protect Document dialog box, choose **R**evisions, **A**nnotations, or **F**orms; you can choose only one. Enter the password and choose OK. Word asks that you confirm the password. Word marks any revisions using revision marks.

To open a password-protected document

1. Choose the **F**ile **O**pen command. The Open dialog box appears.

2. Choose the document file name and choose OK. Word displays the Password dialog box.

3. In the Enter Password for file text box, type the password. Word displays asterisks for each character you enter.

> **Note**
>
> You must enter the exact characters and case for the password.

4. Choose OK. Word opens the document. If you mistyped the password or entered the wrong password, Word displays a message box stating the password is incorrect and that it will not open the document. Choose OK to close the dialog box.

To change or delete a password

1. Open the document.

2. Choose the **F**ile Save **A**s command. The Save As dialog box appears.

3. Choose the **O**ptions button.

4. In the **P**rotection Password text box or the **W**rite Reservation Password text box, select the asterisks representing the password.

   To change the password, type a new one.

   To delete the password, press the Delete key.

5. Choose OK. If you changed the password, Word asks you to retype the word. Type it and choose OK.

6. Word returns to the Save As dialog box. Choose OK to save the document.

Paste

Use the Paste command in conjunction with the Cut or Copy commands. When you cut or copy text or graphics to the Windows Clipboard, you can then paste the item in another location, document, or Windows application. Use the Cut and Paste commands to move items to new locations; use Copy and Paste to duplicate an item in another location.

To paste a cut or copied item

1. After copying or cutting an item, position the insertion point in the location you want the pasted object to appear.
2. Choose the **E**dit **P**aste command.

Shortcut
 Position the insertion point and click the Paste button from the Standard toolbar.

See also **Cut**, **Copy**, and **Clipboard**, as well as the Integration section.

Printing

Not only can you print your Word documents, you can print summary information, annotations, styles, and more. Additionally, Word enables you to print specific pages in a document, print numerous copies, collate those copies, and print to a file.

Word provides other controls for printing, such as choosing paper size and orientation, and designating the paper source. You can also see the document as it will look when printed by using Print Preview.

Print

You can print your document, as well as other elements of a document file, using the Print dialog box.

To print a document

1. Open the document you want to print.
2. Choose the **F**ile **P**rint command. The Print dialog box appears.
3. Choose from the following options:

Option	Description
Print What	Choose the element of the file you want to print: Document (default), Summary Info, Annotations, Styles, AutoText Entries, or Key Assignments. Choosing an option other than Document dims the Page Range option in the dialog box. You can only choose one of the items to print at a time; for example, you can print either the document or the summary info at one time.
Copies	Enter or select the number of copies you want to print
All	Print all pages in document
Curr**e**nt Page	Print the page the insertion point is currently on
Selectio**n**	Print only the selected text (you must select the text before opening the Print dialog box)
Pa**g**es	Enter a page range in the text box using the examples below the option for listing pages
P**r**int	Specify whether to print all pages in the range, odd pages only, or even pages only
Print to Fi**l**e	Prints the document to a file instead of the printer; Word requests a drive and file name. Use this option when taking the file to a computer that does not have the Word program installed; you can print the file from the DOS prompt using the Print command.

Option	Description
Collate Copies	Prints multiple copies of the document in order; for example, prints two copies of three pages as page 1, 2, 3, 1, 2, 3 instead of 1, 1, 2, 2, 3, 3
Options	Displays the Options dialog box in which you can set preferences for printing documents
Printer	Displays the Print Setup dialog box from which you can choose the printer

4. Choose OK to print.

Shortcut

You can print a document quickly, using the default selections in the Print dialog box, by clicking the Print button in the Standard toolbar.

Display the Print dialog box quickly by pressing Ctrl+P.

Page Setup

The Page Setup dialog box enables you to choose several options for printing. You can change the paper size and orientation (check your printer reference manual to make sure your printer can print different sizes of paper or landscape orientation). You can also change the paper source for printing.

To change paper size and orientation

1. Open an existing document or start a new one.

2. Choose the **F**ile Page Set**u**p command. The Page Setup dialog box appears.

3. Choose the Paper **S**ize tab.

4. In Pape**r** Size, choose the appropriate size for the document. An example of the selected size appears in the Preview dialog box.

> **Note**
>
> Alternatively, you can enter or select the paper size in the **W**idth and H**e**ight text boxes, located below the Pape**r** Size list box in the Paper **S**ize tab.

5. In Orientation, choose either Portra**i**t (default) or Lands**c**ape.

6. Choose OK to close the dialog box.

To change the paper source

1. Open the document or start a new one.

2. Choose the **F**ile Page Set**u**p command. The Page Setup dialog box appears.

3. Choose the **P**aper Source tab.

4. You can choose to print the first page of the document and the other pages from the same or different paper sources. In the **F**irst Page, choose the paper source. In **O**ther Pages, choose the paper source.

5. Choose OK to close the dialog box.

Print Preview

Word enables you to view your document in Print Preview to see what it will look like when printed. You can make last minute margin adjustments, text modifications, and so on in Print Preview.

To view a document in Print Preview

1. Open the document.

2. Choose the **F**ile Print Pre**v**iew command. Word changes the document view so you can see the formatted page as it will print. Word also displays the Print Preview toolbar.

3. The page view is Full Page when you first enter Print Preview. Also, the mouse pointer changes to a magnifying tool. Point the tool at an area in the document and click to enlarge that area.

   Alternatively, click the Magnifier button on the Print Preview toolbar to revert the mouse back to a pointer and I-beam.

Note

In Print Preview, you can adjust the margins using the vertical and horizontal rulers. See **Margins** for more information.

4. After viewing the document and making any adjustments, you can print the document or choose **C**lose to return to the previous view (Normal, Page Layout, or Outline). You can alternatively press Esc to return to the previous view.

Shortcut

Click the Print button on the Print Preview toolbar to print the document.

Repeat

The Repeat command enables you to reproduce your last action, whether it is typing or formatting text, entering page numbers, checking spelling, or some other task. You can repeat the text you just typed, for example, by using Word's Repeat command. Word stores the characters or commands you just typed until you perform another action, such as formatting text.

> **Note**
>
> Some tasks, such as changing views or performing a word count, cannot be repeated. The **E**dit **R**epeat command displays the last repeatable task or command as part of the command, such as "**R**epeat Thesaurus..." or "**R**epeat Font Format...".

To repeat a command or task

Choose the **E**dit **R**epeat command. The menu closes and Word repeats the last task or action you performed.

Alternatively, you can press Ctrl+Y to repeat the last repeatable action; however, if you use the **E**dit **R**epeat command, you can see which action Word will repeat.

> **Note**
>
> Word also includes a Redo button on the Standard toolbar. The Redo button only repeats a command or action that has been reversed using the Undo command or Undo button on the Standard toolbar.

Shortcut

Click the Redo button to repeat the last action, or click the arrow to the right of the button to display a list of actions from which to choose.

Press F4 to repeat your last action.

Alternatively, press Ctrl+Y to repeat the last action.

Revision Marks

Revision marks enable you to keep a record of changes and then decide whether to accept or reject those changes. Use the revision marks feature to make it easy to tell where the revisions occurred. Additionally, you can use revision marks to more efficiently incorporate revisions after reviewing them.

Word uses special formatting for revised text: underlining for added text, strike-through for deleted text, borders in the margins, and different colors to specify each revision.

To use revision marks

1. Open the document to be revised.
2. Choose the **T**ools Re**v**isions command. The Revisions dialog box appears.
3. In the Document Revisions area, choose **M**ark Revisions While Editing.

Note

You can choose to check either of two other options: Show Revisions on **S**creen makes it easier to see the revisions as you make them, and Show Revisions in **P**rinted Document gives you a record of the revisions when you print the document.

4. Choose OK to close the dialog box. Position the insertion point and edit the document; the revisions appear as you make them.

Note

The MRK indicator in the Status bar is bold when revision marking is on.

Shortcut

Double-click the MRK indicator to display the Revisions dialog box.

To review revision marks

1. Open the document.
2. Choose the **T**ools Re**v**isions command. The Revisions dialog box appears.
3. Choose the **R**eview button. If the Review button is dimmed, there are no revisions to review in the document. The Review Revisions dialog box appears. The insertion point moves to the nearest revision in the document. In Description, Word displays the name of the person who made the revision and the date and time the revision was made.

> **Tip**
>
> If the command buttons in the Review Revisions dialog box are dimmed, choose the Show **M**arks button. The commands appear and the Show **M**arks button changes to the Hide **M**arks button.

4. Choose any of the following options in the Review Revisions dialog box:

Option	**Description**
F**i**nd (left arrow)	Move to the preceding revision
Find (right arrow)	Move to the next revision
Accept	Accepts the revision; use the Find button to move to the next
Reject	Rejects the revision; use the button to move to the next.
Find **N**ext After Accept/Reject	Automatically finds the next revision after you accept or reject one
Undo Last	Reverses the last accept or reject

5. Choose Close to close the dialog box.

See also **Compare Versions**.

Ruler

You can use the horizontal ruler in any view to format selected paragraphs of text and page margins in your document. You can set tabs and indents or change the page margins and column widths using the horizontal ruler. Additionally, you can use the vertical ruler, in Page Layout and Print Preview views, to adjust the top and bottom margins of a document.

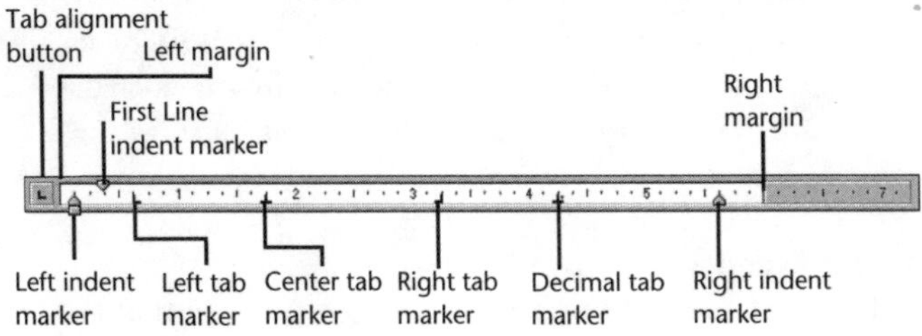

To display or hide the ruler

Choose the **V**iew **R**uler command. The menu closes and the horizontal ruler appears (in all views but Outline view). Both the horizontal and vertical rulers appear in Page Layout and Print Preview view.

To set tabs

1. Select the text, or position the insertion point at the place you are entering the text.
2. Click the tab alignment marker, located in the left corner of the horizontal ruler, to change the tab alignment.

Tip

When you click the tab alignment button, the left tab symbol changes to the center. You can then apply a center-aligned tab to the ruler and the text. Each time you click the tab alignment button, the tab alignment changes: left to center to right to decimal and back to left.

3. Position the mouse pointer on the lower part of the ruler at the point you want the tab stop located. Click the mouse.

Note

You can drag a tab marker on the ruler to a new location. A dotted, vertical line follows the tab marker through the document so you can align tab stops with other text.

To set indents

1. Select the text or position the insertion point at the place you want to enter text.
2. To indent the left edge of the text, drag the left indent marker (the small box on the left end of the ruler) on the ruler to the new position.

   To indent the right edge of text, drag the right indent marker (the triangle on the right edge of the ruler) on the ruler to a new position.

   To indent the first line of text, drag the first line indent marker (the top triangle on the left edge of the ruler) to a new position on the ruler.

To modify the margins

1. On the ruler, position the mouse pointer over the border between the white and gray of the ruler until the pointer changes to a double-headed arrow.

2. Drag the arrow and the margin along the ruler. A dotted vertical guideline follows as you drag the margin. Release the mouse button when the margin is correct.

> **Tip**
>
> When using columns, each column is indicated on the ruler with left, right, and first line markers and margin markers. Follow preceding directions for adjusting margins, tabs, and indents to adjust column measurements.

See also **Page Setup**, **Section Breaks**.

Save/Save As

See the Common Features section.

Section Breaks

To create sections in your document, you must enter a break after the first section and after every subsequent section. Breaks can start on a new page or coexist within one page.

> **Tip**
>
> Section breaks, like paragraph marks, hold the formatting for the preceding section. If you delete a section break, the formatting reverts to the same formatting as in the following section.

To insert a section break

1. Position the insertion point at the location you want to insert the section break.
2. Choose the **I**nsert **B**reak command. The Break dialog box appears.
3. In the Section Breaks area, choose from one of the following options:

Option	Description
Next Page	Creates a new section at the top of the page after the insertion point
Continuous	Creates a new section at the insertion point
Even Page	Creates a new section at the next even page
Odd Page	Creates a new section at the next odd page

4. Choose OK to close the dialog box. Word inserts the section break.

Tip

You can view the section break in Normal view. It appears as a double line with the words "End of Section" in the center of the line. To delete a section break, position the insertion point on the section break and press Delete.

Section Layout

You can format elements of each section in a document differently. You can, for example, change the page size, margins, and page orientation of one section without affecting the other sections in the document. Remember, Word stores all section formatting at the end of the section, in the section break.

To format a section

1. Position the insertion point in the section to be formatted. You can also select multiple sections or select specific text to be formatted.

2. The following table describes which commands contain which special options for section formatting:

Command	Tab or Option button	Section Formatting
File Page Set**u**p	**M**argins	Margins
File Page Set**u**p	Paper **S**ize	Paper size, page orientation
F**o**rmat **C**olumns		Columns
File Page Set**u**p	**L**ayout	Vertical text alignment
File Page Set**u**p	**L**ayout	Line numbers
Insert Foot**n**ote	**O**ptions button	Endnotes, footnotes
File Page Set**u**p	**L**ayout	Headers and footers
Insert Page N**u**mbers	**F**ormat button	Page numbers

3. In the **A**pply to area, choose from the following:

Option	Description
Selected Sections	Applies changes to only selected sections
This Section	Applies change to the current section only
This Point Forward	Applies change to the current section and continues with all following sections
Whole Document	Applies change to all sections in document
Selected Text	Inserts section breaks before and after the selected text and applies changes to this new section

4. Choose OK to close the dialog box.

See also **Margins**, **Printing**, **Numbering Lines**, **Headers and Footers**, **Numbering Pages**, **Centering Text**, and **Columns**.

Select Text

You can select text and graphics—frames, pictures, and other objects—using the keyboard or mouse, or a combination of the two. You select text to perform various commands or actions, such as formatting characters and paragraphs, moving and copying text, and so on. You select graphics to move or copy them or to add shading and borders, for example.

To select using the mouse

Use any of the following techniques for selecting text or graphics with the mouse:

To select	Do this
Any amount of text	Drag the mouse I-beam across the text: thus changing the text to reverse video
One word	Double-click the word; the space following the word is also selected
One or several lines of text	Click the mouse pointer in the Selection bar (an invisible area on the left edge of the document area where the mouse I-beam changes to a pointer); drag the pointer to select more than one line of text.
One sentence	Ctrl+click the sentence
One paragraph	Triple-click the paragraph or double-click in the selection bar
A graphic	Click the graphic to reveal selection handles
Multiple graphics	Click the first graphic, hold the Shift key, and click the next
The entire document	Triple-click the selection bar

To select using the keyboard

Use any of the following techniques for selecting text or graphics with the keyboard:

To select	Press
One character to the right/left	Shift+right/left arrow
To the beginning/end of a word	Ctrl+Shift+left/right arrow
To the beginning/end of a line	Ctrl+Shift+up/down arrow
One screen up/down	Shift+PageUp/PageDown
Entire document	Ctrl+A

Shading

See **Borders and Shading**.

Sort Text

You can sort text alphabetically, numerically, or by date—in ascending or descending order. Word sorts items (separated by paragraph returns) by first sorting symbols, then numbers, and finally letters. To sort those words beginning with the same character, Word uses the second character, then the third, and so on.

To sort a list

1. Select the text to be sorted.
2. Choose the T**a**ble Sor**t** Text command. The Sort Text dialog box appears.
3. In **S**ort By, the default is Paragraphs. In T**y**pe, choose Text, Number, or Date.
4. Choose either **A**scending or **D**escending as the sort order.

5. Choose OK to close the dialog box and sort the list.

Note

When sorting by Number or Date, the number or date can be anywhere in the paragraph.

Tip

If Word sorts a numbered list, it sorts the items regardless of the numbers; then Word automatically renumbers the sorted items.

Special Characters

You can insert symbols and other special characters, such as the trademark symbol, various bullet shapes, or an em dash. Additionally, you can insert various other font symbols you may have received with other Windows programs, including Wingdings (a font that includes scissors, pointing hands, and many others), Monotype Sorts (includes symbols such as stars, check marks, numbers in circles, and arrows), and so on.

To insert a symbol

1. Position the insertion point.
2. Choose the **I**nsert **S**ymbol command. The Symbol dialog box appears.
3. Choose the **S**ymbols tab.
4. In **F**ont, choose Symbol. You can click the down arrow and choose a different font to view various symbols.

Tip

Select any symbol by clicking it once with the mouse; the symbol enlarges so you can see it better.

5. Select the symbol you want and choose **I**nsert. Word places the symbol in the text at the insertion point. The Symbol dialog box remains open.

6. Choose another symbol to insert or choose Close to close the dialog box.

To insert a special character

1. Position the insertion point

2. Choose the **I**nsert **S**ymbol command. The Symbol dialog box appears.

3. Choose the S**p**ecial Characters tab.

4. In **C**haracter, select the special character you want to insert.

> **Tip**
>
> Notice the shortcut key beside an often-used symbol. Word assigns key combinations to the most commonly used symbols. The next time you need that particular symbol, press the shortcut key instead of opening the Symbol dialog box.

5. Choose **I**nsert. Word inserts the special character, but leaves the Symbol dialog box open. You can insert another character or choose Close to close the dialog box.

Spelling

Word checks your spelling and queries any words it finds that are not listed in the main or custom dictionary. You can choose whether to ignore the word, correct it, or add it to the custom dictionary. Word also finds and queries instances of repeated words, such as "a a" or "there there," and capitalization errors, such as "THe."

Note

Word can also use other installed dictionaries, such as a foreign language dictionary, a technical dictionary, a legal dictionary, and so on. You can use dictionaries packaged with other applications or purchase special dictionaries wherever software applications are sold.

To spell check the document

1. Position the insertion point at the top of the document by pressing Ctrl+Home.

   Note

   You can, alternatively, select a word, paragraph, or section, and spell check only the selection.

2. Choose the **T**ools **S**pelling command. Word begins to check the spelling.

   If it finds no misspelled words, Word displays a message box notifying you the spelling check is complete. Choose OK to close the box.

   If Word finds a misspelled or questionable word, it displays the Spelling dialog box. The questionable word is highlighted in the document and displayed in the Not in Dictionar**y** text box.

   Tip

   You can click the document window to edit the document and the Spelling dialog box remains on-screen. When you are ready to resume the spelling check, choose the **S**tart button in the Spelling dialog box.

3. Choose one of the following options:

Option	Description
Change **T**o	Enter the correct spelling in this text box
Suggestio**n**s	Choose the correct spelling from the list of suggested words; the word you select from the list moves to the Change **T**o text box
Ignore	Skips this one incidence of the word's spelling
I**g**nore All	Skips all occurrences of this word's spelling in this document
Change	Replaces this one instance of the misspelled word with the one in the Change **T**o text box
Change A**l**l	Replaces all instances of the misspelled word with the one in the Change **T**o text box
Add	Adds the new word to the dictionary
Suggest	Lists some suggestions in the Suggestio**n**s list box
AutoCo**r**rect	Adds the word to the AutoCorrect list so Word automatically corrects the misspelling as you type
Options	Sets preferences for the Spelling checker
Undo Last	Reverts the last correction to its original state

Shortcut

Press F7 to display the Spelling dialog box.

See also **AutoCorrect**.

Starting Word for Windows

See the Common Features section.

Styles

Assign styles to the text in your document to quickly format the text and to create consistency within the document and among related documents. Using styles not only makes your documents look professional, it saves you time and energy. You can use the styles contained in Word templates or create your own styles. You can modify styles, delete and add styles, and copy styles to other documents.

A style contains character and paragraph formatting, such as 18-point Times New Roman, center-aligned. Each time you assign that style to text, the text automatically takes on that formatting. If you change the style's formatting to 24-point, for example, all text assigned to that style changes to 24-point.

To apply a style

1. If the Formatting toolbar is not already displayed, display it by choosing **V**iew **T**oolbars and choosing Formatting from the list of **T**oolbars. Choose OK.

2. Select the text to which you want to apply a style or position the insertion point at the beginning of the text you plan to type.

3. In the Style box on the Formatting toolbar, click the down arrow. From the list, choose a style to assign. The list closes and the text takes on the style characteristics.

To change a style

1. Select or position the insertion point in the text you want to change.

2. Choose the F**o**rmat **S**tyle command. The Style dialog box appears.

Note

You can change the font, size, alignment, or other formatting of the selected text; however, changing formatting without using the F**o**rmat **S**tyle command changes only the selected text. Other text assigned to that style will not be changed.

3. In **S**tyles, make sure the style you want to change is selected.

Tip

In the Description area of the dialog box, Word displays the character and paragraph formatting assigned to the specific style so you can review the formatting before modifying it.

4. Choose the **M**odify button to edit the style. The Modify Style dialog box appears.
5. Choose the F**o**rmat button. A menu list appears, containing the elements you can choose to modify: **F**ont, **P**aragraph, **T**abs, **B**order, **L**anguage, Fra**m**e, and **N**umbering.
6. Select any of these elements from the Format menu and a corresponding dialog box appears.
7. From the dialog box, choose the options you want to change and then choose OK.
8. Choose OK in the Modify Style dialog box and choose **A**pply in the Style dialog box. Word returns to the document with the selected style modified.

To create a style

1. Select the text.

2. Using the Formatting toolbar and/or the F**o**rmat menu, change any formatting, such as font, type size, spacing, alignment, bullets, tabs, or borders.

3. Position the insertion point in the Style box in the Formatting toolbar. Delete the text and enter a new style name. Press Enter. Word assigns the formatting of the selected text to the new style name.

To copy a style to the Normal template

1. Save the document containing the style you want to copy.

2. Choose the F**o**rmat **S**tyle command. The Style dialog box appears.

3. Choose the **O**rganizer button. The Organizer dialog box appears with the **S**tyles tab selected.

4. In the **I**n (document name) list on the left, select the style you want to copy.

> **Tip**
>
> You can copy multiple styles by holding the Ctrl key as you select the style names.

5. Choose the **C**opy button. The selected style copies to the **T**o NORMAL.DOT, the normal template, for use with other documents.

6. Choose Close. Word returns to the document.

> **Note**
>
> You can also delete and rename styles using the Organizer dialog box. Select the style and choose either the **D**elete or **R**ename button. If you choose **D**elete, Word displays a confirmation dialog box; choose **Y**es to delete the selected style. If you choose **R**ename, Word displays the Rename dialog box; enter a new name and choose OK.

See also **Templates**.

Summary Info

See **Document Summary**.

Table of Authorities

A table of authorities lists both long and short citations in a legal document. Citations are references to rules, statutes, and so on, within the brief or legal document. First, you must mark the citations; Word provides most common categories under which you can organize the citations.

When you compile the table of authorities, Word lists all of the long citations and includes page numbers for all long and short citations marked.

To mark citations

1. Press Ctrl+Home to move to the beginning of the document.
2. Locate the first citation and select it.

> **Tip**
>
> The first occurrence of a citation should be a long citation, including text such as "Frost v. Davis, 25 Wn. 3d 345 (1982)." After the first occurrence, the citation is shortened: "Frost v. Davis," for example.

3. Press Alt+Shift+I. The Mark Citation dialog box appears. The selected text appears in the Selected **T**ext text box.
4. Edit the text as you want it to appear in the table of authorities.
5. Click the Cate**g**ory button. The Edit Category dialog box appears.

6. In the **C**ategory box, select the category that applies to the citation and choose OK to return to the Mark Citation dialog box.

7. In the **S**hort Citation box, edit the text so it matches the short citation as it reads in the text.

8. Choose one of the following options:

Option	Description
Mark	Marks only the long citation
Mark **A**ll	Marks all long and short citations that match those in the Mark Citation dialog box.

Tip

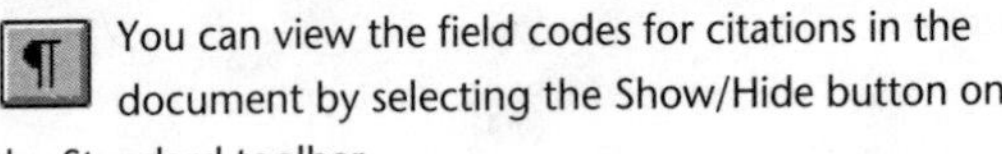

You can view the field codes for citations in the document by selecting the Show/Hide button on the Standard toolbar.

9. You can find the next citation by choosing the **N**ext Citation button. Word searches the document for text normally found in a citation, such as “in re” or “v.” Continue to mark citations until you have marked them all.

10. Choose the Close button when you are done.

To compile the table of authorities

1. Position the insertion point where you want to insert the table of authorities.

2. Choose the **I**nsert Inde**x** and Tables command. The Index and Tables dialog box appears.

3. Select the Table of **A**uthorities tab.

Word

4. In the Category box, select the category you want to compile; alternatively, you can choose the All option to compile all categories.

5. Choose from the following options:

Option	**Description**
Use **P**assim	Replaces five or more page references to the same authority with "passim"
Keep Original Fo**r**matting	Retains the formatting of the citation as it is in the document
Ta**b** Leader	Inserts a tab leader between entries and page numbers

6. In the Forma**t**s box, choose the format for the table. You can view an example of each format in the Pre**v**iew box.

7. Choose OK to compile the table of authorities. Word inserts the formatted table at the insertion point.

Table of Contents

You can create a table of contents using Word's built-in styles or by marking your own entries for the table. To use Word's styles, apply Headings 1 through 9 to the headings in your document. Word then uses the style headings as entries in the table of contents.

After you mark the entries in the text, you compile the table of contents.

To use built-in styles

1. Format your document using the built-in Heading styles.

2. Position the insertion point where you want to insert the table of contents.

3. Choose the **I**nsert Inde**x** and Tables command. The Index and Tables dialog box appears.

4. Choose the Table of **C**ontents tab.

5. In the Forma**t**s box, select the format you want for the table of contents. View examples of the different formats in the Pre**v**iew box.

6. Choose any of the following options:

Option	Description
Show Page Numbers	Displays page numbers in the table of contents
Right Align Page Numbers	Places page numbers along the right edge of the column or page
Show **L**evels	Enters or selects the number of heading levels you want to display
Ta**b** Leader	Selects a tab leader to separate the entry from the page number

7. Choose OK to compile the table of contents. Word inserts the formatted table at the insertion point.

Note

You can also add entries that are not formatted with a heading style. See the following section.

Marking your own entries

1. Select the text you want to mark as an entry. Press Alt+Shift+O. The Mark Table of Contents Entry dialog box appears.

2. The selected text appears in the **E**ntry text box. Edit the text if you want.

> **Note**
>
> In Table **I**dentifier, C is the default choice; C stands for table of contents.

3. In **L**evel, choose the level you want the marked text to be in the table of contents.
4. Choose **M**ark. The dialog box remains open so you can continue to mark entries.
5. Click the mouse in the document window and select another entry for the table of contents. Click the Mark Table of Contents Entry and select the options.
6. Choose **M**ark and continue to mark any other entries.
7. When finished, choose Close.

To compile your own entries

1. Position the insertion point where you want to insert the table.
2. Choose the **I**nsert Inde**x** and Tables command. The Index and Tables dialog box appears.
3. Choose the Table of **C**ontents tab.
4. In Forma**t**s, choose a style and view the style in the Pre**v**iew dialog box.
5. Choose any of the following options:

Option	Description
Show Page Numbers	Displays page numbers in the table of contents
Right Align Page Numbers	Places page numbers along the right edge of the column or page

(continues)

Option	Description
Show **L**evels	Enters or selects the number of heading levels you want to display
Ta**b** Leader	Selects a tab leader to separate the entry from the page number

6. Choose the **O**ptions button. The Table of Contents Options dialog box appears.

7. Choose the Table **E**ntry fields option at the bottom of the dialog box so it has an X in the check box. Deselect the **S**tyles option at the top of the dialog box, unless you want to combine your marked entries with the headings style entries.

8. Choose OK to return to the Index and Tables dialog box. Choose OK to compile the table of contents. Word compiles the table and inserts it into the document at the insertion point.

To update a table of contents

1. Mark the entry or entries you want to add to the table.

2. Point the mouse at the table of contents and press the right mouse button. The quick menu appears.

3. Choose the Update Field command. The Update Table of Contents dialog box appears.

4. Choose Update **E**ntire Table and choose OK. Word adds the entries to the table of contents.

Table of Figures

After adding numbered captions to your figures, you can compile a table of figures. Additionally, you can compile a different list for each type of figure drawings, clip art, graphs, and so on.

To compile a table of figures

1. Insert captions to the figures you want to include in the table.
2. Position the insertion point where you want to insert the table.
3. Choose the **I**nsert Inde**x** and Tables command. The Index and Tables dialog box appears.
4. Choose the Table of **F**igures tab.
5. In the Caption **L**abel, choose the caption label you used in your figures.
6. In Forma**t**s, choose a format for the table. View an example of each format in the Pre**v**iew box.
7. Choose any of the following options:

Option	Description
Show Page Numbers	Displays page numbers in the table of contents
Right Align Page Numbers	Places page numbers along the right edge of the column or page
Show **L**evels	Enters or selects the number of heading levels you want to display
Ta**b** Leader	Selects a tab leader to separate the entry from the page number

8. Choose OK to compile the table. Word inserts the table at the insertion point.

Tip

You can use the quick menu to update the table of figures if you change, add, or delete captions and figures. Point the mouse at the table and press the right mouse button. Choose the Update Fields command. In the Update Fields dialog box, choose **E**ntire table, and then choose OK.

See also **Captions**.

Tables

Use tables to organize information such as text or numbers. Data presented in table format is easy for the reader to understand at a glance. Additionally, you can format the text in tables using styles or character formatting; you can add borders and shading to specific cells or the entire table.

To create a table

1. Position the insertion point where you want to insert the table.
2. Choose the T**a**ble **I**nsert Table command. The Insert Table dialog box appears.
3. In Number of **C**olumns, enter or select the number of columns for your table.
4. In Number of **R**ows, enter or select the number of rows.
5. You can change the Column **W**idth by entering or selecting a measurement, in inches or other set measurement.

Note

Selecting Auto Column Width inserts equal width columns between the left and right margins.

Tip

In the Insert Table dialog box, choose the Wi**z**ard button to help format the table. The Wizard displays various table styles, heading styles for rows and columns, text and number alignment choices, and so on.

Alternatively, you can choose the **A**utoFormat button to choose from several different table formats, borders, shading, fonts, and so on.

6. Choose OK when you are finished. Word inserts the table at the insertion point.

Note

If you do not see the table gridlines, choose the T**a**ble **G**ridlines command to turn the gridlines on. This is a toggle command; you can turn the gridlines off by selecting the command again.

Shortcut

You can also create a table by clicking the Insert Table button on the Standard toolbar. A grid of cells appears; choose the number of columns and rows you want by dragging the mouse over the cells. When you release the mouse button, Word inserts the table.

To add columns or rows

1. Select one or more rows or columns. The number of rows or columns you select indicates how many rows or columns you want to add; for example, select one row to insert one row, select four columns to insert four columns.

Note

The inserted rows or columns are added above the selected rows or to the left of the selected columns.

2. Choose the T**a**ble **I**nsert Rows/Columns command. Word inserts the row or columns.

To delete rows or columns

1. Select the rows or columns to be deleted.

2. Choose the T**a**ble **D**elete Rows/Columns command. Word deletes the selected rows or columns.

See also **Borders and Shading**, **Formatting Characters**, and **Styles**.

Tabs

Tabs are one method of organizing text or numbers in a document. If you use tabs to separate the text, for example, it appears to be divided into columns. Tabs, however, are easier to change and move than columns. When setting tabs, you can choose from a variety of alignments for each tab stop. Additionally, you can choose from three tab leaders.

To set tabs

1. Select the text to be tabbed or position the insertion point.
2. Choose the F**o**rmat **T**abs command. The Tabs dialog box appears.
3. In **T**ab Stop Position, enter a measurement, in inches, for the first tab stop.
4. In Alignment, choose from one of the following:

Option	Description
Left	Aligns the text or number on the left, beginning at the tab stop
Center	Aligns the text or number centered on the tab stop
Right	Aligns the text or number on the right on the tab stop
Decimal	Aligns all numbers on the decimal point at the tab stop; if the number has no decimal, the number extends to the left of the tab stop
Bar	Places a vertical line through the selected text at the ruler position you specify, whether you enter a tab on that line of text or not

5. In Leader, choose from the following:

Option	Description
1	No leader
2	Dotted line leader
3	Dashed line leader
4	Solid line leader

6. Choose the **S**et button to set the tab. The measurement moves to the list below **T**ab Stop Position. You can enter the next tab stop in the text box.

> **Note**
>
> Although the measurement remains in the **T**ab Stop Position text box, the number is selected. When you enter the measurement for the next tab stop, you delete the selected number. As long as you choose the **S**et button, the first tab setting remains active.

7. When finished entering the tab stops, choose OK to close the dialog box.

> **Note**
>
> Word sets tab stops every 1/2 inch by default. To change the distance between the default tab stops, change the measurement in the Default Tab Stops box in the Tabs dialog box.

See also **Ruler**.

Templates

A template is a foundation for creating documents with similar styles, contents, and so on. Word includes many templates—including memo, letter, resume, newsletter, and so on—that you can use as a base for your documents. Additionally, you can modify or edit any of the elements in a template, including margins, page size, font, paragraph, and formatting, to make it better suit your document. You can also create your own templates.

To use a template to create a new document

1. Choose the **F**ile **N**ew command. Word displays the New dialog box.

2. Choose **T**emplates, and select from the list which template you want to use.

> **Tip**
>
> Select a template and view its description in the Description area of the dialog box.

3. Choose OK to close the dialog box. Word displays the template as the basis for your new document.

> **Note**
>
> To get an idea of what the template contains, first change to Page Layout view. Display the Formatting toolbar and look over the styles in the Style box. You can also view the margins, page size, and page orientation (**F**ile Page Set**u**p command) for an idea of the template's contents.

To create a template

1. Choose the **F**ile **N**ew command. The New dialog box appears.

2. Choose any of the templates that offers a foundation close to the template you plan to create. Alternatively, you can choose the Normal template, which is very basic with few styles and formatting. With the Normal template, you can start from scratch.

3. In the New area, choose T**e**mplate and choose OK. Word opens the template.

4. Make any changes, including margins, paper size, columns, and so on; create styles for the text you plan to use and add any text you want to remain in the template.

5. Choose the **F**ile Save **A**s command. The Save As dialog box appears.

6. In File **N**ame, enter a name for the template. If you enter an extension, make sure you enter the DOT template extension. Choose OK to save the template.

7. Choose the **F**ile **C**lose command. To use the template, choose the **F**ile **N**ew command and select your template from the list of templates. Choose OK.

> **Note**
>
> You can attach a template to an existing document by choosing the **F**ile **T**emplates command. In the Templates and Add-ins dialog box, choose the **A**ttach button and select the template you want to use. Choose OK twice to close the dialog boxes. The added template changes none of the styles already assigned but adds new styles to the template for you to use.

See also **Wizards**, **Styles**.

Thesaurus

Word's thesaurus offers synonyms, antonyms, and related words for many words in your documents. You can also look up other words after opening the thesaurus.

To use the thesaurus

1. Select the word or position the insertion point within the word you want to look up.

2. Choose the **T**ools **T**hesaurus command. The Thesaurus dialog box appears with the selected word in the Loo**k**ed Up text box.

3. The **M**eanings list displays the various meanings and parts of speech the word could represent. Select the meaning that is closest to your word.

Note

Some words you look up will include Antonyms and Related words as choices in the **M**eanings list. Select either of these options to view a detailed list in the Synonyms list box.

4. A list of synonyms appears below the Replace with **S**ynonyms text box. Scroll through the list and select the synonym you want.

Tip

You can also double-click any word in either the **M**eanings or **S**ynonyms list to display synonyms for that word.

Alternatively, you can enter a new word in the Replace with **S**ynonym text box and choose the **L**ook Up button. Word displays a new list of meanings and synonyms.

You also can move back through the choices you have viewed by choosing the Previous button.

5. The selected synonym appears in the Replace with **S**ynonym text box. Choose the **R**eplace button to close the dialog box and replace the selected word with the synonym.

Note

If you want to close the Thesaurus dialog box without selecting a synonym or other word, choose the Cancel button.

Shortcut

Select a word and press Shift+F7 to look that word up in the Thesaurus dialog box.

Toolbars

See the Integration section.

Underline

See **Formatting Characters**.

Undo

See the Common Features section.

Views

Word enables you to choose from a variety of views so you can see the various elements you need to work with in your document. Some views are better for entering and editing text without worrying about page and text formatting; other views work better for viewing the entire page as it will print, or for adjusting margins and columns. You can change views easily and quickly so you can always see your document in a way that suits your work best.

To change views

Choose the **V**iew menu, and then choose from one of the following options:

Option	Description
Normal	Presents the text in a draft view—no columns or margins are formatted. Gives you quick screen redraw and makes text editing fast and easy. The default view.

(continues)

Option	Description
Outline	Provides the Outlining toolbar and displays text in outline formatting: indents, headings formatted, and so on
Page Layout	Presents text on a page that shows margins, columns, graphics, and text the way it will be printed
Master Document	Shows text in a view similar to Outline view, including the Outlining toolbar with additional buttons for Master Document view; Enables you to work in a single document while seeing all parts of the document
F**u**ll Screen	Removes all screen elements—status bar, menu, title bar, scroll bars, and so on—so you can view just the document. Press Esc to return to the previous view

Shortcuts

You can choose one of the following buttons on the Horizontal toolbar to change views quickly:

 Normal view

 Page Layout view

 Outline view

Wizards

Wizards are a series of dialog boxes that ask you questions about the document you are about to create. Word designs and formats the document for you, based on your specifications. All you have to do is enter the text. You can use any of Word's document wizards: Agenda Wizard, Award Wizard, Calendar Wizard, Fax Wizard, Letter Wizard, Memo Wizard, Newsletter Wizard, Pleading Wizard, Resume Wizard, or Table Wizard.

To open a wizard

1. Choose the **F**ile **N**ew command. The New dialog box appears.

2. In **T**emplate, choose the wizard that represents the document you want to create.

3. Choose OK. Word displays a series of Wizard dialog boxes; the number of dialog boxes depends on the wizard you choose.

   Each dialog box asks questions about the style, format, and design of the selected document. The wizard dialog boxes are easy to understand and follow. Answer the questions presented to you in each dialog box.

4. After answering the questions in each dialog box, you can choose any of the following options:

Option	Description
Cancel	Cancel the wizard and the document
Next	Proceed to the next dialog box
Back	Move to the previous dialog box
Finish	Stop the process at this point; Word creates and formats the document with whatever information you entered and displays the document for you to complete

5. At the end of the wizard, Word notifies you that it is finished. When Word displays the last dialog box, choose **F**inish and Word creates the document for you.

Note

When Word notifies you it is done, it gives you two options: display help as you work or just display the document. You can choose to display help and Word guides you to completing the document, step-by-step.

See also the Common Features section.

Word Count

Word can count the number of words in your document or in the selected text quickly. At the same time, Word counts the number of words, characters, paragraphs, and lines.

To count the words in a document

1. Choose the **T**ools **W**ord Count command. Word counts the elements in the document and displays the Word Count dialog box with the numbers of pages, words, characters, paragraphs, and lines in your document.

2. Choose Close to close the dialog box.

See also **Summary Info**, **Statistics**.

WordArt

See the Integration section.

Zoom

You can choose to reduce or enlarge the elements on-screen so that you can better see the text, a graphic, or the entire document. In addition to choosing one of the views from the **V**iew menu, you can choose to view a document in a variety of magnifications.

To magnify the view

1. Choose the **V**iew **Z**oom command; the Zoom dialog box appears with these options:

> **Note**
>
> If you use Page Layout view, you have two additional options for zoom: **W**hole Page and **M**any Pages.

Option	Description
200%	Double the magnification of the default (100%) view
100%	Shows the document at actual size
75%	Displays the document at 75 percent of actual size
Page Width	Shows the page from left margin to right margin
Whole Page	Reduces the display so you can see the entire page on-screen
Many Pages	Reduces the view of the pages, enabling you to view two or more pages of the document in print preview; click the monitor and drag the mouse to the number of pages you want to view
P**e**rcent	Enter or select the percentage of magnification

Note

When you choose an option in the Zoom dialog box, view the sample in the Preview box. Additionally, sample text sizes appear in the text box below the Preview box.

2. Choose OK.

Shortcuts

You can choose the Zoom control down arrow on the Standard toolbar to change views of the document. Select a zoom percentage between 10 and 200 percent or other view from the drop-down list.

See also **Views**.

Excel

Excel is the powerful, full-featured spreadsheet program that comes with Microsoft Office. Use Excel to organize data and to assist in your financial planning. Additionally, you can create graphic representations of your financial data in the form of graphs or charts, such as bar charts, area charts, line graphs, and pie graphs.

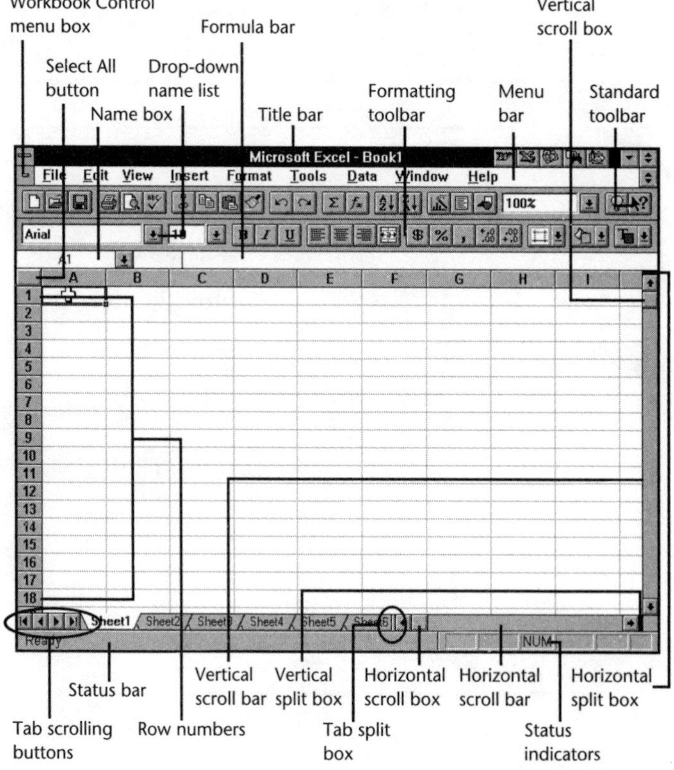

Alignment

Alignment refers to the way text is organized within a cell. You can align text between the left and right cell edges, between the top and bottom cell edges, and change the text orientation within a cell.

To change the horizontal alignment

1. Select the cell you want to align.
2. Choose the Format Cells command. The Format Cells dialog box appears.
3. Choose the Alignment tab.
4. In the Horizontal area, choose one of the following options:

Option	Description
General	Automatically aligns text to the left, numbers to the right, and logical and error values in the center
Left	Aligns cell contents to the left
Center	Centers cell contents
Right	Aligns cell contents to the right
Fill	Fills the cell by repeating the text in the selected cell; additionally, if blank cells to the right of the selected cell also have the Fill alignment, they are filled with the selected text.
Justify	Gives text in a cell even left and right edges
Center **a**cross selection	Centers the entry across the selected cells

> **Tip**
>
> Choose the **W**rap Text option if you have more text than will fit in one cell; the cell enlarges as you enter the text and the text wraps to the next line.

5. Choose OK to close the dialog box.

To change the vertical alignment

1. Select the text you want to align.
2. Choose the Format Cells command. The Format Cells dialog box appears.
3. Choose the Alignment tab.
4. In the Vertical area, choose one of the following options:

Option	Description
Top	Aligns the cell contents along the top of the cell
C**e**nter	Aligns the cell contents in the center, or middle, of the cell
Bottom	Aligns the cell contents along the bottom of the cell
Justify	Aligns the cell so the contents are equally spaced from top to bottom
Center **a**cross selection	Centers the contents of the cell across selected cells

5. Choose OK to close the dialog box.

To change text orientation within a cell

1. Select the text you want to align.

2. Choose the Format Cells command. The Format Cells dialog box appears.

3. Choose the Alignment tab.

4. In Orientation, choose one of the four options, as shown in the examples. You can choose to orient text horizontally or in any of three vertical orientations: vertically from top to bottom, vertically from left to right, or vertically from right to left.

5. Choose OK to close the dialog box.

Shortcuts

 Click the Align Right button in the Formatting toolbar.

 Click the Align Left button in the Formatting toolbar.

 Click the Center button on the Formatting toolbar.

Auditing Worksheets

Excel provides tracers that enable you to find precedents, dependents, and errors related to any cell in the worksheet. A precedent is the cell referred to by the formula in the active cell; a dependent is a cell containing the formula referring to the active cell.

To trace dependents

1. Choose the Tools Options command; select the View tab. Make sure the Hide All command is *not* selected by removing the X.

2. Select the cell you want to trace.

3. Choose the Tools Auditing command. A secondary menu appears.

4. Choose Trace Dependents. Excel will display arrows pointing from the selected area to any dependent cells.

5. Double-click any arrow to select the cell at the other end of the arrow — the cell the arrow is pointing to.

To trace precedent data and formulas

1. Choose the Tools Options command; select the View tab. Make sure the Hide All command is *not* selected.
2. Select the cell containing the formula you want to trace.
3. Choose the Tools Auditing command. A secondary menu appears.
4. Choose Trace Precedents. Excel will display arrows pointing to the selected cell from any precedent cells.
5. Double-click an arrow to select the cell at the other end of the arrow — the cell the arrow is pointing to.

> **Note**
>
> You must position the mouse pointer over the arrow so that it changes from the cross to a pointer.

> **Note**
>
> Blue or solid arrows indicate the direct precedents; red or dotted arrows show formulas that refer to error values. Dashed arrows with a spreadsheet icon refer to a separate spreadsheet.

To find error values visually

1. Choose the Tools Options command; select the View tab. Make sure the Hide All command is *not* selected.
2. Select the cell you want to trace.

Tip

The following are error values: #DIV/0!, #NAME?, #NULL!, #NUM!, #N/A, #REF!, and #VALUE!.

3. Choose the Tools Auditing command. A secondary menu appears.

Note

Blue or solid arrows show the precedents of the first error-producing cell. Red or dotted arrows show the path of the first error value through successive formulas.

4. Choose Trace Error.

Note

Choose Trace **E**rror again to display the next step of precedents until you reach the initial values.

5. Double-click an arrow to select the cell at the other end— the cell the arrow is pointing to. When the cell is selected, you can correct the error.

To Remove tracer arrows

1. Choose the Tools Auditing command. A secondary menu appears.

2. Choose Remove All Arrows. The arrows disappear.

Shortcuts

To display the Auditing toolbar, choose the **T**ools **A**uditing command, and then select **S**how Auditing toolbar.

To trace dependents, click the Trace Dependents button on the Auditing toolbar.

To trace precedents, click the Trace Precedents button on the Auditing toolbar.

To trace errors, click the Trace Errors button on the Auditing toolbar.

To remove all tracer arrows, click the Remove All Arrows button on the Auditing toolbar.

Excel

Bold

See **Formatting**.

Borders

You can apply any one of various border styles to a cell, row, column, or table. You can also apply a border to only the left, right, top, or bottom of a cell or group of selected cells.

To apply borders

1. Select the cell or cells where you want to place a border.
2. Choose the Format Cells command. The Format Cells dialog box appears.
3. Choose the Border tab.
4. In the Border area, choose the placement of the border: Outline, Left, Right, Top, or Bottom. The border applies to all selected cells. The selected Line style will be displayed beside the choice line.

5. In the Style area, choose the style of line: dotted, dashed, solid, thick, thin, double, and so on, from the style boxes.

Tip

You can also choose a color other than black (the default color). Click the **C**olor down arrow to display a box of available colors.

Note

To remove a border, select it from the Border choice box so that the sample line disappears from beside it.

6. Choose OK to close the dialog box.

Shortcut

To apply a border (default thickness), click the Borders button on the Formatting toolbar and choose the border and placement from the drop-down border box.

Alternatively, Press Ctrl+1 to display the Format Cells dialog box.

Calculating Worksheets

Excel performs many recalculations automatically as you work; if you change the data in a cell, Excel recalculates the results of the formulas and functions. Some calculations, however, must be done manually—certain date functions, for example.

To calculate a worksheet

1. Select the worksheet you want to calculate.

2. Choose the Tools Options command. The Options dialog box appears.

3. Choose the Calculation tab.

4. Choose the Calc Sheet button and choose OK to close the dialog box.

Shortcut

To calculate the formulas in all open documents, click the Calculate Now button.

Note

The Calculate Now button can be added to any toolbar. To reveal the quick menu, right-click on any toolbar. Choose the Customize command. In the Customize dialog box, choose the Utility category. The Calculate Now button is stored in this category. Drag the button out of the dialog box and place it on any displayed toolbar.

Centering

In addition to centering text within a cell or group of cells, you can center a report within the margins of the page for printing. When centering the report, you can center it between the left and right margins and/or the top and bottom margins.

To center a report on the page

1. Choose the File Page Setup command. The Page Setup dialog box appears.

2. Choose the Margins tab.

3. In the Center on Page area, choose one or both of the following options:

Option	Description
Horizontally	Divides the white space around the cells between the left and right margins
Vertically	Divides the white space around the cells between the top and bottom margins

4. Choose OK to close the dialog box; alternatively, you can choose Print to print the report.

See also **Alignment**.

Charts

You can choose from the many chart types and formats that Excel provides. By selecting any amount of data in your worksheet, you can create a chart, and with the ChartWizard's help, you can produce attractive, professional-looking additions to your documents. You can edit the data and chart elements easily, so you produce the exact representation of your data that you need.

To create a chart

1. Select the data you want to include in the chart, including labels.
2. Choose the Insert Chart command. A secondary menu appears.
3. Choose from one of the following options:

Option	Description
On This Sheet	Draw and create the chart on the current worksheet
As New Sheet	Draw and create the chart on a new sheet, created by Excel

4. The mouse pointer changes to the chart tool (a cross with a small chart icon attached) if you choose On this Chart. Drag the tool to define the size and shape of the chart you are creating. Alternatively, you can place the cross-hair pointer to position the upper left corner of the chart and click to have Excel insert a default-sized chart.

   If you chose As New Sheet, Excel displays the ChartWizard.

5. Excel displays the first of five ChartWizard dialog boxes. This first box confirms the selected range for the chart. If the range is not correct, enter the correct range in the Range text box. Choose the Next button.

6. The ChartWizard Step 2 of 5 dialog box appears. Fifteen chart types are displayed; select the type of chart you want to use.

7. Click the Next button. The ChartWizard Step 3 of 5 dialog box appears. Select any of 10 formats for the chart. The formats displayed relate specifically to the chart type you chose in the last dialog box.

Tip

Click the **B**ack button if you want to review (or change) a previously selected option.

8. Choose the Next button. The ChartWizard Step 4 of 5 appears displaying a Sample Chart. In the dialog box, choose from the following options:

Option	Description
Data Series in **R**ows	Specifies the data series displays in rows
Data Series in **C**olumns	Displays data series in columns

(continues)

Option	Description
Use First Rows	Specifies which rows/columns are used as the axis or labels text, depending on the selected chart type
U**s**e First Columns	Specifies which rows/columns are used for legend or titles text, depending on the selected chart type

Tip

After selecting options from the ChartWizard, view the results in the Sample Chart box. You can change the options until you are satisfied with the sample chart.

9. Click the Next button. The ChartWizard Step 5 of 5 dialog box appears. Choose from the following options:

Option	Description
Add a Legend?	If you want to add a legend to the chart, choose Y**e**s; if not, choose **N**o. Yes is the default.
Chart Title	Enter a title in the text box
Axis Titles	Enter a title for the X-axis in the **X** text box; enter a title for the Y-axis in the **Y** text box, if applicable

10. Click Finish to complete the chart. Excel creates the chart and displays it on-screen. Excel also displays the Chart toolbar.

Tip

You can move the chart around on the page by clicking it to display the black selection handles. Position the mouse pointer anywhere inside the chart box and drag the box to a new position.

Editing the Chart Data

You will probably edit the data in your worksheet many times before you are finished with it. You can add, remove, or modify chart data so your chart is up to date with your figures.

To add data to the chart

1. Select the data in the worksheet that you want to add to the chart.
2. Select the Edit Copy command; alternatively, you can press Ctrl+C.
3. Select the chart, whether it is on the same sheet or a separate sheet. Select the Edit Paste command; alternatively, press Ctrl+V. The new data is represented in the chart.

Shortcut

You can use the Copy and Paste buttons from the Standard toolbar to copy the selected data and paste it in the worksheet.

To remove data from the chart

1. Double-click the chart to edit it.
2. Click the column, bar, line, or other representative mark you want to delete.
3. Press the Delete key. The data series is deleted from the chart.

Note

The data is not deleted from the worksheet if you delete the series from the chart. You can select and delete the data from the worksheet and Excel deletes it from the chart automatically.

To modify chart data

1. In the worksheet, change any of the numbers you need to modify.
2. The chart adjusts automatically.

Editing the Chart Elements

Excel enables you to change the chart type and adjust other options within the chart, such as the marker (or column in a column or bar chart) placement, series order, and chart subtype.

To change the chart type

1. Double-click the chart to activate it. A screened border appears around the outer edge of the chart to indicate it is activated.
2. Choose the Format Chart Type command. The Chart Type dialog box appears.
3. In Chart Dimension, choose either 2-D or 3-D. When you select one of the two options, examples of the charts appear in the boxes below.

Tip

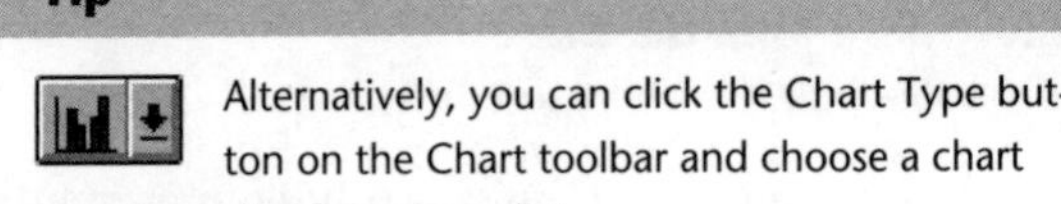

Alternatively, you can click the Chart Type button on the Chart toolbar and choose a chart type from the drop-down list.

4. Select any of the examples and choose OK. Excel changes the chart type.

To format markers and clusters

1. Double-click the chart to activate it. The screened border appears around the chart frame.
2. Choose the Format 1 Column Group command. The Format Column Group dialog box appears.

Note

The **1** Column Group command defines that the chart is a column chart. If the chart is a bar chart, for example, the command would then be **1** Bar Group. The name of the dialog box also changes with the chart type.

3. Select from the following tabs:

- *Subtype tab.* To fine-tune the chart, choose from the displayed variations of chart types.
- *Series Order tab.* Select one of the labels in the Series Order list and choose to move it Up or Down. As the label moves on the list, an example box shows how the corresponding data point moves in the chart.
- *Options tab.* The options appearing in this tab varyaccording to the chart type you have chosen. The most commonly-used options follow:

  2-D Bar and Column Charts. Choose the Over lap option and enter a value of 0 to 100 to overlap the markers within a cluster; enter a value between 0 and -100 to set a gap between markers in a cluster.

  3-D Bar, 3-D Column, Bar, Column, Line Charts. Choose the Gap Width option and enter a value of 0 to 500 to set a gap between clusters.

  Stacked Bar, Stacked Column Charts. Choose the Series Lines option to connect the tops of the data markers with lines.

  All Charts. Choose the Vary Colors By Point/ Slice option if your chart has only one data series. This option assigns a different color or marker to each data marker.

  3-D Charts. Enter a value of 0 to 500 in Gap Depth to change the distance between data markers. If using a column chart, the range is 20 to2,000.

3-D Charts. Enter a value of 0 to 500 to determine the depth of a 3-D chart relative to its width, thus changing the spacing between the clusters.

- *Axis tab*. Assigns a primary or secondary axis to the data series or to all data series of one chart type.

4. Click OK when finished.

Editing the chart frame

You can change the thickness and style of the frame border. Additionally, you can add a shadow or change the corners of the frame to rounded.

To format the chart frame

1. Click the chart once to select the frame. Handles appear around the edge of the frame to indicate it is selected.
2. Choose the Format Object command; alternatively, press Ctrl+1. The Format Object dialog box appears.
3. Choose the Patterns tab.
4. In Border, choose Custom.
5. In Style, choose the style of line, such as dashed, dotted, solid, screened, and so on.
6. Choose a Color.
7. In Weight, choose the thickness you want for the border line.
8. If you wish, choose the Shadow or Round Corners options.
9. Choose OK to close the dialog box and apply the border.

Changing Colors and Fonts

You can change any of the colors of any chart element, including the legend, the chart walls, the plot area, and so on. Additionally, you can change the font used in the legend and axes. The dialog boxes are similar, as is the procedure for changing fonts and colors.

To change the fonts and colors

1. Double-click the chart. A screened border appears around the chart.

2. Double-click the mouse on the element you want to modify: the legend, an axis, the plot area or wall, and so on. The Format Axis dialog box appears.

> **Note**
>
> Depending on the element you double-click, the dialog box may be titled the Format Legend dialog box, Format Walls, and so on.

3. In the Patterns tab, choose either the Border or Area sections. Make changes in the style, color, and/or pattern.

   In the Font tab, choose the Font, Font Style, Size, and other attributes and make the necessary changes.

4. Choose OK to close the dialog box.

Modifying Axes

You can change the alignment, number, or scale of the chart axes. Alignment refers to the orientation of the text, number refers to the format in which the data is displayed, and the scale indicates the minimum, maximum, and increment values that appear on the axes.

To change the alignment

1. Double-click the chart to edit it; then select the axis you want to modify.

2. Choose the Format Selected Axis command; alternatively, press Ctrl+1. The Format Axis dialog box appears.

3. Choose the Alignment tab.

4. In Orientation, choose the format you want to use. Choosing Automatic (the default option) enables Excel to align the axis text the way it best fits the chart.

5. Choose OK to close the dialog box.

To change the number formats

1. Double-click the chart to edit it, and then select the axis you want to modify.

2. Choose the Format Selected Axis command; alternatively, press Ctrl+1. The Format Axis dialog box appears.

3. Choose the Number tab.

4. In Category, choose the number, date, or time format you want to use.

5. In Format Codes, choose the format you want to use. View the sample below the list box.

6. Choose OK to close the dialog box.

To change the scale

1. Double-click the chart to edit it; then select the axis you want to modify.

2. Choose the Format Selected Axis command; alternatively, press Ctrl+1. The Format Axis dialog box appears.

3. Choose the Scale tab.

4. Enter the value for the following options (for a selected Y-axis, Z-axis, or both axes in a radar chart):

Option	**Description**
Mi**n**imum	Specifies the smallest data value to appear on the axis; if the Auto box is checked, displays lowest value of all data series
Ma**x**imum	Specifies the highest data value on the axis; if Auto is checked, displays the highest value of all data series
M**a**jor Unit	Specifies the major tick mark increment and major gridlines; if Auto is checked, automatically calculates increment
M**i**nor Unit	Specifies the minor tick mark increment and minor gridlines; Auto automatically calculates the increment
Floor **C**rosses At	Specifies the point where a 3-D floor crosses the Z-axis or where a 2-D floor crosses at the X-axis

For a selected X-axis, enter values for these options:

Number of Categories between Tick Mark Labels	Specifies which categories are labeled: 1 labels every category; 2 labels every second category; and so on
Number of Categories between Tick Mar**k**s	Specifies the number of categories between each pair of tick marks
Categories in **R**everse Order	Reverses the displayed order of the categories

5. Choose OK to close the dialog box.

Shortcut

Select the data range and click the ChartWizard button on the Standard toolbar to display the first ChartWizard dialog box.

You can double-click on various parts of the chart to display certain formatting dialog boxes. For example, double-click the legend to display the Format Legend dialog box.

Use the Chart toolbar to change chart types and to edit gridlines and legends.

Closing Files

See the Common Features section.

Color

Excel enables you to assign color to text, cells, charts, and even to different types of data on the page. Excel also offers several different patterns and various pattern colors. Colors and patterns in your Excel spreadsheets and charts add a brilliant touch when printed on a color printer; when Excel spreadsheets are used in PowerPoint presentations, color can add just the right amount of emphasis to a slide.

To change the color of a font

1. Select the cells containing the text you want to change.
2. Choose the Format Cells command. The Format Cells dialog box appears.
3. Choose the Font tab.
4. In Color, click the down arrow and a palette appears. Select the color you want to use for the text.
5. Choose OK to close the dialog box.

To change the color of cells

1. Select the cell or cells you want to change.
2. Choose the Format Cells command. The Format Cells dialog box appears.
3. Choose the Patterns tab.
4. In the Cell Shading area, choose a color form the Color palette.
5. Additionally, you can choose a Pattern to apply to the cell.
6. Choose OK to close the dialog box.

To change the color of chart elements

1. Double-click the chart.
2. Double-click on the element you want to change. The corresponding dialog box appears.
3. Choose the Patterns tab.
4. In the Border area, choose Color and select a color from the palette.

   In the Area section, choose a Color from the palette and/or a pattern in the Pattern palette.
5. Choose OK to close the dialog box.

Shortcuts

Select the object or cell and click the down arrow to the right of the Color button on the Formatting toolbar to display a palette of color boxes. Select the color to apply.

Select the cells containing the text and then click the Font Color button from the Formatting toolbar. Choose a color to apply to the text.

Press Ctrl+1 to display the Format Cells dialog box.

Column Widths

You can change the width of one or all columns in the worksheet to a specific measurement, to automatically fit the selection, or to the standard width.

To change the column width to a specific measurement

1. Select a cell or cells in the column you want to change, or select the entire column or columns.
2. Choose the Format Column command. A secondary menu appears.
3. Choose the Width command. The Column Width dialog box appears.
4. In the Column Width box, enter the number of characters that can be displayed in the cell.
5. Choose OK to close the dialog box. Excel adjusts the width of the selected columns.

Shortcut

Drag the right border of the column heading to the desired width.

To set the column to AutoFit

1. Select the column or columns you want to change; alternatively, select a cell or cells in the column you want to change.
2. Choose the Format Column command. A secondary menu appears.
3. Choose the AutoFit Selection command. Excel adjusts the column width to fit the selected text or number.

Shortcut

Position the mouse pointer on the right border of the column heading you want to change and double-click to AutoFit the column width.

To reset the standard width

1. Select the column or columns.
2. Choose the Format Column command. A secondary menu appears.
3. Choose Standard Width. The Standard Width dialog box appears with the default width entered in the Standard Column Width text box.
4. Choose OK. Excel adjusts the column or columns.

Consolidation

Use consolidation to summarize the data from one or more source areas; a source area can be one or more worksheets in the same or different workbooks. You can consolidate data by position or by category. Consolidate by position when the source areas are the same in layout; consolidate by category when the source areas are different in layout.

To consolidate by position

Use this option when the data in all source areas is arranged exactly the same.

1. Select the destination area—a range of cells to hold the summarized data.
2. Click the Data Consolidate command. The Consolidate dialog box appears.
3. In the Function list box, select the summary function you want to use; SUM is default.
4. In the Reference text box, enter the cell range of the source area to be consolidated.

> **Tip**
>
> You can select the Reference box and then select the source area on the open worksheet instead of typing in the range.

5. Click the Add button.

6. Repeat steps 4 and 5 until all source areas are defined.

> **Note**
>
> Choose the Create Links to **S**ource Data check box if you want Excel to automatically update the table for you as data changes.

7. Choose OK to close the dialog box. Excel inserts the consolidated data in the selected destination area.

To consolidate by category

Use this option if the consolidation areas are not the same size and layout.

1. Select the destination area.

2. Choose the Data Consolidate command.

3. In the Function text box, select the Summary function.

4. In the Reference box, enter the range for the source area.

5. Choose the Add button.

6. Repeat steps 4 and 5 until all source areas are defined.

7. In the Use Labels In area, select the Top Row check box if the category labels are in the top row of the source area.

   Select the Left Column check box if the category labels are in the left column of the source area.

8. Choose OK to close the dialog box. Excel inserts the consolidated data in the selected destination area.

Converting

You can convert a variety of files from other applications for use in Excel, including text files, Lotus 1-2-3, Quattro Pro for DOS, MS Works, dBASE, and Excel 4.0 files.

To convert another file to Excel

1. Choose the File Open command. The Open dialog box appears.
2. In the List Files of Type drop-down list, choose the file type you want to convert.
3. In Drives, change drives if necessary.
4. In Directories, choose the directory containing the file.
5. Select or enter the file name and choose OK. Excel converts the file. Excel may display a conversion dialog box and ask for more information. If so, follow the directions in the dialog boxes.

Shortcut

Click the Open button on the Standard toolbar to display the Open dialog box.

You can also double-click the file name; Excel asks if you want to convert the file.

Copying

You can copy the contents of one cell to another, an entire worksheet to another workbook, or even copy a worksheet to another application, such as Word or PowerPoint. Using the copy command, Excel enables you to duplicate existing figures and data easily and quickly. Use the Edit Copy command in conjunction with the Edit Paste command.

To copy data to the Clipboard

1. Select the data to be copied by dragging the mouse cursor over the data.
2. Choose the Edit Copy command; alternatively, press Ctrl+C. Excel places the data on the Windows Clipboard, where it remains until you copy or cut another selected item.

To copy data or an object to another location on the same page

1. Select the text or object to be copied.
2. Press and hold the Ctrl key while positioning the mouse pointer on the border of the selected cell or on the object. The mouse cursor changes to a pointer. Drag the cell or object to its new location.
3. Release the mouse button and Excel copies the text or object to the new location.

Shortcut

Select the data and click the Copy button on the Standard toolbar.

See also **Paste**, as well as the Integration section.

Cross Tabulation

See **Pivot Tables.**

Currency

See **Formatting.**

Database Management

You can set up a database in Excel by creating a list. A list consists of data entered into a worksheet; using a list is easier than defining fields and creating data entry screens. Each row of the worksheet represents a single record listing. For instance, name, company, address, city, state, and zip code would all be within the cells in one row. Each item, or field, in the record is recorded in one cell; therefore, the entries in each column are similar: Name, Company, Address, and so on.

After creating the database in Excel, you can add and delete records, find specific records, and sort the records so one will be easier to find. Additionally, you can use the AutoFilter feature to display and work with subsets of data.

To set up a database

1. In a worksheet, begin in cell A-1. Enter the column headings, in a row, for the database, such as NAME, COMPANY NAME, ADDRESS, CITY, STATE, ZIP, pressing the Tab key between each heading.

   See also **Column Widths**, **Borders**, and **Formatting**.

2. In cell A-2, enter a name. Press Tab and enter a company name in cell B-2. Continue to enter the rest of the record, adjusting the column widths if necessary.

Note

Don't leave a blank row between the column titles.

Note

You can add other data to the worksheet: figures, charts, and so on; however, leave at least one blank row around the database data to separate it from other worksheet data.

To add records with a data form

1. Select any cell within the database.

2. Choose the Data Form command. The data form appears, titled with the name of the active worksheet. The column labels you created in the database appear as field names in the data form.

3. Choose the New button; the text in the text boxes disappears and you can enter a new record. Press the Tab key to move from one text box to the next; press Shift+Tab to move to the previous text box.

4. Choose the New button to add each record. When finished, choose Close. The new records are added to the database worksheet.

To filter a list with AutoFilter

Filtering displays only rows in your list that contain a certain value or meet a specific set of criteria, while hiding the other rows.

1. Choose the Data Filter command. A secondary menu appears.

2. Choose the AutoFilter command so it has a check mark beside the command. Excel displays a down arrow button beside each column head. You can click the down arrow in the Zip column, for example, and select any zip code. Excel then displays only records containing that zip code. Any item you choose in the list remains selected, so you can activate filters in other columns to narrow the list even further.

> **Note**
>
> The AutoFilter command is a toggle command; each time you select it you either activate or deactivate the command. A check mark beside the command means it is active.

3. After selecting an element in one of the filter lists, the down arrow in the column heading changes color to

indicate that a filter is in effect. Choose the down arrow and select All if you want to turn the filter off.

Note

You can choose the Custom filter in any AutoFilter list. You can enter your own custom filter in the Custom AutoFilter dialog box. In the Zip column head, for example, you can choose to filter all but two zip codes, or use a wildcard character to narrow a filter field.

To search a database

1. Select any cell in the database.
2. Choose the Data Form command. The data form appears.
3. Choose the Criteria button. The data form changes slightly: the Criteria button changes to Form and the Delete button changes to Clear.
4. In any of the field text boxes, enter the criteria for a search: a name, address, company name, or other criteria. You do not need to fill all fields.

Tip

The number of found records is shown in the top right corner of the dialog box; 2 of 70 means the second record out of 70 agreed with the criteria.

5. Choose Find Next to search for occurrences of the criteria. The data form changes back so that the Criteria button replaces the Form button. You can now edit the form. Press Enter to save the changes and move to the next record.
6. Choose the Close button to close the dialog box when you are finished.

To delete a record

1. Select any cell in the database.
2. Choose the Data Form command. The data form appears.
3. Display the record on the data form by browsing through the records or using the Criteria search.
4. Choose Delete. Excel displays a confirmation box. Choose OK to delete the record or Cancel to return to the data form.
5. Choose Close to return to the worksheet.

See also **Sorting**.

Date Math

Excel sets the date and time using numeric values. The dates are stored as serial numbers and times are stored as decimal fractions. Since Excel sees dates and times as numbers, you can also add, subtract, and otherwise calculate them. Use date math to calculate the difference between two dates, to add days or weeks to a date, and so on.

To determine the difference between two dates

1. Enter the equal sign (=) as the first part of the formula.
2. Enter the first date in quotation marks, such as "9/15/94".

> **Tip**
>
> You must include each date in quotation marks for the formula. You can use either slashes (/) or hyphens (-) in the date format.

3. Enter a minus sign and enter the second date in quotation marks. The final formula may look something like this:

   ="9-15-94"-"10-12-94"

4. Press Enter. Excel displays -27 in the cell while displaying the formula in the Formula bar.

Tip

You can also calculate between years, for example:

="12-1-93"-"1-12-94" yields the answer -42.

See also **Functions.**

Decimal Places

Excel can display up to 16 decimal places, including the decimal point. You can choose to display any number of decimal places while still enabling Excel to use the entire number in its calculations. You can also choose to display rounded values.

Note

You can override the fixed decimal by typing a decimal point in your number.

To set a fixed number of decimal places for the worksheet

1. Choose the Tools Options command.
2. Choose the Edit tab.
3. Choose the Fixed Decimal check box. Select or enter the number of decimal places in the Places box.
4. Choose OK to close the dialog box. Numbers you add now automatically contain the specified number of decimal places and you don't have to type the decimal point.

To change decimal place formats for a specified cell or cells

1. Select the cells you want to format.

2.  Click the Increase Decimal button on the Formatting toolbar to add one decimal place to the number format each time you click the button.

   Click the Decrease Decimal button on the Formatting toolbar to remove one decimal place at a time each time you click the button.

To round a number

1. Select the cell you want to format.

2. In the formula bar, enter the formula in the following syntax: round(number, num_digits). To round the number 2.345 to two decimal places, enter: **round(2.345, 2)**

> **Note**
>
> Rounding only affects how the value is displayed; the full stored value is used in calculations.

Deleting

You can delete any element you add to a worksheet or chart, including cells, columns, data, rows, and text.

To delete cells

1. Select the cell or cells to be deleted.

2. Choose the Edit Delete command. The Delete dialog box appears.

3. Choose either the Shift Cells Left or Shift Cells Up option button.

4. Choose OK.

To delete cell, column, or row contents

1. Select the cell(s), row(s), or column(s) to clear.
2. Choose the Edit Clear command. A secondary menu appears.
3. Choose All, Contents, Formats, or Notes.

To delete rows or columns

1. Select the row(s) or column(s).
2. Choose the Edit Delete command. Excel deletes the selected row or column.

Note

If you select only a cell and choose the **E**dit **D**elete command, the Delete dialog box appears. Choose the appropriate option, and choose OK to close the dialog box and delete the entire row or column.

Shortcuts

Press Ctrl+minus sign (-) to delete selected cells, rows, or columns.

Press the Delete key to clear the contents from selected cells.

See also **Charts**.

Drag and Drop

See the Integration section.

Drawing

See the Integration section.

Editing Groups of Worksheets

When formatting, you can select two or more worksheets and treat them as a group. When grouped, you can make the same changes on several worksheets at the same time, including data entry, formatting, editing, and so on.

To group worksheets

1. Click the sheet tab for the first worksheet in the group.
2. Hold the Ctrl key while clicking each of the other sheet tabs to add to the group.
3. To move from sheet to sheet, click the sheet tab you want to move to.
4. To ungroup the worksheets, hold the Shift key and click the Sheet tab for the active document. All other sheets are ungrouped as well. Alternatively, you can point the mouse at the sheet tabs and select Ungroup Sheets from the shortcut menu.

Entering Data

There are two types of data you can enter in an Excel worksheet: constant values or text and formulas. Constant values are data typed directly into a cell, including numbers, text, annotations, and so on. Constant values do not change unless you select the cell and edit it yourself. Formulas consist of a sequence of values, cell references, functions, and operators that perform a calculation using the contents of other cells.

To enter data in a cell

1. Select the cell or cells in which you want to enter data.
2. Type the data.

> **Tip**
>
> You can enter decimal points, commas, minus signs, any text character, spaces, and so on.

3. Press Enter, Tab, Shift+Tab, Shift+Enter, or a directional arrow to enter the data and move to the next cell.

> **Note**
>
> By default numbers are right-aligned; text is left-aligned.

To enter a formula

1. Select the cell in which you want to enter the formula.
2. Begin the formula with the equal sign (=). The equal sign activates the formula bar.

> **Tip**
>
> If you begin entering a formula by pasting a name or function, Excel automatically enters the equal sign for you.

3. Type the formula. Alternatively, you can use another formula technique.
4. Press Enter to complete the formula.

> **Note**
>
> To enter a formula as text, type a single quotation mark before the entry.

See also **Formulas**.

Exiting Excel

See the Common Features section.

Filling a Range with Values

Excel includes a feature, AutoFill, that enters sequences of numbers for you automatically. You start the sequence, and

AutoFill analyzes the sequence and continues it for you. You can use AutoFill for dates, months, years, positive and negative numbers, and so on.

To fill a range with a sequence of numbers

1. Enter the first two numbers in the first two cells of the range.
2. Select the two cells.
3. Position the mouse over the handle in the lower right corner of the selected cells; the pointer changes to a cross.

   Drag the cross to the right to the end of the column range you want to fill with the sequence.

   Drag the cross to the left or up to create a reversed order to the sequence.
4. Release the mouse button; AutoFill completes the sequence of numbers.

> **Tip**
>
> If you want to use dates instead of values, enter the first two dates of the sequence. 1/1/94, 2/1/94 as a sequence will continue on a monthly basis; 1/94, 1/95 as a sequence continues on a yearly basis.

To fill a range with the same numbers

1. Enter the numbers in the cells and select the cells.
2. Hold the Ctrl key while clicking the bottom right corner handle and dragging the selection to the right (column) or down (row).

Finding and Replacing Data

You can search a worksheet for specific text, numbers, formulas, or other data. Excel searches for the data and selects the cell containing the data, so you can easily find it on-screen. After finding the data, you can edit it or replace it with something else. The Find and Replace dialog boxes remain on-screen; you can click the mouse in the worksheet and edit data and then resume the Find and Replace functions. When replacing data, you can replace each instance one at a time, or choose to replace all.

To find data

1. Click the A-1 cell to begin the search at the beginning of the worksheet; alternatively, click the cell in which you want to begin the search.
2. Choose the Edit Find command. The Find dialog box appears.
3. In the Find What text box, type the data you want to find.

> **Note**
>
> You can use wildcard characters—the question mark (?) and asterisk (*)—to widen the search. For example, if searching for all files with a .DOC extension, use the asterisk wildcard—*.DOC.

4. You can choose to narrow the search by choosing the following options:

Option	Description
Search	Choose to search By Rows (across) or By Columns (down) to determine the direction of the search
Look in	Search Formulas, Values, or Notes for the data or text
Match Case	Finds exactly the case you enter (upper- or lowercase) in the Find What text box

(continues)

Option	Description
Find Entire Cells **O**nly	Searches for only cells containing exactly the data you typed

5. Choose the Find Next button. Excel moves to the next occurrence of the specified data. You can choose to edit the data by clicking in the document window, or you can choose to Replace (see next set of steps).

6. When finished, choose the Close button.

Tip

You can choose the **E**dit **R**epeat Find command (or press F4) to duplicate the last find.

To replace data

1. Select the cell from which you want to begin the Find and Replace process.

2. Choose the Edit Replace command. The Replace dialog box appears.

Note

Alternatively, you can choose the **R**eplace button in the Find dialog box.

3. Enter the data or text you want to find in the Find What text box.

4. Enter the text you want to substitute in the Replace with text box.

5. Choose one of the following options:

Option	Description
Search	Choose to search By Rows (across) or By Columns (down) to determine the direction of the search
Match **C**ase	Finds exactly the case you enter (upper or lowercase) in the Fi**n**d What text box
Find Entire Cells **O**nly	Searches for only cells containing exactly the data you typed

6. Click one of the following buttons:

Button	Description
Find Next	Searches the worksheet and stops on the next occurrence of the specified text or data
Replace	Substitutes the specified data for the current occurrence of found data
Replace **A**ll	Replaces all occurrences without confirmation on each one

7. Click Close when finished.

Fonts

You can assign any fonts available to you through Windows and other Windows applications. Format the text and numbers in your worksheets using various fonts, font sizes, styles, and colors.

To change fonts

1. Select the cell or cells containing the font you want to change.

Note

You can also double-click a cell containing a constant value, then select specific text within the cell to format.

2. Choose the Format Cells command (or press Ctrl+1). The Format Cells dialog box appears.
3. Choose the Font tab.
4. In Font, scroll through the list and choose the font you want to apply to the selected cells.
5. In Font Style, choose from the available styles, such as italic, bold, regular, and so on.
6. In Size, choose the size font you want.
7. You can also choose from the following options:

Option	Description
Underline	Choose to underline the text with None, Single, Double, Single Accounting, or Double Accounting underlines
Effects	Choose to Strikethrough, Superscript, or Subscript the selected text
Color	Select a color from the drop-down palette
Normal Font	Sets all attributes back to the Normal style which is the style used on all worksheets until another style is applied

> **Note**
>
> Use the Single or Double Accounting underlines when you format numbers in a cell or cells; accounting underlines fall on the baseline of the number.

8. Choose OK when finished. Excel formats the selected text to the specified font, size, and style.

To change the default font

1. Choose the Tools Options command. The Options dialog box appears.
2. Choose the General tab.
3. In Standard Font, choose a font.
4. In Size, choose a size.
5. Choose OK to close the dialog box. Excel displays a message box stating you must exit Excel and restart it for the changes to take place. Choose OK.

See also **Formatting** and **Styles**.

Shortcuts

Select a cell or text and click the down arrow to the right of the Font box on the Formatting toolbar; select the font you want to assign.

Select a cell or text and click the down arrow to the right of the Font Size box on the Formatting toolbar; select the size you want to assign.

Press Ctrl+U to underline the selection, or click the Underline button on the Formatting toolbar.

Press Ctrl+B to boldface the selection, or click the Bold button on the Formatting toolbar.

Press Ctrl+I to italicize the selection, or click the Italic button on the Formatting toolbar.

Formatting

You can format selected text by changing it to bold, italic, or underlined. You can format selected numbers by applying the currency, percentage, or comma style to the numbers. The easiest way to apply any of these styles is to use the Formatting toolbar.

> **Note**
>
> To display the Formatting toolbar, point the mouse at any current toolbar and press the right mouse button. The toolbar quick menu appears; select Formatting and the Formatting toolbar appears.

To assign text styles

1. Select the text or cells containing the text to be formatted.
2. Click the Bold, Italic, and/or Underline button on the Formatting toolbar.

> **Note**
>
> You can assign other formats and text styles by choosing the F**o**rmat C**e**lls command and selecting the Font tab.

To assign numbering styles

1. Select the data or cells to be formatted.
2. Click one of the following buttons on the Formatting toolbar to assign a style:

Button	Format
[$] Currency Style	Adds a dollar sign, decimal point, and two decimal places to the number—456 becomes $456.00

Button		Format
%	Percent Style	Changes a value to a percentage and adds the percent sign—.75 becomes 75%
,	Comma Style	Inserts commas in the proper places and adds a decimal point plus two decimal places—45678 becomes 45,678.00

Note

You can assign other formats to numbers by choosing the Format Cells command and choosing the Number tab.

Shortcuts

Select the text and press Ctrl+B to boldface it, Ctrl+I to italicize it, or Ctrl+U to underline it.

See also **Decimal Places** and **Fonts**.

Formulas

Use formulas to perform operations, such as addition and multiplication, and to calculate or analyze data in a worksheet. Formulas can contain operators, cell references, values, worksheet functions, and names. To enter a formula in a cell, you type a combination of these elements into the formula bar.

To enter a formula

1. Select the cell in which you want to enter the formula.
2. Begin the formula with the equal sign (=). The equal sign activates the formula bar.

Tip

If you begin by pasting a name or function into the formula bar, Excel automatically enters the equal sign for you.

3. Type the formula into the cell or formula bar. To enter cell addresses, you can select the cells on the worksheet (Excel enters the references in the formula). You can also cut/copy and paste existing formulas.

4. When you've finished entering the formula in the formula bar, press Enter.

Shortcut

Choose the Function Wizard on the Standard toolbar. The Function Wizard-Step 1 of 2 dialog box appears. Follow the directions in the two dialog boxes.

See also **Entering Data**.

Fractions

You can enter and work with fractions in Excel instead of using decimal values to indicate fractional values. Additionally, you can convert a fraction to a decimal or decimal to a fraction.

To enter a fraction

1. Type the integer first; if there is no integer, type a zero. Follow the integer with a space.

2. Type the numerator, a slash, and then the denominator—such as 2 1/2 or 0 1/7.

3. Press Enter.

To convert fractions and decimals

1. Select the cell containing the fraction or decimal.

2. Choose the Format Cells command. The Format Cells dialog box appears.

3. Choose the Number tab.

4. In Category, choose Number or Currency if you want to convert a fraction to a decimal.

   Choose Fraction if you want to convert a decimal to a fraction.

   Note

   The converted value appears in the sample box near the bottom of the dialog box.

5. In the Format Codes box, choose a format.

6. Choose OK to close the dialog box.

Freeze Panes

When you want to keep row or column titles on the screen while scrolling through a long list in a worksheet, freeze the pane. The Freeze Pane command splits the active window.

To freeze panes

1. To freeze horizontal titles, select the row below the titles.

   To freeze vertical titles, select the column to the right of the titles.

2. Choose the Window Freeze Panes command. You can now scroll through the worksheet while the titles remain in place.

To unfreeze panes

Choose the Window Unfreeze Panes command.

See also **Split-Window**.

Functions

Functions are commands you enter into a formula to make complex operations simple. Functions perform mathematical processes with a single command; use functions to perform financial processes, such as calculating the internal rate of return for a series of cash flows, or finding the subtotal in a list or database.

You can enter a function by typing directly into the cell and Function bar, or you can use the Function Wizard. If you type the function yourself, you must be careful to use the correct syntax.

Excel's Function Wizard provides quick and easy use of Excel's functions. In the Function Wizard, you can choose a function category, and then select the exact function you want to use. For your convenience, the Function Wizard provides a description of the functions.

To enter a function directly

1. Select the cell.
2. Type an equal sign (=). The Formula bar appears.
3. Enter the function name and a left parenthesis. Enter any arguments and then a right parenthesis.

> **Note**
>
> An argument is information the function uses to create a new value or perform an action; arguments can be numbers, text, logical values, error values, references, or arrays.

4. Press Enter. The cell contents change to the result of the function. When the cell is active, the formula appears in the Formula bar.

To enter a function using the Function Wizard

1. Select the cell in which the formula will appear.

2. Choose the Insert Function command. The Function Wizard-Step 1 of 2 dialog box appears.

> **Tip**
>
> The Function Wizard will enter the equal sign at the beginning of the formula, automatically, if you did not already enter it.

3. In the Function Category list, choose the category.
4. In the Function Name list, choose the function. A description of the function appears below the lists.
5. Choose the Next button. The Function Wizard-Step 2 of 2 dialog box appears. Fill in the required function values. Requests for information in the second dialog box depends on the function selected. Directions are included to help you enter the correct information. You can enter the required values by typing directly into the box, or by selecting cells with the mouse.
6. Choose the Finish button to enter the function in the current cell. You can make any changes, such as adding expressions. Press Enter when finished.

> **Shortcut**
>
> 
> Click the Function Wizard button on the Standard toolbar to display the Function Wizard dialog box.

Gridlines

The gridlines on-screen define the cells for you as you work, but they can be hidden. The gridlines also print by default; you can choose not to print them.

To hide the gridlines

1. Choose the Tools Options command. The Options dialog box appears.

2. Choose the View tab.
3. In the Windows Options group, choose Gridlines. An X in the option's box indicates the option is active; no X indicates the option is deactivated. Click on the option to change its state.
4. Choose OK to close the dialog box. The grids are hidden from view.

To print without gridlines

1. Choose the File Page Setup command. The Page Setup dialog box appears.
2. Choose the Sheet tab.
3. In the Print area, choose Gridlines. The X in the option's box indicates the option is active; no X indicates the option is deactivated.
4. Choose OK to close the dialog box, or choose Print to print the worksheet.

Headers and Footers

Use headers and footers to help define your printed worksheet. Headers and footers include information that appears on the top (header) or bottom (footer) of every printed page. You can incorporate titles, dates, your name or your company's name, page numbers, or other information in a header or footer.

Excel's default is to print the header one-half-inch from the top of the page and to print the name of the worksheet as the header text. The default footer contains the page number printed one-half-inch from the bottom of the page.

To use a built-in header or footer

1. Select the sheets in which you want the header or footer to appear.

2. Choose the File Page Setup command. The Page Setup dialog box appears.

3. Choose the Header/Footer tab.

4. To set a header, in the Header list select one of the predefined headers. If you want a footer, choose a predefined footer from the footer drop-down list.

5. Choose OK to close the dialog box, or choose Print to print the worksheets.

To create a custom header or footer

1. Select the sheets in which you want the header or footer to appear.

2. Choose the File Page Setup command. The Page Setup dialog box appears.

3. Choose the Header/Footer tab.

4. Choose either the Custom Header or Custom Footer button. The corresponding dialog boxes look and behave similarly.

5. Enter the text you want in the three text boxes: Left Section, Center Section, and Right Section.

Note

You can also use the available tool buttons: Font, Page Number, Total Pages, Date, Time, Filename, or Sheet Name to enter and format the text.

6. Choose OK to close the Header or Footer dialog box and choose OK to close the Page Setup dialog box.

To delete a header or footer

1. Select the sheets where you want to remove the header or footer.

2. Choose the File Page Setup command. The Page Setup dialog box appears.
3. Choose the Header/Footer tab.
4. In Header or Footer, click the down arrow and choose [none] from the drop-down list.
5. Choose OK to close the dialog box.

Help

See the Common Features section.

Hiding Data

You can hide the data in a cell, a row, a column, or an entire sheet. Hidden elements do not print with the worksheet.

To hide a sheet

1. Select the sheet you want to hide.

> **Tip**
>
> You can only hide a sheet if the workbook contains more than one sheet.

2. Choose the Format Sheet command. A secondary menu appears.
3. Choose Hide.

To show a sheet

1. Choose the Format Sheet menu. A secondary menu appears.
2. Choose Unhide. The Unhide dialog box appears.
3. From the list of hidden sheets, choose the sheet you want to show.
4. Choose OK.

To hide data in cells

1. Select the cells containing the data you want to hide.
2. Choose the Format Cells command.
3. Choose the Number tab.
4. In the Code box, type three semicolons.

> **Tip**
>
> To show the data in the selected cells again, open the Format Cells dialog box, choose the Number tab, and type **General** in the cell or choose a different format.

5. Choose OK to close the dialog box.

To hide a column or row

1. Select the columns or rows to be hidden.
2. Choose the Format Row or Column command. A secondary menu appears.
3. Choose Hide.

> **Shortcut**
>
> Right-click the mouse on the row label—1, 2, 3, and so on—and choose Hide from the shortcut menu.

To show a column or row

1. Select the rows or columns on both sides of the hidden row or column.
2. Choose the Format Row or Column command.
3. Choose Unhide.

Shortcut

Right-click the mouse on the column label—A, B, C, and so on—and choose Unhide from the shortcut menu.

In-Cell Editing

You can use the Formula bar for editing data or you can edit data in a cell directly in the cell. Add, remove, or change data previously entered just by double-clicking the cell.

To edit data in a cell

1. Double-click the cell to be edited. The I-beam appears in the cell.
2. Move the I-beam using the arrow keys or mouse; then enter, delete, or otherwise modify the data in the cell.
3. Press Enter when done.

Tip

You can break a line in a cell to start a new line by positioning the cursor and pressing Alt+Enter. Excel starts a new line at the insertion point and enlarges the cell accordingly.

Inserting

When editing your worksheet, you may find the need to insert data. Excel enables you to insert rows, columns, cells, ranges, and worksheets into your workbook.

To insert rows or columns

1. Select a row or column. The inserted row appears before, or above, the selected row; the inserted column appears before, or to the left of, the selected column.

2. Choose the Insert Rows or Columns command. The rows or columns are inserted.

To insert cells or ranges

1. Select the cell where you want to insert a new cell.
2. Choose the Insert Cells command. The Insert dialog box appears.
3. Choose from the following options:

Option	Description
Shift Cells R**i**ght	Shifts the existing cells to the right and inserts one new cell
Shift Cells **D**own	Shifts existing cells down and inserts one new cell
Entire **R**ow	Shifts row down and inserts new row
Entire **C**olumn	Shift column to right and inserts new column

4. Choose OK to close the dialog box.

To insert worksheets

1. Select the sheet in front of which you want to insert a new worksheet.
2. Choose the Insert Worksheet command.

Shortcut
To insert a worksheet, press Shift+F11.

Italic

See Formatting.

Lines

See **Borders**.

Linking Dynamically

See the Integration section.

List

See **Database Management**.

Macros

See the Integration section.

Margins

Excel's default margins are 1-inch top and bottom and 3/4-inch left and right. You can change the margins, however, to suit your purposes. You can also change the headers and footers margin from the default 1/2-inch to a setting more fitting to the worksheet margins.

To change the margins

1. Choose the File Page Setup command. The Page Setup dialog box appears.
2. Choose the Margins tab.
3. Select or enter the new margin measurement in the Top, Bottom, Left, and/or Right text boxes.

> **Note**
>
> You can choose to change the Header or Footer margins by selecting or entering a measurement in those text boxes.

4. Choose OK to close the dialog box.

See also **Centering**.

Menus

See the Common Features section.

Moving Around the Worksheet

To work successfully in a worksheet, you must be able to move around in the worksheet. You may want to move quickly to a specific cell or to another sheet. You can move around using the mouse or the keyboard; additionally, you can use a combination of both methods.

To move with the mouse
Move to a cell by clicking the mouse in the specific cell.

Move the worksheet within the window by using the horizontal and vertical scroll bars.

Move between sheets by clicking the Sheet tabs above the Status bar.

To move with the keyboard

Press	To
Arrow key	Move in the direction of the arrow, one cell at a time
Ctrl+Up/Down Arrow	Move up/down to the edge of the current data region
Ctrl+Left/Right Arrow	Move left/right to the edge of the current data region
Tab	Move to the cell on the right
Home	Move to the beginning of the row
Ctrl+Home	Move to the beginning of the worksheet
Ctrl+End	Move to the end of a worksheet
Page Up/Down	Move up/down one screen

(continues)

Press	To
Alt+Page Up/Down	Move left/right one screen
Ctrl+Page Up/Down	Move to the previous/next sheet in workbook

End mode is an alternate method of moving between and within adjacent blocks. The End Mode key combinations follow:

Press	To
End	Turn End Mode on or off
End, Up/Down/ Left/Right Arrow	Move one block of data within a row or column
End, Home	Move to last cell in the worksheet
End, Enter	Move to last cell in current row

Moving Elements

You can move elements within a worksheet and between worksheets, so that you can better organize your data and documents. You can move data from cell to cell and from worksheet to worksheet; you can also move data from Excel to another application. Move charts, pictures, and other objects within the same worksheet or between worksheets; you can even move sheets from workbook to workbook.

To move data or objects between sheets or applications

1. Select the data or object you want to move.

2. Choose the Edit Cut command, or press Ctrl+X.

3. Reposition the insertion point in the cell where you want to paste the data or object.

4. Choose the Edit Paste command, or press Ctrl+V.

To move data or objects within the same sheet

1. Select the data or object you want to move.

2. To move data, position the pointer over the selected data cell border; the pointer changes to an arrow.

   To move an object, position the pointer in the center of the object.

3. Drag the pointer to the new location and release the mouse button.

> **Note**
>
> If drag-and-drop does not work, choose the **T**ools **O**ption command and the Edit tab. In Settings, make sure the Allow Cell **D**rag and Drop option is active. The option is active when it has an X in the check box.

To move a sheet within the workbook

1. Click the sheet tab to be moved.

2. Drag the sheet tab to a new location.

To move a sheet between workbooks

1. Click the sheet to be moved.

2. Choose the Edit Move or Copy Sheet command. The Move or Copy dialog box appears.

3. In To Book, select the workbook you want to move the sheet to.

4. In Before Sheet, choose the location for the new sheet.

Tip

You can copy the sheet instead of moving it by choosing the **C**reate a Copy option at the bottom of the Move or Copy dialog box.

5. Choose OK to close the dialog box.

Shortcut

  Select the data, click the Cut button on the Standard toolbar, then position the insertion point and click the Paste button.

See also **Charts**, as well as the Integration section.

Naming Cells and Ranges

Name a cell or range of cells to make it easier to move to a specified area in the worksheet, print a specified area, replace references, and so on.

To assign a name

1. Select the cell or range of cells you want to name.
2. Choose the Insert Name command. A secondary menu appears.
3. Choose Define. The Define Name dialog box appears.
4. In the Names in Workbook text box, enter a name for the cell or range.
5. Choose OK.

To insert a name for a cell or range

1. Select the cell or cell range where you want to insert the name.
2. Choose the Insert Name command. The secondary menu appears.

3. Choose Paste. The Paste Name dialog box appears.

4. In the Paste Name list, choose the name you want to use.

5. Choose OK.

Shortcuts
Press Ctrl+F3 to display the Define Name dialog box. Select a cell or cell range and click the name box at the left end of the Formula bar. Type the name for the cell or range and press Enter.

Notes

You can add notes to a worksheet that remind you of layout, explain formulas, and so on. Notes are handy to use, especially when you share files with others; use notes to explain or point out certain important features of the worksheet.

To insert a note

1. Select the cell you want to attach the note to.

2. Choose the Insert Note command. The Cell Note dialog box appears.

3. In the Text Note text box, enter the note.

4. Choose OK to close the dialog box. A small red box appears in the upper right corner of a cell containing a note.

To read a note

1. Select the cell containing the note.

2. Choose the Insert Note command. The Cell Note dialog box appears with the note in the Text Note text box.

Note

The selected cell's address appears in the **C**ell text box. A list of all notes in the sheet appears in the Notes in **S**heet list box, along with the cell addresses. Select a note from the Notes in **S**heet list and read the note in the **T**ext Note box.

Tip

You can also edit the note in the **T**ext Note text box; simply modify the text in any way and click the **A**dd button when done.

3. Choose Close when finished reading the notes.

To delete a note

1. Select the cell containing the note.

2. Choose the Insert Note command. The Cell Note dialog box appears with the note in the Text Note text box.

3. Choose the Delete button. A confirmation dialog box appears.

4. Choose OK to confirm the deletion and OK to close the dialog box.

Shortcut

Press Shift+F2 to display the Cell Note dialog box.

Note

You can also print the notes for a worksheet by selecting Print Notes in the Page Setup dialog box.

Opening Files

See the Common Features section.

Outlines

You can outline the worksheet data to create a summary report that is easy to read and analyze. Additionally, you can outline a range of data as well as the entire worksheet. After you produce the outline, you can show or hide various levels within the outline.

To create an outline automatically

1. Select the range you want to outline; to select the entire worksheet, select any cell.
2. Choose the Data Group and Outline command. A secondary menu appears.
3. Choose the Auto Outline command. Excel creates the outline and displays the symbols on-screen.

To create an outline manually

1. Select the rows or columns subordinate to the summary row or column.
2. Choose the Data Group and Outline command. A secondary menu appears.
3. Choose Group. Excel creates an outline and displays the outline symbols, such as show detail, hide detail, column and row levels, on-screen.
4. Continue selecting rows or columns and grouping them until you have created the outline levels.

To remove an outline

1. Select the rows or columns that contain the groups; alternatively, select all cells in the worksheet to remove the entire outline.

2. Choose the Data Group and Outline command.
   A secondary menu appears.

3. Choose Clear Outline.

See also **Subtotals.**

Page Breaks

You can insert horizontal and vertical page breaks in a worksheet to control the data that prints on a worksheet.

To insert a vertical and horizontal page break

1. Select the cell where you want to insert the page break.

2. Choose the Insert Page Break command. Excel inserts the page break above and to the left of the selected cell.

To insert a horizontal page break

1. Select the row where you want to insert the page break.

2. Choose the Insert Page Break command and Excel inserts a break above the selected row.

> **Tip**
>
> Excel marks the page break with a dashed horizontal and/or vertical line.

To remove a page break

1. Select the cell or row after the page break.

2. Choose the Insert Remove Page Break command and Excel removes the page break.

Page Setup

You can change the orientation of the page, scaling, paper size, print quality, and other elements of the working document. Additionally, you can control other aspects of the page and page layout as far as printing is concerned; for example, you can choose whether to print gridlines, notes, row headings, and so on.

Note

The Page Setup dialog box contains four tabs: Page, Margins, Header/Footer, and Sheet. For more information about two of these tabs: Margins and Header/Footer, see theses tasks: **Margins** and **Headers and Footers**.

To change page options

1. Choose the File Page Setup command. The Page Setup dialog box appears.
2. Choose the Page tab.
3. In Orientation, choose either Portrait (default) or Landscape.
4. In Scaling, choose one of the following options:

Option	Description
Adjust to	Enter a percentage to reduce or enlarge the printed worksheet.
Fit to	Enter a number of pages to which the sheet or selection prints; the number of pages wide and tall do not have to be the same. The sheet or selection is scaled proportionally.

5. Select a Paper Size from the drop-down list.
6. Choose High, Medium, Low, or Draft print quality.

Tip

In the First Page Number box, you can enter a starting page number. Enter **Auto** to print the next sequential number, if it is not the first page in the print job.

> **Tip**
>
> You can select multiple worksheets before opening the Page Setup dialog box to apply changes to all selected sheets at the same time.

7. Click OK to close the dialog box, or choose Print to print the document.

To change the Sheet options

1. Choose the File Page Setup command. The Page Setup dialog box appears.
2. Choose the Sheet tab.
3. In the Print Area, indicate the range that you will want to print, if it will always be the same range in the worksheet.
4. Choose whether to Print Titles at the top or left of every page by selecting one of the following options:

Option	Description
Rows to Repeat at Top	Select the option; on the worksheet, select the row (or enter a cell range) to use as titles
Columns to Repeat at Left	Select the option; on the worksheet, select the column (or enter a cell range) to use as titles

5. In the Print area, choose from the following options:

Option	Description
Gridlines	Prints the cell gridlines
Notes	Prints cell notes on additional pages

Option	Description
Draft **Q**uality	Reduces printing time by printing fewer graphics and no gridlines
Black and White	Use if data is in color, but the printer only prints in black and white
Row and Co**l**umn Headings	Prints or hides headings

6. In Page Order, choose one of the following options if printing more than one page:

Down, then Across	Sheets print and number from first page to pages below; then printing and numbering move to the top right and continue printing down
Across, then Down	Sheets print and number from first page to right, then move down and right again, and so on

7. Choose OK to close the dialog box, or **Print** if you want to print the workbook.

See also **Margins, Centering,** and **Headers and Footers.**

Passwords

See **Protecting Files.**

Percentages

You can choose the percentage formatting you want to use for selected data. You can choose from two different percentage formats.

To format in percentages

1. Select the cell or range you want to format.

2. Choose the Format Cells command (or press Ctrl+1). The Format Cells dialog box appears.
3. Choose the Number tab.
4. In Category, choose Percentage.
5. In Format Codes, select the formatting you want.
6. Choose OK to close the dialog box. Excel applies the selected formatting.

Shortcut

% Click the Percent Style button on the Formatting toolbar to apply the percentage format as defined in the Style dialog box (default is no decimal places).

See also **Formatting**.

Pivot Tables

Create a pivot table from a list or database, either in Excel or from an external source. A pivot table is an interactive table that enables you to summarize, analyze, and manipulate the data in a list easily. The pivot table can be updated whenever the data changes, and the pivot table stays with the worksheet on which you created it. The original data remains intact, no matter how the pivot table data changes.

Tip

You cannot directly enter or edit data in a pivot table; the cells of the table are read-only.

You specify the data as fields—row, column, and page—when you create the pivot table. Excel analyzes and organizes the data and forms it into the pivot table. Excel provides the Pivot Table Wizard to make creating the table easy.

To create a pivot table

1. Select any cell within the list or database. The list or database must contain column titles.

2. Choose the Data PivotTable command. The PivotTable Wizard-Step 1 of 4 dialog box appears.

3. In Create PivotTable from data in, choose the source of the data. If you selected a cell within an Excel worksheet, use the default option Microsoft Excel List or Database.

4. Choose the Next button. The PivotTable Wizard-Step 2 of 4 dialog box appears.

> **Tip**
>
> If you want to change an option or view the previous dialog boxes, choose the **B**ack button.

5. Type the cell range of the data, including the column titles, in the Range text box; alternatively, select the cells on the worksheet and Excel enters the range for you.

6. Choose the Next button. The PivotTable Wizard-Step 3 of 4 dialog box appears.

7. To design the pivot table layout, select and drag the field button representing your data (located on the right) to its position in the pivot table: Page, Row, Column, and Data. For example, drag the Time button to appear in the Row area of the pivot table and drag the Date button to appear in the Column area of the table.

> **Tip**
>
> Make sure you drag one or more data buttons to the **D**ata area.

8. Choose Next. The PivotTable Wizard-Step 4 of 4 dialog box appears.

9. In PivotTable Starting Cell, specify the starting cell for the table. You also can choose to change the PivotTable Name or leave the name Excel has assigned.

Note

Excel activates four pivot table options, by default. You can choose to turn any of the options off by selecting that option. If the X does not appear beside the option, the option is off.

10. Choose the Finish button. Excel creates the pivot table and inserts it at the specified location.

Tip

Excel displays the Query and Pivot toolbar from which you can choose shortcuts for commands in the **D**ata menu.

To edit a pivot table

1. Select the field or item you want to change.

Note

You can only edit table fields and items; you cannot change information or data within the table.

2. Type the new name and press Enter.

Tip

If you do change data in the source list or database, the pivot table does not automatically update. To update the pivot table, select any cell in the table, and click the Refresh Data button on the Query and Pivot toolbar.

To format a pivot table

1. Select any cell in the pivot table.
2. Choose the Format AutoFormat command. The AutoFormat dialog box appears.
3. In the Table Format box, choose the style you want. View the style in the Sample box.
4. Choose OK. Excel applies the selected style.

To delete a pivot table

1. Select the entire pivot table.
2. Choose the Edit Clear command. A secondary menu appears.
3. Choose All. Only the pivot table is deleted; the source data is still intact.

Printing

After completing a worksheet or workbook, charts, tables, lists, databases, and so on, you will want to print your work to create a record. You can preview the document before printing to make last minute adjustments. Additionally, you can format certain aspects, such as margins, page breaks, header and footers, specially for printing. You can print selected areas of the worksheet or the entire worksheet, and you can choose to print your work to an alternate printer, port, resolution, and so on.

To preview a page

1. Choose the File Print Preview command. Excel displays the page in print preview.

> **Tip**
>
> The status bar indicates which page you are viewing out of the total number of pages in the document.

2. Following is a list of buttons you can click to issue commands while in print preview:

Button	Description
Next	Displays the next page
Previous	Displays the previous page
Zoom	Switches between the full page view and a magnified view
Prin**t**	Displays the Print dialog box
Setup	Displays the Page Setup dialog box
Margins	Turns on or off the page margin handles, header/footer margins, and column widths. Use the handles to adjust the margins on the page
Close	Closes the preview and returns to the active sheet
Help	Displays help on the Print Preview command

To specify the print area

1. Choose the File Page Setup command. The Page Setup dialog box appears.

2. Choose the Sheet tab.

3. In the Print Area text box, enter the cell range or type the given names of the areas you want to print.

   Alternatively, you can move the Page Setup dialog box out of the way and select the range you want to print in the worksheet.

4. Choose OK to close the dialog box, or choose Print to print the specified area.

To print column and row headings

1. Select the sheet or sheets for which you want to print headings.
2. Choose the File Page Setup command.
3. Choose the Row and Column Headings option so there is an X in the check box.
4. Choose OK to close the dialog box or Print to print the sheet now.

To set up to print

1. Choose the File Print command. The Print dialog box appears.
2. In the Print What area, choose one of the following options:

Option	Description
Selection	Print only the selected cells or ranges
Selected Sheet(s)	Print only the selected sheets
Entire Workbook	Print all sheets in workbook

3. Select or type the number of Copies you want.
4. In the Page Range area, choose to print either All or choose Page(s). If you choose Page(s), enter the pages you want to print in the From and To text boxes.
5. Choose the Printer Setup button to change printers or set up different printing options. The Printer Setup dialog box appears.
6. In Printer, choose the printer you want to print to.
7. You can also choose the Setup button which may display a dialog box relating to the selected printer.

Change any options—such as paper size, orientation, and fonts—and then choose OK to return to the Print dialog box.

Note

Each printer displays a different type of Setup dialog box, and some printers do not display the box. An HP LaserJet III printer, for example, displays a dialog box that enables you to choose paper size and source, graphics resolution, copies, memory, orientation, and cartridges. Additionally, you can use the HP Font Installer to add more fonts and the Options dialog box to choose gray scales and other graphic options.

8. Choose OK to print the specified sheet or sheets.

Note

The Print dialog box also contains two buttons: Page Set**u**p and Print Previe**w**. Choose either button to display a corresponding dialog box and to help make changes to the worksheet before printing.

See also **Headers and Footers**, **Notes**, **Gridlines**, **Margins**, **Page Setup**, and **Page Breaks**.

Shortcuts

Click the Print Preview button on the Standard toolbar to change views.

Click the Print button on the Standard toolbar, or press Ctrl+P to display the Print dialog box.

Protecting Files

You can protect your files so the data cannot be changed. Excel enables you to protect worksheets, workbooks, windows, the structure of your workbook as well as the contents of a worksheet. Protecting the sheet prevents unauthorized changes to your work. Additionally, you can lock individual cells, cell ranges, objects, and so on, to prevent changes to the contents, whether the contents are data or formulas.

To lock cells

1. Select the cell or cell range you want to lock.
2. Choose the Format Cells command. The Format Cells dialog box appears.
3. Choose the Protection tab.
4. Choose the Locked option. An X appears in the check box.

> **Tip**
>
> All cells are locked by default and remain locked unless you unlock them. Locking, however, has no effect unless you protect the worksheet.

5. Choose OK to close the dialog box.
6. Follow the instructions to protect the worksheet.

To lock charts and objects

1. Select the chart or other object.
2. Choose the Format Object command. The Format Object dialog box appears.
3. Choose the Protection tab.
4. Choose the Locked option. An X appears in the check box.

5. Choose OK.

6. Follow the steps to protect the worksheet.

To protect worksheets

1. Select the sheet you want to protect.

2. Choose the Tools Protection command. A secondary menu appears.

3. Choose Protect Sheet. The Protect Sheet dialog box appears.

4. In Password, you can optionally enter a password. Only those users who know the password can remove sheet protection and access the sheet's data.

> **Note**
>
> A password can consist of letters, numbers, symbols, and spaces; a password is case-sensitive. If you enter "WhyMe" as a password, for example; the file will not open if you type "whyme" or Whyme."

5. Choose any of the following options:

Contents	Protects cells, macros, chart items
Objects	Protects graphic objects from being moved, sized, edited, or deleted
Scenarios	Protects against changes to scenario definitions

6. Choose OK.

7. If you entered a password, Excel displays the Confirm Password dialog box. In Reenter Protection Password, type the same password and choose OK.

> **Note**
>
> If you lose or forget the password, you can no longer access the protected worksheet.

To protect the workbook

1. Choose the Tools Protection command. A secondary menu appears.
2. Choose Protect Workbook. The Protect Workbook dialog box appears.
3. In the Password text box, enter a password (this step is optional).
4. Choose one or both of the following options:

Structure	Prevents changes to workbook: sheets cannot be deleted, moved, hidden, renamed; new sheets cannot be inserted
Windows	Windows cannot be moved or resized; minimize, maximize, control menu box, and windows borders are all hidden

5. Choose OK to close the dialog box.
6. If you entered a password, Excel displays the Confirm Password dialog box. Enter the password again and choose OK.

To remove protection from a sheet or workbook

1. Open the sheet or workbook.
2. Choose the Tool Protection command. A secondary menu appears.
3. Choose either the Unprotect Sheet or Unprotect Workbook command.

4. The Unprotect dialog box appears if you used a password. In Password, enter the assigned password and choose OK.

To unlock a cell range

1. Choose the Tools Protection command.
2. Choose Unprotect Sheet.
3. Select the cell or range you want to unlock.
4. Choose the Format Cells command. The Format Cells dialog box appears.
5. Choose the Protection tab.
6. Choose the Locked option so no X appears in the check box.
7. Choose OK. Now you can choose Tools Protection and Protect Sheet to protect the worksheet.

Records

See **Database Management**.

Replace

See **Finding and Replacing**.

Reports

A report is a combination of sheets, views, and scenarios gathered and printed together for your convenience. Any reports you create with a workbook are saved with the workbook file.

To create a report

1. Choose the File Print Report command. The Print Report dialog box appears.

2. Choose the Add button. The Add Report dialog box appears.
3. In the Report Name text box, enter the name of the report you are creating.
4. In the Section to Add area, choose the Sheet, View, and Scenario you want to include in the report from the drop-down lists.
5. Choose the Add button and continue to add more sections to the report. The Sections in this Report area displays each section as you specify it.

> **Tip**
>
> You can check the Use Continuous Page Numbers option to number the report.

6. Choose OK to close the dialog box and return to the Print Report dialog box.
7. Choose Close to return to the worksheet or Print to print the report.

To print a report

1. Choose the File Print Report command. The Print Report dialog box appears.
2. In the Reports list, choose the report you want to print.
3. Choose the Print button. The Print dialog box appears.
4. Select or enter the number of Copies you want and choose OK.

Rounding

You can round a number or numbers by changing the numeric format. When Excel rounds a number, the entire number is still used in calculations.

To round numbers

1. Select the cell or range containing the numbers you want to round.
2. Choose the Format Cells command. The Format Cells dialog box appears.
3. Choose the Number tab.
4. In the Format Codes list, choose the format you want. 0.00, for example, displays the number rounded to two decimal places.
5. Choose OK to close the dialog box.

See also **Functions**.

Row Heights

You can adjust the height of the rows in your worksheet to fit the tallest entry or to a specified amount.

To adjust height automatically

1. Select the row you want to change.
2. Choose the Format Row command. A secondary menu appears.
3. Choose AutoFit. Excel adjusts the height of the row to fit the tallest character in the row.

> **Tip**
>
> You can also double-click the bottom border of a row heading to AutoFit the row height.

To adjust height manually

1. Select the row to change.
2. Choose the Format Row command. A secondary menu appears.

3. Choose Height. The Row Height dialog box appears.
4. In Row Height, enter a value in points for the row height.
5. Choose OK. Excel adjusts the row height.

Tip

You can also drag the bottom border of a row heading to manually adjust row height.

Saving Files

See the Common Features section.

Search

See **Finding and Replacing** and **Database Management.**

Selecting

Before you can edit, format, delete, move, and perform other actions on data and objects in your worksheet, you must first select the item. Excel enables you to select items with the mouse and the keyboard.

To select with the mouse

To select	Do this
Cell	Click it
Range	Click the first cell and drag the mouse across the cells in the range
Non-contiguous range	Select the first range, then hold the Ctrl key while selecting the next range. Continue to hold the Ctrl key and select as many ranges as you want

(continues)

To select	Do this
Row	Click the row heading number
Column	Click the column heading number
Worksheet	Click the Select all button (blank rectangle forming the cell where the row and column heading numbers meet)
Object	Click it
Sheet	Click the sheet tab
Several sheets	Select the first sheet tab, hold Shift, and click next
All sheets	Point the mouse at the sheet tabs and press the right mouse button; choose Select All Sheets
Chart	Double-click the chart; a screened border appears around the chart to indicate it is selected
Chart elements	Click the element

To select using the keyboard

Press	To select
Shift+Arrow key	One cell at a time in direction of the arrow
Ctrl+Shift+Arrow	To the edge of the current data region in direction of arrow
Shift+Home	To the beginning of row
Ctrl+Shift+End	To last cell in worksheet
Ctrl+spacebar	Entire column
Shift+spacebar	Entire row
Ctrl+A	Entire worksheet
Shift+Page Up/Down	Up/Down one screen

Shading Cells

See Color.

Sorting

You can sort any worksheet information—including numbers, text, logical values, and so on—in either ascending or descending order. You will likely use sorting for organizing lists and databases, but you can use it with any text or data in a worksheet.

To sort information

1. Select the list or information you want to sort.
2. Choose the Data Sort command. The Sort dialog box appears.
3. In Sort By, choose either Ascending or Descending order.
4. You can also choose to sort duplicate items by choosing Then By and an order.
5. In My List Has, choose whether the list has a Header Row or No Header Row.
6. Choose OK to sort the information.

Shortcut

Select the information and choose either the Sort Ascending or Sort Descending button from the Standard toolbar. The sort groups only the first column in the selected range.

Spelling Checker

See the Integration section.

Split-Window

You can view two parts of a worksheet on-screen at the same time. This Windows feature enables you to compare and edit two places at once.

To split the window

1. Position the insertion point in the row where you want the split.
2. Choose the **W**indow **S**plit command. Excel splits the window to the top and left of the selected cell. You can move the splits around to adjust the size of the portions by dragging the split bar.

> **Note**
>
> You can also create and remove splits by dragging the horizontal and vertical split boxes to the desired position. The split boxes are located on the horizontal and vertical scroll bars.

To remove the split

Choose the **W**indow Remove **S**plit command.

Starting Excel

See the Common Features section.

Styles

Styles are formats you create and save to use over and over again. You may, for example, change the column heading text to center-aligned, 10-point bold, Times New Roman text in a worksheet. You can save that formatting as a style and quickly apply that style to the other worksheets. Format the text only once, and save time and energy.

To create a style

1. Format the text as you want, and then select the cell containing the text.
2. Choose the Format Style command. The Style dialog box appears.
3. In the Style Name text box, enter a name for the style.
4. Choose OK.

> **Tip**
>
> You can also edit a style by choosing the **M**odify button in the Style dialog box. The Format Cells dialog box appears, from which you can choose to modify the Number, Alignment, Font, Border, Patterns, and Protection of the selected style.

To apply a style

1. Select the cell or range you want to apply the style to.
2. Choose the Format Style command. The Format Style dialog box appears.
3. In the Style Name drop-down list, select the style you want to apply.
4. Choose OK.

See also **Formatting**.

Subtotals

You can analyze the data in a list by subtotaling it. You can use subtotals to summarize data in a column, row, or in a combination of both. When you insert subtotals, Excel automatically inserts the grand total row at the bottom of the list.

To subtotal a list

1. Sort the list.

> **Tip**
>
> The first row must have column headers; if it does not, Excel displays a message box asking if the top row is a header row. Choose OK if this is so; choose Cancel and add a header if the top row does not contain a header.

2. Choose the Data Su**b**totals command. The Subtotals dialog box appears.
3. In the **A**t Each Change In drop-down list, select the column heading containing the groups you want to subtotal. If you selected only one column, the default heading is that column.
4. In the **U**se Function drop-down list, select the calculation you want to use.
5. In the A**d**d Subtotal To box, select the column or columns you want to add the subtotal to.

> **Note**
>
> You can choose from the three options in the dialog box: Replace **C**urrent Subtotals, **P**age Break Between Groups, and **S**ummary Below Data.

6. Choose OK to close the dialog box. Excel summarizes the data.

To remove subtotals

1. Choose the Data Su**b**totals command. The Subtotal dialog box appears.
2. Choose the **R**emove All button.

Summing

The most common function in a worksheet is the SUM function. You can quickly and easily total a selected row or column using a shortcut button in Excel.

To sum numbers

1. Select the cell you want to contain the sum.
2. Σ Click the AutoSum button on the Standard toolbar. Excel places the sum formula in the cell and formula bar.
3. If Excel's selection of cells is correct, press Enter or click the AutoSum button again. Alternatively, if Excel does not select cells or the selection is not correct, drag the mouse across the cells you want to add and then press Enter. Excel inserts the correct total in the specified cell.

See also **Functions**.

Templates

You can create a template, or foundation workbook, in which you store such information as macros, graphics, text and page formats, and text. After saving the template, you can use it as a base to start other workbooks that will contain the same objects, text, and formatting.

To create a template

1. Create the workbook base. Add all common text, formatting, and graphics and set the margins, orientation, borders, and styles you want to use. Add any macros or other information necessary to the template.
2. Choose the File Save As command. The Save As dialog box appears.
3. In the File Name text box, enter the template name.
4. In Save File as Type, choose Template.

5. In Directories, choose the \msoffice\excel\xlstart directory.

6. Choose OK to save the template.

To use the template

1. Choose the File New command; alternatively, press Ctrl+N. The New dialog box appears.

2. In New, choose the template you saved and choose OK.

Text Boxes

Use a text box to add text to a worksheet without having to enter the text in a cell. You can add notes, annotations, explanatory text, callouts, and other kinds of text additions in a text box. You can format the text in a text box as you would any other text.

To create a text box

1. Click the Text Box button on the Standard toolbar. The mouse pointer changes to a cross when you move it to the worksheet.

2. Position the cross at the point you want the top left corner to appear and then drag the box down and to the right. You can adjust the height and width of the text box as you draw it.

3. Release the mouse button. The text box appears. It hides the gridlines and any text or data in cells behind it.

4. Type the text you want in the text box.

Note

You can select text in a text box and format it using the Formatting toolbar or the Format Object dialog box. For other formatting options, you can select the text box (so the handles appear) and use the Format Object dialog box.

To manipulate the text box

To	Do this
Select	Click once; a gray border with handles indicates the text box is selected
Edit text	Double-click the text box; the cursor appears in the box
Move	Select the box and position the pointer over one of the screened borders; drag the text box to a new position
Resize	Select the box and position the pointer over a handle until the pointer changes to a double-headed arrow; drag the arrow to resize the box

See also **Alignment**, **Formatting**, **Borders**, and **Deleting**.

Toolbars

See the Integration section.

Underlining

See **Formatting**.

Undo

See the Common Features section.

Wizards

See **Charts**, **Functions** and **Pivot Tables**, as well as the Common Features section.

Worksheet Views

Excel enables you to specify which elements you want to view on-screen, and at what magnification you want to view your worksheet. You can, for example, remove the Formula bar, Status bar, and any or all of the toolbars from view. Additionally, Excel enables you to choose from several magnifications, or create your own custom magnification in which to view your worksheet.

To change view options

Note

Options with an X in the check box are activated. Selecting an activated check box removes the X and turns the option off. Selecting the option again adds the X and turns the option back on.

1. Choose the Tools **O**ptions command. The Options dialog box appears.
2. Choose the View tab.
3. In the Show area, you can choose to show the **F**ormula bar, **S**tatus bar, **N**ote Indicator (small red box in a cell containing a note), and or the Info **W**indow.

Tip

You can choose the **V**iew **F**ormula Bar command, the **V**iew **S**tatus Bar command, or the **T**oolbars command to show or hide these elements.

4. In the Objects area, choose whether to Show All, Show Placeholders, or Hi**d**e All.
5. In Window Options, choose the items you want to show or hide from the following list of options:

Option	Description
A**u**tomatic Page Breaks	Displays Excel's automatic page breaks
Fo**r**mulas	Displays formulas in the cell instead of the values produced
Gridlines	Shows or hides the gridlines
Color	Sets a color for the gridlines
Row & Column H**e**aders	Displays row and column headings
Outline Symbols	Displays outlining symbols
Zero Values	Displays all zero values
Horizon**t**al Scroll Bar	Shows or hides the horizontal scroll bar
Vertical Scroll Bar	Shows or hides the vertical scroll bar
Sheet Ta**b**s	Shows or hides the sheet tabs

6. Choose OK to close the dialog box.

Shortcuts

Press Ctrl+6 to switch among displaying all objects, displaying placeholders, and hiding all objects.

Press Ctrl+8 to show or hide the outlining symbols.

Press Ctrl+ ' (left single quotation mark) to show formulas instead of values in cells.

To change magnification

1. Choose the View Zoom command. The Zoom dialog box appears.

2. In Magnification, choose a percentage view option, or you can choose Custom and enter a percentage in the text box.

3. Choose OK to close the dialog box. Excel changes the view to the specified magnification.

Tip

To display a full-screen view in which only the worksheet, scroll bars, sheet tabs, and menu bar show, choose the **V**iew F**u**ll Screen command. To switch back to the normal view, click the Full Screen button in the Full toolbar provided when you switched to full-screen view.

Shortcut

100% Click the down arrow to the right of the Zoom Control box, and select a magnification from the drop-down list.

PowerPoint

PowerPoint, the third component of Microsoft Office, is an effective presentation program. With PowerPoint, you can create slides, overhead transparencies, or printed presentations. Using Word and Excel in conjunction with PowerPoint, you can exchange text and data and present updated information in an organized and effectual way.

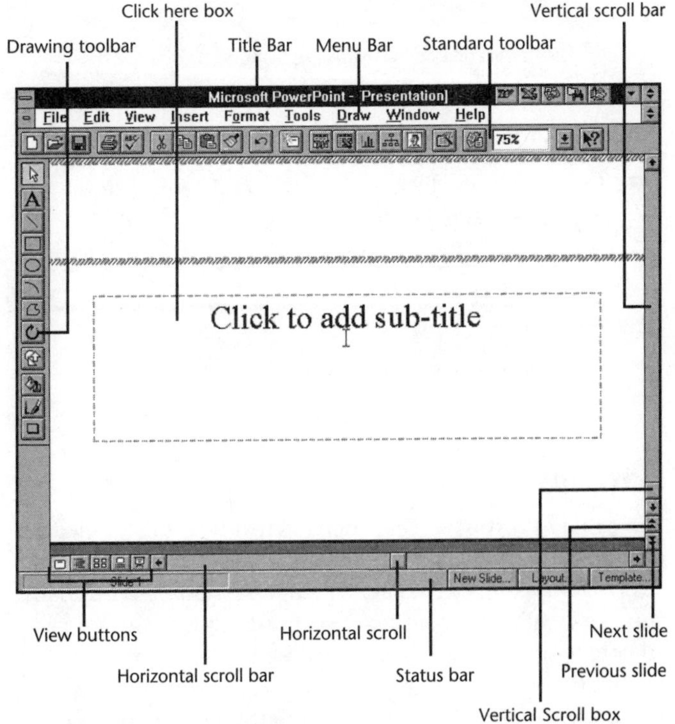

Add Notes

See **Annotate Slide Show.**

Add Slide

You can add a slide at any time; PowerPoint offers a variety of AutoLayouts from which you can choose. An AutoLayout presents you with many different styles of layout to choose from, such as text, chart, graph, bulleted list, and so on.

To add a slide

1. Choose the **I**nsert New **S**lide command, or press Ctrl+M. The New Slide dialog box appears.

> **Tip**
>
> Use the scroll bar to view more layouts.

2. Select the layout you want.
3. Choose OK to close the dialog box. The new slide appears on-screen.

> **Shortcut**
>
> New Slide... Click the New Slide button on the status bar.

Add Text

You can add text in a "Click here..." text box—also called a placeholder—including title text, sub-title text, bullets, and so on, by clicking in the preformatted text box. Additionally, you can create your own text box in which you enter text anywhere on the slide. Text added with a text box is automatically formatted as 24-point Times New Roman. Naturally, you can change text formatting of any text in the presentation.

To add a text box

1. Click the Text Tool on the Drawing toolbar. The pointer changes to an upside down cross when it is pointing to an area where you can draw a text box.

2. Position the Text Tool and drag the tool to create a rectangular box that will hold the text.

> **Tip**
>
> You can drag the Text Tool up or down and to the left or right; the rectangular box follows as you drag.

3. Release the mouse button. The border of the text box appears shaded to indicate it is active, and a blinking cursor appears in the box.

4. Type as you normally would.

> **Note**
>
> You can move the added text box, or any text box, by clicking in the text box, then clicking the screened border of the box. Small black handles appear indicating the box is selected. Position the mouse pointer on the border and drag the box to a new location.

To delete a text block

1. Click the text block and then select it by clicking the screened border.

2. Press the Delete key.

See also **Font, Font Style,** and **Font Size**.

Align Objects

To create an attractive slide presentation, you may want to move objects and text around on the slide. PowerPoint provides several methods of aligning objects—pictures, graphs, tables, clip art, and so on—so you can be sure the finished slide looks attractive and professional. You can use PowerPoint's horizontal and vertical rulers, guides, or automatic align feature to align the objects.

To align objects using the rulers

1. Choose the **V**iew **R**uler command. The horizontal and vertical rulers appear on-screen.

2. Drag the object to a new location. As you drag the pointer, guides appear on each ruler to show its position on the page.

> **Tip**
>
> To hide the rulers, choose the **V**iew **R**uler command again.

To align objects using the guides

1. Choose the **V**iew **G**uides command.

2. PowerPoint displays non-printing horizontal and vertical guidelines that appear as dotted lines on the screen.

> **Tip**
>
> When you move an object close to a guide, the edges or center of the object (whichever is closest) snaps to the guide.

3. To move the guide, drag it with the mouse pointer.

> **Tip**
>
> To hide the guides, choose the **V**iew **G**uides command.

To align objects together

1. Select the objects you want to align by clicking on the first object, holding the Shift key, and then clicking on each successive object.

2. Choose the **D**raw **A**lign command. A cascading menu appears.

> **Note**
>
> The **D**raw **A**lign command is only available for use with two or more selected objects.

3. Choose from the following options:

> **Note**
>
> The Align options align only the rectangles containing the objects—not the objects within the rectangles. Additionally, the Align commands align the selected rectangles in relation to each other, not in relation to the page.

Option	Description
Lefts	Aligns the left sides of each rectangle
Centers	Aligns the rectangles at the vertical center
Rights	Aligns the right sides of each rectangle
Tops	Aligns the tops of the rectangles
Middles	Aligns the rectangles at the horizontal center
Bottoms	Aligns the bottoms of the rectangles

Align Text

You can align the text in any text block to the left, right, center, or fully justified. Text in a text box aligns to the borders of the rectangle containing the text.

To align text

1. Position the insertion point in the text, or select the text box.
2. Choose the F**o**rmat **A**lignment command. A cascading menu appears.
3. Choose from these options: **L**eft, **C**enter, **R**ight, or **J**ustify.

> **Tip**
>
> A bullet to the left of the option indicates that it is the current text alignment.

> **Shortcut**
>
>   Click the Left Alignment or Center Alignment button on the Formatting toolbar to left- or center-align the text.
>
> Alternatively, you can press the alignment shortcut key combinations: Ctrl+L (left), Ctrl+R (right), Ctrl+E (center), or Ctrl+J (justify).

Anchor Text

You can type text within a shape and then anchor the text to the top, middle, or bottom of the shape in order to control the way the text fits into a shape. If you resize or move the object, anchored text will move with the object.

To anchor text

1. Select the text or the object containing the text that you want to anchor.
2. Choose the F**o**rmat **T**ext Anchor command. The Text Anchor dialog box appears.
3. In **A**nchor Point, choose the position of the text within the object.

4. In Box Margins, set a left and right or a top and bottom measurement for the space between the text and the borders of the box.

5. You can also choose from the following options:

   Adjust Object Size to **F**it Text forces the object to enlarge or reduce to fit the text; especially handy for when the text is edited.

   Word-wrap Text in Object forces the text to wrap from one line to the next to fit within the borders of the object.

> **Tip**
>
> Choose the **P**review button to view the changes before accepting them.

6. Choose OK to close the dialog box.

Annotate Slide Show

As you run the slide show, you can use the mouse pointer to draw on the screen to underline, for example, important features of the presentation as you are speaking. Any annotations you make during the slide show are temporary and not saved with the presentation.

To annotate a slide

1. Choose the **V**iew Slide Sho**w** command. The Slide Show dialog box appears.

2. Make any changes and then choose **S**how to start the slide show.

3. Move the mouse and the Freehand annotation button appears. Click the button and the pointer changes to a pencil.

Note

The Freehand button is a toggle button. Click it a second time and the mouse cursor changes back to a pointer.

4. Move the pencil to a location you want to draw in and drag the pen to draw lines, write on the slide, and so on. Press the E key to erase annotations during a slide show.

Tip

Depending on your mouse, you may find it difficult to draw or write with the pencil. Practice using the tool before you give the final presentation.

AutoContent Wizard

The AutoContent wizard takes you step by step through creating a presentation by helping you select a presentation category—such as Selling a Service, a Product, or an Idea. AutoContent creates an outline for you to follow, based upon the purpose of your presentation. Additionally, the wizard creates the slide layouts for you; all you have to do is enter the information.

To use the wizard

1. Choose the **F**ile **N**ew command. The New Presentation dialog box appears.
2. In Create a New Presentation Using, choose the **A**utoContent Wizard.
3. Click OK to start the wizard. The AutoContent Wizard-Step 1 of 4 dialog box appears, containing information about starting the wizard.
4. Click the **N**ext button to continue. The AutoContent Wizard-Step 2 of 4 dialog box appears.

Tip

After the first dialog box, you can choose the **B**ack button to review or change any choices you have made in the previous wizard boxes.

5. Step 2 prompts you to create a title slide for the presentation. Answer the questions in the dialog box.

Note

Some of the information may already be completed using information entered when the program was installed. You can delete and replace this information if you want.

6. Click the **N**ext button. The AutoContent Wizard-Step 3 of 4 dialog box appears.
7. In Step 3, choose the type of presentation you want to create. Select each type and view an outline in the sample box within the dialog box.
8. Click the **N**ext button. The AutoContent Wizard-Step 4 of 4 dialog box appears, notifying you the wizard is complete.
9. Click the **F**inish button. PowerPoint displays the outline for the presentation, plus Cue Cards to help you complete the presentation. Enter the text for the presentation in the Outline mode.

Tip

To view the actual slides, choose the **V**iew **S**lides command. The wizard leaves the presentation in outline view.

See also **Outlines, New Presentation**, as well as the Common Features section.

AutoLayout

See **Layouts**.

AutoShapes

See **Drawing**.

Borders

PowerPoint automatically adds a border to any object you draw, but you can also add borders to text boxes, pictures, and imported art. PowerPoint enables you to delete borders, change border styles and line weights, as well as change the color of the borders around your objects.

To add a border

1. Select the object to which you want to add a border.

2. Choose the F**o**rmat Colors and **L**ines command. The Colors and Lines dialog box appears.

3. In **L**ines, choose a color for the line.

4. In Line **S**tyles, select any of the line styles.

5. In **D**ashed Lines, select a dashed, dotted, or solid pattern for the line.

6. Choose the **P**review button and move the dialog box out of the way to see the border before accepting the changes.

7. Choose OK to close the dialog box and apply the border.

To remove a border

1. Select the object with the border.

2. Choose the F**o**rmat Colors and **L**ines command. The Colors and Lines dialog box appears.

3. In the **L**ine box, choose No Line; choose OK to close the dialog box.

Shortcut

 Click the Line Color tool button on the Drawing+ toolbar to display a palette of available line colors.

 Click the Line Style tool button from the Drawing+ toolbar to display various line styles and thicknesses.

Builds and Transitions

Use builds and transitions to make your slide show more interesting. A *build* is when each successive slide adds one more bulleted item to the previous items until the entire list is displayed on one slide. A *transition* is the method in which you move from one slide to the next. PowerPoint presents several transitions you can use to attract attention; you can use different transitions between each slide in a show.

To build a slide

1. Choose the **T**ools **B**uild command. The Build dialog box appears.

2. Choose from the following options:

Option	Description
Build Body Text	A simple build; one item adds to the previous item
Dim Previous Points	The previous item fades and changes color as the next build item appears; choose a color in the color drop-down list below the option
Effect	Select the special effect from the drop-down list

3. Choose OK to close the dialog box.

To apply transitions

1. Move to the first slide to which you want to assign a transition.
2. Choose the **T**ools **T**ransition command. The Transition dialog box appears.
3. In **E**ffect, choose the effect you want to use.

> **Tip**
>
> Watch the small slide in the right corner of the dialog box to view the specified transition effect when you select it from the list.

4. In Speed, choose **S**low, **M**edium, or **F**ast as the transition rate.
5. In Advance, choose to move to the next slide **O**nly on Mouse Click, or **A**utomatically After and enter a number of seconds.
6. Choose OK to close the dialog box.

> **Note**
>
> To apply the same transition effects to all of the slides in the show, choose the **V**iew Sli**d**e Sorter command. Press Ctrl+A to select all of the slides in the show. Choose the Transition Effects drop-down list on the Slide Sorter toolbar and choose a transition to apply to all of the slides.

Bullets

You can use any of PowerPoint's slide layouts that contain bullet styles—such as Bulleted List, 2 Column Text, and so on—to create bullets in your slides. All you do is click the mouse in the placeholder and enter the text. When you press Enter, the bullet is repeated and you continue to enter text.

Additionally, you can format any text to bullet text and then modify the formatting, if you want.

To format bullet text

1. Enter the text, or position the insertion point where you want the bulleted text to begin.
2. Choose the Format Bullet command. The Bullet dialog box appears.
3. Choose the Use a Bullet option, so an X appears in the check box.
4. In Bullets From, choose a font from the drop-down list. The available characters from that font appear.

> **Tip**
>
> Some fonts offer better bullets than others. Try Symbol, Wingdings, or Dingbats.

5. In Special Color, you can choose a color other than black by selecting the option and then clicking the down arrow. Choose the color from the drop-down palette.
6. In Size, you can scale the bullet to be larger or smaller than the text; 100% is the default.
7. Choose any bullet by clicking it with the mouse pointer; the bullet enlarges so you can be sure it is the right bullet.
8. Choose OK to accept the bullet and close the dialog box.

> **Shortcut**
>
> 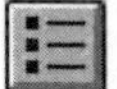 Select text and click the Bullet On/Off button on the Formatting toolbar to add or remove a bullet from the text. The button is a toggle button.

Chart

In PowerPoint, a chart is an organizational chart. PowerPoint provides the applet (a mini-program packaged with another software program) Microsoft Organization Chart to make producing charts simple. The Chart applet enables you to choose from a variety of chart styles and formats; it gives you complete control over the final look of the chart.

To create a chart

1. Move to the slide that will hold the chart.
2. Choose the **I**nsert **O**bject command. The Insert Object dialog box appears.
3. In Object **T**ype, choose Microsoft Organization Chart.
4. Choose OK. PowerPoint displays the Microsoft Organization Chart window containing a sample chart and tool buttons.
5. Click in the first chart box. Enter the name and title to replace the placeholder text.

Tip

Double-click the mouse over a placeholder to display the "comment" areas; add extra text in these areas, if you want.

6. To add a new box to the organization chart, click one of the buttons on the toolbar—Subordinate, Co-worker, Manager, or Assistant—and click the tool on the box you want to attach the new box to. Enter the text.

Tip

A Add a title for your chart. To enter notes, comments, annotations, or any other text, click the Text tool in the toolbar, click where you want the text to go, and begin typing.

7. To insert the chart into your slide, choose the **F**ile **U**pdate Presentation command.

8. To exit the Microsoft Organization Chart applet, choose the **F**ile E**x**it and Return to Presentation command. PowerPoint returns to the presentation and inserts the chart on the current page.

Editing the chart

1. Double-click the chart on the slide; the Organization Chart menus and tools appear.

2. Edit the text by clicking the mouse in the box and typing or deleting.

3. You can use the Microsoft Organization Chart menus to format text, change the style of the chart, align text, and so on. Following are some useful commands and the menus in which you will find them in the Chart applet:

Command	Description
Edit **S**elect	Select all or any group of boxes in a chart, such as All Assistants or All Managers, to perform a task on just that level
Edit Select Le**v**els	Select all boxes between two levels, such as 1 through 3 or 2 through 6
Styles menu	Choose from various chart layouts
Text **F**ont	Select the font, style, and size of the selected text
Text menu	Left, right, or center align the selected text
Boxes Box **B**order	Select from various thicknesses and styles of borders for the chart boxes
Boxes Box Sh**a**dow	Select from various shadow styles

(continues)

Command	Description
Boxes **C**olor	Choose a color for the box
Boxes Line **T**hickness	Choose a line thickness for the connecting line
Boxes Line St**y**le	Choose a solid, dashed, or dotted line style for a connecting line
Line Co**l**or	Choose a color for the connecting line
Chart menu	Choose viewing options, such as 200% or 50% of actual size

4. To update the chart in the slide, choose the **F**ile **U**pdate Presentation command.

5. To exit the Microsoft Organization Chart applet, choose the **F**ile E**x**it and Return to Presentation command. PowerPoint returns to the presentation and inserts the chart on the current page.

Shortcut

Click the Org Chart button on the Standard toolbar; the Microsoft Organization Chart applet appears.

Alternatively, you can click the Layout button on the Status bar and choose the Org Chart layout; the slide is added to the presentation. Double-click the organization chart placeholder and the Microsoft Organization Chart applet appears.

See also the Integration section.

ClipArt Gallery

The ClipArt Gallery is a dialog box that enables you to view all clip art files included with Microsoft Office. From the Gallery files, choose the art you want to insert into a slide.

The slides include over 1,000 images such as animals, people, symbols, and scenic backgrounds. You can also add your own images, or other clip art files to the Gallery.

After inserting a clip art file, you can resize and move the art to suit the design of your slide and presentation. You also can quickly replace one image with another, using the ClipArt Gallery.

Note

The first time you use the Gallery in PowerPoint, you are asked if you want to add the clip art from PowerPoint to the Gallery. Choose OK and from that point on, the Gallery opens without hesitation.

To open and use the Gallery

1. Choose the **I**nsert **C**lip Art command. The Microsoft ClipArt Gallery dialog box appears.
2. In Choose a **C**ategory to View Below, scroll through the available categories and choose one; alternatively, you can leave the default choice, All Categories, and view all clip art in the Gallery.
3. Scroll through the Gallery's pictures and click on any picture you want to insert.
4. Choose OK to insert the picture and close the Gallery.

To replace one image with another

1. Double-click the clip art on the slide. The Microsoft ClipArt Gallery appears.
2. Select the new picture and choose OK. PowerPoint replaces the first image with the second.

To move and resize the clip art

1. Select the clip art by clicking on the image. Handles appear on the corners and sides of the image box to indicate it is selected.

2. To move the art, position the pointer in the center of the art and drag it to its new location.

   To resize the art, position the pointer over one of the handles until a double-headed arrow appears. Drag the double-headed arrow to resize.

> **Shortcut**
>
>  Click the Insert Clip Art button on the Standard toolbar to display the ClipArt Gallery.

Close

See the Common Features section.

Colors

When presenting a slide show on a color monitor, or when printing to a color printer, the color schemes you use must be attractive to make your presentation pleasing to the eye. You must also consider text color for readability, and fill and line colors for contrast as well as emphasis. Color is one of the most important factors of a presentation, and PowerPoint enables you to change the color of most elements in a slide.

To change text color

1. Select the text or the text box to be changed.
2. Choose the F**o**rmat **F**ont command. The Font dialog box appears.
3. In **C**olor, click the down arrow, and a limited color palette appears. Choose a color from the palette or choose "Other Color."
4. The Other Color dialog box appears with a larger Color Palette. Choose a color from the palette, or choose the **M**ore Colors button.

5. The More Colors dialog box appears. You can choose a color from the color swatch, and fine-tune it with the color bar.

   You can also select or enter values in the following text boxes to mix a custom color:

Text box	Description
H**u**e	Changes the color
Sat	Changes the intensity (saturation) of the color; a larger number in the value box represents a more intense color
Lum	Adds black or white to the color to affect the luminance; the larger the number, the more black that is added
Red	Increases or decreases the amount of red in the color
Green	Increases or decreases the amount of green in the color
Blue	Increases or decreases the amount of blue in the color

> **Tip**
>
> The Color and Solid boxes preview the color.

6. When you are finished choosing colors, choose OK in each successive dialog box to close the boxes.

> **Note**
>
> You can also change the color of the bullets in any text by choosing the F**o**rmat **B**ullet command. In the Bullet dialog box, choose the Special **C**olor down arrow to reveal a color palette like the one used in the Font dialog box. You can choose Other Color and **M**ore colors to display more color choices.

Fill and Line Color

1. Select the object, table cell, chart item, AutoShape, or other item you want to fill or change line color.

2. Choose the F**o**rmat Colors and **L**ines command. The Colors and Lines dialog box appears.

3. In **F**ill, click the down arrow to display the color palette. Choose a color or choose one of the following options:

Option	Description
No Fill	No fill in the selected object
Background	Matches the fill color of the background
Shaded	Displays the Shaded Fill dialog box; define a graduated fill for the selected object
Pattern	Displays the Pattern Fill dialog box; define a pattern to fill the object
Other Color	Displays the Other Color dialog box

4. To change the line, click the **L**ine down arrow. The color palette appears. Choose a color or select Other Color to display the Other Color dialog box.

5. Choose OK to close the Colors and Lines dialog box.

Note

You can also change the color of a shadow added to a box or other object by choosing the F**o**rmat S**h**adow command. In the Shadow dialog box, choose **C**olor. Choose a color from the drop-down palette or choose Other Color to display the Other Color dialog box.

Shortcut

   Select an object and click the Fill Color, Line Color, or Shadow Color button on the Drawing+ toolbar.

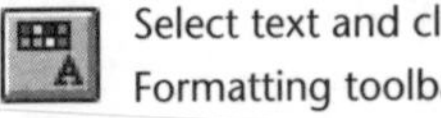 Select text and click the Text Color button on the Formatting toolbar to choose a color from the palette or to display the Other Color dialog box.

  Select an object and click the Apply Fill or the Line buttons from the Drawing toolbar to show or hide the fill or line for that object.

To change an element in a color scheme

1. Choose the F**o**rmat Slide **C**olor Scheme command. The Slide Color Scheme dialog box appears.
2. To change the color of one or two elements in the slide, you can select each element and change its color. In the **C**hange Scheme Colors area, select the color square representing the area of color you want to change. For example, select Background if you want to change the color of the background of the slide.
3. Choose the Change C**o**lor button. The (Background) Color dialog box appears.
4. In the Color **P**alette, choose a new color for the selected element and choose OK to return to the Slide Color Scheme dialog box.

To change an entire color scheme

1. To change the entire color scheme, in the Slide Color Scheme dialog box, choose the Choose **S**cheme button to display the Choose Scheme dialog box.
2. In **B**ackground Color, choose the background color of the slide. Corresponding colors appear in the **T**ext & Line Color list.

3. Select a color for the text and line. Samples appear in the **O**ther Scheme Colors area.

4. Select a sample from the **O**ther Scheme Colors area to complete the color scheme.

5. Choose OK to close the dialog box and return to the Slide Color Scheme box.

6. Choose the **A**pply button to apply the new color scheme to just one slide, or choose the Apply **t**o All button to change all slides in the presentation.

The dialog box closes and PowerPoint applies the new color scheme.

> **Tip**
>
> If you change your mind about the new colors, choose the **F**ollow Master button in the Slide Color Scheme dialog box. PowerPoint changes the presentation back to the original colors.

Copy and Paste Text

Use the Copy and Paste commands to insert text from one slide to another, or from one application to another. When you copy text in any Windows program, a duplicate of the text is placed on the Clipboard. After copying text, you can reposition the insertion point and then paste the copy in another location. Additionally, you can continue to paste the same duplicated text over and over again, until another cut or copied selection replaces it on the Clipboard.

To copy and paste text

1. Select the text to be copied.

2. Choose the **E**dit **C**opy command, or press Ctrl+C. The text is duplicated on the Clipboard.

3. Reposition the insertion point.

Note

You can reposition the insertion point in the same slide, on another slide, in a different presentation, or in a Word or Excel document.

4. Choose the **E**dit **P**aste command, or press Ctrl+V. The copied text is placed at the insertion point.

Note

As an alternative to using the Copy and Paste commands, you can select the text you want to copy and hold the Ctrl key while you drag the text to a new location on the same slide.

Shortcut

Select the text and click the Copy button on the Standard toolbar; reposition the insertion point and click the Paste button.

See also the Integration section.

Delete Objects

You can easily delete objects, such as a text block, clip art, chart, graph, or other element. When you delete an object, you do not transfer the object to the Clipboard; the object is cleared from the slide completely.

To delete an object

1. Select the object.

2. Choose the **E**dit Cle**a**r command, or press the Delete key. The object is erased from the slide.

> **Tip**
>
> If you change your mind, choose the **E**dit **U**ndo command or press Ctrl+Z to undo the clear. You must, however, perform the Undo before you perform another task or you cannot undo the deletion.

Delete Slides

You can delete one or more slides from a presentation. You can also Undo the deletion, but only if you undo before performing another task.

To delete a slide

1. Choose the **V**iew Sli**d**e Sorter command.

> **Note**
>
> You can also delete a slide in Outline view. To change to Outline view, choose the **V**iew **O**utline command. Additionally, you can delete a slide from Slide view by displaying the slide and choosing the **E**dit Delete Sl**i**de command.

2. Select the slide.
3. Choose the **E**dit Cle**a**r command, or press the Delete key.

Delete Text

You can delete an entire block of text, or you can select one or more characters from a text box to delete.

To delete text

1. Click on the text box.
2. Select the text you want to delete.
3. Choose the **E**dit Cle**a**r command, or press the Delete key.

See also **Delete Objects**.

Drag and Drop

See the Integration section.

Drawing

PowerPoint includes many drawing tools and features that enable you to add shapes, lines, and objects to a slide for emphasis, ornamentation, or illustration purposes. PowerPoint includes two drawing toolbars: Drawing and Drawing+. Use the toolbars to draw shapes and lines, enter text, add AutoShapes, alter fill and line color, and manipulate drawn objects.

You can also use the drawing tools to add to clip art or other files you import to your slides. You can, for example, add an AutoShape with text to a graph imported from Excel or draw an arrow pointing to a particular item in a Word table placed in your presentation.

Following are the drawing tools on the Drawing toolbar:

Button	Tool	Description
	Selection	Use to select objects, lines, shapes, and so on
A	Text	Use to draw a text box and enter text anywhere on the slide
	Line	Use to draw one straight line; you must click the tool again to draw another line
	Rectangle	Use to draw a square or rectangle; hold the Shift key while using the tool to create a perfect square
	Ellipse	Use to draw an oval or circle; hold Shift while drawing to create a perfect circle

(continues)

Button	Tool	Description
	Arc	Use to draw arcs and curves
	Freeform	Use to draw freehand lines, moving the mouse the way you move the pencil and the freeform line follows; double-click to end the line
	Free Rotate	Select a line or shape, and then click this tool and drag to rotate the object
	AutoShapes	Displays the AutoShape toolbar; click a tool and drag the mouse on the slide, the specified shape draws as you drag
	Fill On/Off	Changes the fill of the selected object between the background color and the default color
	Line On/Off	Shows or hides the line of the selected object
	Shadow	Displays or hides a shadow around On/Off object

The following are tools on the Drawing+ toolbar:

Button	Tool	Description
	Fill Color	Assign a color to a shape; choose a color from the palette or select Other Color to view more colors
	Line Color	Assign a color to a selected line; choose a color from the palette or select Other Color to view more colors
	Shadow Color	Assign a shadow to a selected shape or line; choose a color from the palette or select Other Color

Button	Tool	Description
	Line Style	Assign a line thickness or style to the selected line or border
	Dashed Lines	Choose from dashed, dotted, or solid line for the selected line or border
	Arrowheads	Apply an arrowhead style to a selected line
	Bring Forward	Places the selected line or object in front of all others in the drawing
	Send Backward	Places the selected line or object behind all others
	Group	Groups all selected objects or lines together so you can perform various tasks, such as changing line style, applying fill color, deleting, and moving
	Ungroup	Ungroups a selected group of objects or lines
	Rotate Left	Rotates the selected line or shape 90 degrees to the left
	Rotate Right	Rotates the selected line or shape 90 degrees to the right
	Flip Horizontal	Flips the selected line or object 180 degrees horizontally
	Flip Vertical	Flips the selected line or object 180 degrees vertically

To use the drawing tools

1. Display the Drawing toolbar. Point the mouse at the current toolbar and click the right mouse button. A quick menu appears. Choose the Drawing toolbar.

> **Tip**
>
> PowerPoint also includes the Drawing+ toolbar with additional tools. To display the toolbar, repeat step one and choose the Drawing+ option.

2. Click the tool you want to use and move the tool to the slide.

3. Drag the tool to the size you want the line or shape to be.

> **Note**
>
> To move a line or shape, select it and then drag the line or shape to a new location.
>
> To enlarge or reduce a line or shape, select it and then drag a selection handle.

4. Using other tools in the toolbars, you can change the line, fill, line style, rotation, and other attributes of the lines or shapes you draw.

Drawing AutoShapes

1. Click the AutoShapes button on the Drawing toolbar. The AutoShapes toolbar appears.

2. Click the AutoShape you want to draw. The mouse pointer changes to a cross.

> **Tip**
>
> ToolTips display the name of a tool button beside the button when you hold the mouse pointer over any tool in the AutoShapes toolbar, just as with any toolbar.

3. Drag the cross on the slide to create the shape. As you drag, the shape changes size. Release the mouse button when finished.

4. Click the AutoShapes button again to hide the AutoShapes toolbar.

Drawing perfect shapes

1. Select any shape tool: AutoShapes, Rectangle, or Ellipse.

2. Hold the Shift key while you drag the cross to the size you want the shape.

> **Tip**
>
> Be sure to release the mouse button first and the Shift key second, or the shape distorts.

Drawing freeform shapes

1. Click the Freeform tool. The mouse changes to a cross.

2. Drag the tool (which changes to a pencil when you drag it) around on the slide as if you were drawing with an actual pencil.

3. Double-click the mouse when you want to stop the line.

Editing Slides

PowerPoint supplies many slide layouts you can use to create your slides. Additionally, you can change the slide layout after you enter text, objects, pictures, and so on. When you change a slide's layout, you can also resize and move objects on the slide to better fit the new layout.

To edit a slide layout

1. Choose the F**o**rmat Slide Lay**o**ut command. The Slide Layout dialog box appears.

2. In **R**eapply the current master styles, choose a style you want to use for the slide.

3. Choose the **A**pply button. PowerPoint moves the existing text and objects on the slide and adds new placeholders representing the new layout.

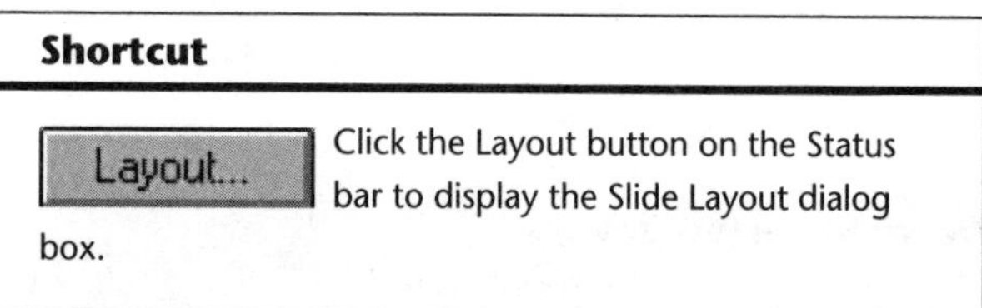

Shortcut

Click the Layout button on the Status bar to display the Slide Layout dialog box.

Exiting PowerPoint

See the Common Features section.

Fills and Patterns

You can fill an object with a solid color, a two-color pattern, shaded colors, or the same color as the background of the slide. When filling an object with a pattern, you assign a color to the foreground and another color to the background. PowerPoint also enables you to choose a graduated (shaded with one color from light to dark) fill for objects.

To fill with a pattern

1. Select the object to be filled.

2. Choose the F**o**rmat Colors and **L**ines command. The Colors and Lines dialog box appears.

3. In the **F**ill drop-down list, choose Pattern. The Pattern Fill dialog box appears.

4. Choose a pattern, and then choose a color for the **F**oreground and a color for the **B**ackground.

Tip

You can preview the pattern by clicking the **P**review button, so you can see the change before accepting it. If you cannot see the object, move the dialog box by dragging its title bar.

5. Choose OK to close the Pattern Fill dialog box and OK again to close the Colors and Lines dialog box.

To use a shaded fill

1. Select the object to be filled.
2. Choose the Format Colors and **L**ines command. The Colors and Lines dialog box appears.

Note

You can choose Background in the **F**ill drop-down list to change the color of the object's background to that of the slide.

3. In the **F**ill drop-down list, choose Shaded. The Shaded Fill dialog box appears.
4. In Shade Styles, choose the direction of the fill. When you choose a direction, examples appear in the Var**i**ants area.
5. When you find a direction you like, select a Var**i**ant.
6. In C**o**lor, choose the color you want to use and in **D**ark/Light, click an arrow or use the scroll box to make the shading lighter or darker.

Tip

Choose the **P**review button if you want to view the shaded fill before accepting or changing it.

7. Choose OK to close the Shaded Fill dialog box. Choose OK again to close the Colors and Lines dialog box.

To remove fills and patterns

1. Select the object.

2. Choose the F**o**rmat Colors and **L**ines command. The Colors and Lines dialog box appears.

3. In the **F**ill drop-down list, choose No Fill.

4. Choose OK to close the dialog box.

Shortcut

Select the object and click the Fill On/Off tool button on the Drawing toolbar to fill the object with the default color fill or to toggle to no fill.

Select the object and click the Fill Color tool on the Drawing+ toolbar to display the color palette.

See also **Colors**.

Font

Font refers to the typeface of the text. You can use any font offered by your Windows programs or printer, or you can use any add-on fonts in your collection.

To change a font

1. Select the text.

2. Choose the F**o**rmat **F**ont command. The Font dialog box appears.

3. In **F**ont, select the font you want to use.

4. Choose OK to close the dialog box.

Shortcut

Times New Roman  You can select the text and click the down-arrow to the right of the Font box on the Formatting toolbar. Select a font from the drop-down list.

Font Size

You can change the size of selected text to any size that your printer is capable of printing.

To change font size

1. Select the text.
2. Choose the F**o**rmat **F**ont command. The Font dialog box appears.
3. In **S**ize, type a size in the text box or select a size from the list below.

Tip

While in the Font dialog box, choose any other options you want, such as font, color, and font style, to save time when formatting text.

4. Choose OK to close the dialog box.

Shortcut

Select the text; click the down arrow to the right of the Font Size drop-down list on the Formatting toolbar and choose a font size.

  Select the text and click the Increase Font Size button or the Decrease Font Size button on the Formatting toolbar to make the selected text larger or smaller; the size of the selected text changes by two to four points for each click.

Font Style

PowerPoint enables you to change the style of any selected text. You can make the text bold, italic, or underlined (or any combination of those three). You can also apply a shadowed or embossed effect to selected text.

To change the font style

1. Select the text.

> **Tip**
>
> To apply the Bold style, press Ctrl+B; to apply Italic, press Ctrl+I; to apply an underline, press Ctrl+U. Similarly, select the text and press the shortcut keys again to remove the formatting.

2. Choose the F**o**rmat **F**ont command. The Font dialog box appears.

3. In F**o**nt Style, select a style. You can select any of the other styles in the Effects area of the dialog box as described below:

Effect	Description
Underline	Underlines selected text
Sh**a**dow	Places a shadow slightly to the right of the selected text
Emboss	Gives the text an embossed appearance
Supe**r**script	Raises the baseline of selected text
Su**b**script	Lowers the baseline of selected text
Offse**t**	Enter a value in percentage form to offset the text; a positive number superscripts the text and a negative number subscripts it

4. Choose OK to accept the changes.

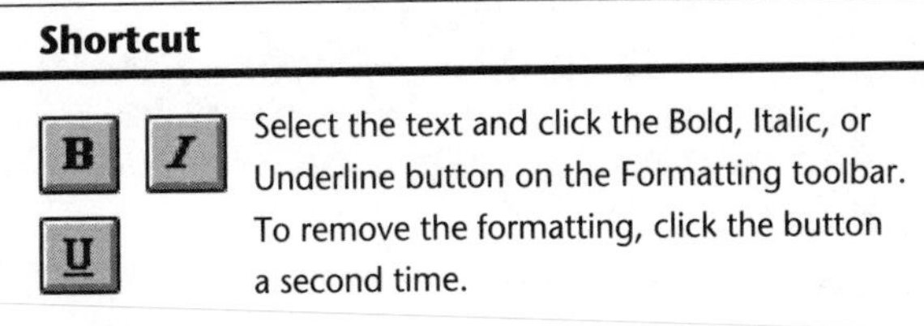

Shortcut

Select the text and click the Bold, Italic, or Underline button on the Formatting toolbar. To remove the formatting, click the button a second time.

Finding and Replacing Text

See **Find and Replace** in the Word section.

Format Painter

The Format Painter copies the format—font, style, alignment, borders, fills, and so on—from selected text and applies that format to other text.

Tip

The Format Painter does not work with graphs and pictures, but it does work with objects—shapes and lines—that you draw in PowerPoint.

To use the Format Painter

1. Select the text or object whose format you want to copy.
2. Click the Format Painter button on the Standard toolbar. The pointer changes to a pointer (object) or an I-beam (text) with a paint brush attached.
3. Click the text or object to which you want to transfer the format. The format is copied and the pointer changes back to a normal mouse pointer.

Tip

If you want to "paint" the format to several selections, double-click the Format painter button—it will remain active until you click the Format Painter button again, or press Esc.

Formatting Text

See **Font**, **Font Size**, **Font Style,** and **Line Spacing**.

Grids and Guidelines

Use grids and guidelines to help place objects or text on a slide. The grid is a series of invisible, horizontal and vertical lines that help you place objects precisely. The gridlines are about one-twelfth of an inch apart. The gridlines also present a snap to effect, so when you move an object near the line, the object snaps to the line.

To turn the grid on/off

1. Choose the **D**raw **S**nap to Grid command. A check mark appears next to the command when it is on.

Note

You do not see the grid on-screen; however, it helps guide objects when you draw or move them.

2. Choose the command again to turn the command off. The check mark disappears.

Tip

To turn the grid off temporarily, hold the Alt key as you move an object.

To use guidelines

1. Choose the **V**iew **G**uides command. The guides appear on-screen.
2. To move the guide, drag it with the mouse pointer.

To move objects

1. Click the text or object to select it. Small handles appear on the sides and corners of a box to indicate it is selected.
2. If the object is filled, click anywhere inside it, and drag it to a new position.

   If the object is not filled, click and drag the border of the object and drag it to a new location.

> **Tip**
>
> Objects moved close to a guideline also snap to the line. When moving objects, hold the Shift key to constrain the movement to horizontal or vertical direction.

See also **Align Objects** and **Align Text**.

Handouts

PowerPoint enables you to print handouts to support your presentation. Handouts, in PowerPoint, are small printed versions of your slide presentation.

To create a handout

1. Choose the **V**iew **M**aster command. A secondary menu appears.
2. Choose Han**d**out Master. The Handout Master appears.
3. [A] Select the Text tool button on the Drawing toolbar. Click on the Master, outside the outlined boxes, and enter any text you want to include on the handout.

Tip

You can change the text format and slide attributes on the notes page just as you can on a slide.

To add the date, time, or page number to a handout

1. Choose the **I**nsert D**a**te, **T**ime, or Page N**u**mber command. PowerPoint inserts the element.

2. Drag the element to the location you want it to appear.

To print a handout

1. Choose the **F**ile **P**rint command. The Print dialog box appears.

2. In the Print **W**hat box, choose the Handouts option. You can choose to print 2, 3, or 6 slide images per each handout page.

3. Choose the number of **C**opies and select the Slide Range.

4. Click OK to print the handouts.

Help

See the Common Features section.

Layouts

PowerPoint provides over twenty slide layouts from which you can choose. Each layout contains placeholders for elements you can add to the presentation; for example, you can add title and sub-title text, a graph, organizational chart, bulleted text, table, clip art, and several combinations of these elements. These layouts help you format your slides so they look attractive and professional. You can also choose a Blank slide layout—the last choice in the Slide Layout dialog box—and design your own layout.

To add a new slide

1. Choose the **I**nsert New **S**lide command, or press Ctrl+M. The New Slide dialog box appears.
2. In Choose an **A**utoLayout, select the slide layout you want to use for the new slide.
3. Choose OK to accept the layout and close the dialog box.

> **Shortcut**
>
> Click the New Slide button on the Status bar to display the Slide Layout dialog box. Choose a layout and choose OK to create a new slide.
>
> Click the Layout button from the Status bar to choose a layout to substitute for the current layout.

See also **Editing Slides**.

Line Spacing

You can adjust the spacing between lines of text within the same paragraph, or the spacing between paragraphs.

To change line spacing

1. Select the text to be changed.
2. Choose the F**o**rmat Line **S**pacing command. The Line Spacing dialog box appears.
3. Choose any or all of the following options:

Option	Description
Line Spacing	Enter or select the number of lines or points you want to apply between the lines of the selected lines of text. From the units box to the right of the number, choose either Lines or Points

(continues)

Option	Description
Before Paragraph	Enter or select the number of lines or points you want to add above the selected paragraphs of text
After Paragraph	Enter or select the number of lines or points you want to add after the selected paragraphs of text

4. Choose OK to close the dialog box.

Line Styles

See **Drawing** and **Borders.**

Masters

See **Slide Masters.**

Moving Around in PowerPoint

You can move around in PowerPoint by using either the mouse or the keyboard; many people find it convenient to use a combination of the two.

To move using the mouse

To move	Click or drag
Up or down	Vertical scroll bar, arrows, and box
Left or right	Horizontal scroll bar, arrows, and box
To a line or character	Position the mouse and click the left mouse button
To next or previous slide	Click the next or previous slide button on the vertical scroll bar

To move around using the keyboard

To move	Press
One character left	Left arrow
One character right	Right arrow
One line up	Up arrow
One line down	Up down
One word left	Ctrl+left arrow
One word right	Ctrl+right arrow
One paragraph up	Ctrl+up arrow
One paragraph down	Ctrl+down arrow
Beginning of the line	Home key
End of the line	End key
Beginning of presentation	Ctrl+Home
End of presentation	Ctrl+End
To previous object	Tab
To next object	Shift+Tab

Moving Text

See **Clipboard** and **Drag and Drop** in the Integration section.

New Presentation

When you choose to start a new presentation in PowerPoint, the program gives you several choices. You can let a PowerPoint wizard guide you to create a presentation, or you can create your own presentation from a template or from a blank presentation. Following is a summary of the choices for starting a new presentation:

- *AutoContent Wizard.* Creates a presentation foundation based on information you enter in the dialog boxes. Included in the presentation is an outline that guides you through each slide. When finished, PowerPoint displays an outline, with guides, in which you can enter your text and Cue Cards to further help you complete the presentation. (See also **AutoContent Wizard**.)

- *Pick a Look Wizard.* A nine-step wizard guides you through the creation of a design for your presentation, including such elements as template designs, choices for printing slides, contents of the master slide, notes, handouts, and outline.

- *Template.* Choose from any of PowerPoint's built-in templates to start your presentation. The template you choose includes a background design, formatted text, and placeholders. PowerPoint also displays the New Presentation dialog box from which you choose a slide layout for the first slide.

- *Blank Presentation.* Create a presentation with a blank, white background. From the New Presentation dialog box, choose a slide layout, or none, for the new presentation.

- *Current Presentation Format.* Choose to create a new presentation based on the template, background, and other attributes of the current presentation.

To use the AutoContent Wizard

1. Choose the **F**ile **N**ew command, or press Ctrl+N. The New Presentation dialog box appears.

2. Choose the **A**utoContent Wizard option, and choose OK. The AutoContent Wizard-Step 1 of 4 dialog box appears.

3. Follow the directions and answer the questions in each dialog box. Click the **N**ext button to continue, the

Back button to go to the previous dialog box, or the **F**inish button to complete the wizard.

To use the Pick a Look Wizard

1. Choose the **F**ile **N**ew command, or press Ctrl+N. The New Presentation dialog box appears.
2. Choose the **P**ick a Look Wizard option and click OK. PowerPoint displays the Pick a Look Wizard-Step 1 of 9 dialog box.
3. Follow the directions in each box to help the wizard create your presentation. Click the **N**ext button to continue through the dialog boxes, the **B**ack button to move to the previous dialog box, or the **F**inish button when you are through with the wizard.

To use the Template

1. Choose the **F**ile **N**ew command, or press Ctrl+N. The New Presentation dialog box appears.
2. Choose the **T**emplate option and choose OK. PowerPoint displays the Presentation Template.
3. In File **N**ame, choose a template. An example displays in the example box in the lower right corner of the dialog box.
4. Click the **A**pply button to close the dialog box. The New Slide dialog box appears.
5. Choose a layout for the slide, or choose Cancel for none, and click the OK button. PowerPoint adds a new slide with the selected template design.

To use the Blank Presentation

1. Choose the **F**ile **N**ew command, or press Ctrl+N. The New Presentation dialog box appears.
2. Choose the **B**lank Presentation option, and choose OK. The New Slide dialog box appears.

3. Choose a slide layout, or choose Cancel for none, and click OK to close the dialog box. The new slide appears.

To use the Current Presentation Format

1. Choose the **F**ile **N**ew command, or press Ctrl+N. The New Presentation dialog box appears.

2. Choose the **C**urrent Presentation Format option and click OK. PowerPoint creates a new presentation based on the current one.

Notes

See **Annotate Slide Show.**

Objects

Using the **I**nsert **O**bjects command, you can insert any number of objects in your presentation, including clip art, charts, graphs, worksheets, tables, document files, and more. After you have inserted objects, you can control where the objects are placed, their size, and other factors regarding how the objects are presented.

To create a caption for an object

1. A Click the Text Tool button on the Drawing toolbar.

2. Drag the tool to create a rectangle in which you will type the caption.

Tip

You must drag the Text tool if you want the text in the caption to wrap; if you just click the tool, the text you enter continues in one long line.

3. Enter the text and format it as a caption; for example, change the text to 9-point Arial centered. You can move and adjust the size of the text box after you type it.

See also **Add Text**.

To select an object

To select an object with fill, touch the object with the mouse pointer and click.

To select an object with no fill, such as a text box, click the border of the object.

To deselect an object, click anywhere on the slide where there is no object.

To select several objects, click the first object, hold the Shift key, and select subsequent objects.

To deselect one out of several selected objects, hold the Shift key and click on the object you want to deselect.

Press Ctrl+A to select all objects on a slide.

To group selected objects

> **Note**
>
> Group objects so you can perform tasks on the objects as if they were a single object—such as delete, copy, paste, and change attributes, in addition to flipping, rotating, and resizing.

1. Select two or more objects.
2. Choose the **D**raw **G**roup command.

   To ungroup the objects, choose the **D**raw **U**ngroup command.

Shortcut

  Select the objects and click the Group button on the Drawing+ toolbar to group them; select the Ungroup button to ungroup the objects.

To copy, move, paste, and duplicate objects

To copy an object, select it; then choose the **E**dit **C**opy command. Move to another page or presentation and choose the **E**dit **P**aste command to paste a copy of the object.

To move an object, select it; then choose the **E**dit Cu**t** command. Move to another page or presentation and choose the **E**dit **P**aste command to paste the object.

To duplicate an object, select it; then choose the **E**dit **D**uplicate command. PowerPoint pastes a duplicate of the object on top of the original.

Shortcut

   Select an object and click the Cut or Copy buttons from the Standard toolbar. Move to the new location and click the Paste button on the Standard toolbar.

To duplicate an object, select the object and hold the Ctrl key as you drag a copy of the object to the new location.

To resize an object

1. Select the object.
2. Position the mouse pointer over one of the selection handles until the pointer changes to a two-headed arrow.
3. Drag the handle away from the center of the object to enlarge, or toward the center of the object to reduce the size.

To constrain an object as you resize it

- To resize from one corner to maintain the aspect ratio (height-to-width relationship), hold Shift as you drag a corner handle.
- To resize an object from the center out, hold Ctrl as you drag a handle.
- To resize from the center outward while maintaining the aspect ratio, hold Ctrl+Shift while dragging a corner handle.

To stack objects

1. Select the object.
2. Choose the **D**raw Bring to Fron**t** command to bring the selected object to the top of the stack.

   Choose the **D**raw Send to Bac**k** command to send the object to the bottom of the stack.

   Choose the **D**raw Bring **F**orward command to bring the object forward by one object.

   Choose the **D**raw Send **B**ackward command to send the object backward by one object.

Tip

If you have trouble selecting an object in a stack, you can cycle through the objects by using the tab key. Each object is selected in turn, from the back to the front. To move from front to back, press Shift+Tab.

Shortcut

Select an object and click the Bring Forward button on the Drawing+ toolbar.

Select an object and click the Send Backward button on the Drawing+ toolbar.

To rotate and flip an object

1. Select the object or group.
2. Choose the **D**raw Rotate/Fli**p** command. A secondary menu appears.
3. Choose one of the following options:
   - Free Rotate rotates the object as much or as little as you want. With the rotation pointer, drag a handle on the selected object to the left or right. When finished, click the object to change the pointer back.
   - Rotate Left rotates the object to the left 90 degrees.
   - Rotate Right rotates the object to the right 90 degrees.
   - Flip Horizontal flips the object horizontally 180 degrees.
   - Flip Vertical flips the object vertically 180 degrees.

Note

You cannot rotate or flip an object or group that contains an imported picture.

Open

See the Common Features section.

Organization Chart

See **Chart**, as well as the Integration section.

Outlines

PowerPoint enables you to outline your presentation, either in another application, or in the PowerPoint program. PowerPoint uses your outline to create slides by using each main topic as a different slide. Text levels below each main topic are used as subtitles and other text on each slide. Additionally, PowerPoint includes an outline view, plus several handy features that make organizing the presentation easier.

> **Tip**
>
> Objects do not appear in outline view except as small picture icons.

To change to outline view

Choose the **V**iew **O**utline command. PowerPoint changes to the outline view and adds an Outline toolbar for your use.

To create the outline

1. Enter the text for the title of the first slide. Press Enter, thus creating the next slide.

   > **Tip**
   >
   > To select the text in one slide, click the slide icon or the slide number. All of the text in the slide is selected; drag the selected slide to change its position in the outline and in the presentation.

2. If you want to add another slide, enter the title.

   If you want to create subtext to the first slide, click the Demote button on the Outlining toolbar, or press the Tab key.

3. If you want to change a lower level to a higher one, select the text or position the insertion point in the text and click the Promote button on the Outlining toolbar, or press Shift+Tab.

To manipulate the outline	
	Move Up
	Move Down
	Collapse Selection
	Expand Selection

- Select the text and click the Move Up button on the Outlining toolbar to move a slide title and its subtext up one topic, thus placing it in front of the previous slide.
- Select the text and click the Move Down button on the Outlining toolbar to move a slide title and its subtext down one topic, thus placing it after the previous slide.
- Select the text and click the Collapse Selection button to view only the title of the slide; the rest of the text is hidden.
- Select the text and click the Expand Selection button to view all subtext contained within a collapsed title.

To change to slide view

Choose the **V**iew **S**lides command. PowerPoint creates a slide for every title on the outline and places subtext for each slide under the title text.

See also **AutoContent Wizard**.

Patterns

See **Fills and Patterns**.

Pick a Look Wizard

See **New Presentation**.

Pictures

See the Integration section.

Printing

You can print slides or other various components of your presentation, including handouts, outlines, and speaker's notes. No matter which component you are printing, the process is generally the same.

To print

1. Choose the **F**ile **P**rint command, or press Ctrl+P. The Print dialog box appears.
2. In the Print **W**hat drop-down list, choose to print Slides, Notes Page, Handouts (2, 3, or 6 slides per page), or the Outline View.
3. In **C**opies, enter or select the number of copies you want to print.
4. In Slide Range, choose from the following options:

Option	Description
All	Print all slides, notes, handouts, or pages in the presentation.
C**u**rrent Slide	Print only the current slide or the notes, handouts, or outline for the current slide.
Sel**e**ction	Print currently selected item in presentation; you must select the item before choosing the **F**ile **P**rint command.
Slides	Enter the number representing specific slides you want to print. Separate slides by a comma if not in succession, as in 1, 3, 5; or by a hyphen if the slides are in succession, as in 3-5 or 1-5. You can mix references, as well, as in 1, 3, 5-7.

5. Additionally, you can choose from the following options:

Option	**Description**
Print to **F**ile	Prints to a file you save on diskette; for use when sending files to a service bureau.
Print H**i**dden Slides	Prints all slides, even if you have hidden them.
Black & White	Prints all fills as white, patterns as black and white, and adds a thin border to unbordered objects.
C**o**llate Copies	Prints multiple copies in order; for example, it prints all pages of the first copy, in sequence, before printing the second copy.
Scale to Fit **P**aper	Prints the slides scaled to fit the paper size specified in the Print Setup dialog box.
Pure B**l**ack & White	Prints all color fills as white and all text and lines as black; pictures are rendered in gray scale.

6. Click OK to print the selection.

Shortcut

Click the Print button on the Standard toolbar to print using the default selections in the Print dialog box.

Rehearse Presentation

While rehearsing your presentation, you can set the amount of time that you want each slide to display during your presentation. When you choose to set timing in this manner, PowerPoint keeps track of the time each slide shows, displaying the time in seconds in the lower left corner of the slide show during the rehearsal. Then, PowerPoint sets the timing for you.

To set time while rehearsing the presentation

1. Choose the **V**iew Slide Sho**w** command. The Slide Show dialog box appears.
2. In the Advance area, choose **R**ehearse New Timings.
3. Click the **S**how button. The first slide appears, with a small counter in the lower right corner. The counter counts the number of seconds the slide is showing. When ready to advance to the next slide, click anywhere in the slide.
4. Continue to rehearse and set the time for each slide. When finished, PowerPoint displays a message box stating the total time for the show and asking if you want to record the new timings. Choose **Y**es if the timings seemed right; choose **N**o if you want to try again.

See also **Timings**.

Rulers

Use the horizontal and vertical rulers to move and align objects on the slide, measure distance on the slide, and to set tabs and indents. When you are working with text, such as a placeholder text box, the rulers show the point of origin (0 on the ruler) at the left; however, when you are using drawing tools, the point of origin is in the center.

As you move the mouse pointer, a dotted line moves along both rulers identifying the exact position of the pointer.

To display the rulers

Choose the **V**iew **R**uler command. The horizontal and vertical rulers appear on-screen.

To hide the rulers, choose the **V**iew **R**ulers command again.

To use the ruler to set tabs and indents

1. Select the text or position the insertion point in the text area.

2. To set a tab, choose the tab alignment using the tab alignment button, located to the left of the horizontal ruler and at the top of the vertical ruler. The tab alignment button is a small gray box containing a left tab marker (L) until you click the button to change alignment.

3. Click the pointer on the horizontal ruler, at the position you want the tab. A tab marker appears.

> **Tip**
>
> If the marker is not in the correct place, you can drag it on the ruler to move it. Drag the marker down and off of the ruler to delete the tab stop.

4. To set a left or first line indent, drag the indent markers on the horizontal ruler to the new position.

See also **Align Text** and **Align Objects**.

Run Slide Show

When you are ready to run the slide show, you can choose which slides to run and how to advance the slides. You can also choose various effects to make the show more interesting.

To run a slide show

1. Choose the **V**iew Slide Sho**w** command. The Slide Show dialog box appears.

2. In Slides, choose to view **A**ll, or choose **F**rom and fill in the numbers of the slides you want to view.

3. In Advance, choose from the following:

Option	Description
Manual Advance	Click the mouse during the show to advance the slide
Use Slide Timings	Automatically advances to the preset timings
Rehearse New Timings	Set new timings for each slide
Run **C**ontinuously Until 'Esc'	The show runs over and over until you press the Esc key

4. Click the **S**how button to show the presentation.

Tip

You can press the Esc key at any time in the presentation to stop the show and return to the PowerPoint screen.

See also **Rehearse Presentation**, **Builds and Transitions**, and **Timings**.

Save/Save As

See the Common Features section.

Set Up Slides

PowerPoint enables you to set size and orientation for your slides, as well as for notes, handouts, and outlines. Using Slide Setup, you can also choose whether to design your slides for an on-screen show, printer, or actual 35mm slides.

To set up slides

1. Choose the **F**ile Slide Set**u**p command. The Slide Setup dialog box appears.

2. In **S**lides Sized for, choose what you will print to. The default is an on-screen show; however, you may choose to print to an 8 1/2-by-11 inch sheet, or create your own custom size. If you choose Custom as the size, enter the size in the **W**idth and H**e**ight text boxes.

> **Tip**
>
> When you choose Custom in the Slides Sized for drop-down list, the size that appears in **W**idth and H**e**ight is the printable area of your printer. If you change the size, make sure the designated printer can print the page size.

3. In **N**umber Slides From, enter or select the beginning page number.

4. In Orientation, choose either **P**ortrait or **L**andscape in the Slides area, and then in the Notes, Handouts, Outline area.

5. Choose OK to close the dialog box.

Shading

You can add a shaded background to slides in your presentation. Additionally, you can shade a fill or color in an object.

To shade a slide background

1. Choose the F**o**rmat Slide Back**g**round command. The Slide Background dialog box appears.

2. In Shade Styles, choose any of the options and view the result in the Var**i**ants area.

3. Choose the Chan**g**e Color button to reveal the Background Color dialog box.

4. In Color **P**alette, choose the color to which you want to change the background.

> **Tip**
>
> Choose the **M**ore Colors button to display the More Colors dialog box, in which you can create or mix your own colors. See **Colors** for more information.

5. Choose OK to close the Background Color dialog box and return to the Slide Background dialog box.
6. In the **D**ark/Light area, click the left arrow to make the shading darker, or click the right arrow to make the shading lighter.
7. When you find a variant you like, select it in the Var**i**ants area.
8. Choose one of the following options:

Option	Description
Appl**y** to All	Applies the background change to all slides in the presentation
Apply	Applies the change to only the current slide
Preview	Enables you to see the change before accepting it; you may need to move the dialog box out of the way
Cancel	Close the box without making any changes

See also **Fills and Patterns** and **Colors**.

Shadows

You can add shadows to text or objects to add depth and dimension to a slide. You can also change the color and offset of the shadow, thus customizing it to your own slide designs.

To add a shadow

1. Select the object.
2. Choose the F**o**rmat S**h**adow command. The Shadow dialog box appears.
3. In the **C**olor drop-down list, choose a color for the shadow.
4. In the Offset area, choose from the following options:

Option	Description
Up or **D**own	Offsets the shadow on the top or bottom of the object; enter or select a value in the P**o**ints text box to offset the shadow.
Left or **R**ight	Offsets the shadow on the left or right side of the object; enter or select a value in the P**o**ints text box as the amount to offset the shadow.

5. Click OK to close the dialog box, or **P**review to view the change before accepting it.

To remove a shadow

1. Select the object.
2. Choose the F**o**rmat S**h**adow command. The Shadow dialog box appears.
3. In **C**olor, choose No Shadow and choose OK.

Shortcut

Click the Shadow On/Off tool on the Drawing toolbar to apply the default (6 points offset on right and bottom) shadow to a selected object.

Click the Shadow Color button on the Drawing+ toolbar to change the color of the shadow on a selected object.

See also **Colors** and **Font Style**.

Slide Layouts

See **Layouts**.

Slide Masters

The Slide Master is a slide that contains text formatting and background items common to all slides in the presentation: the name of your company, a logo, colors, font, and so on. A change to the Slide Master affects all slides in the presentation. You can change the Slide Master at any time while creating your presentation.

> **Note**
>
> Text in placeholders on the master is only for formatting text for each slide. If you want specific text to appear on every slide, you must create a text box and enter the text on the Master Slide.

To change a slide master

1. Choose the **V**iew **M**aster command. A secondary menu appears.
2. Choose **S**lide Master. The Slide Master appears.

> **Tip**
>
> You can switch to any of the Masters by holding the Shift key and selecting one of the View buttons on the horizontal scroll bar.

> **Note**
>
> You can also choose to change the outline, handout, or notes masters from the same secondary Master menu.

3. Work on the slide master as if it was a slide. Change the format, colors, text formatting, and so on. Any changes you make apply to the entire presentation.

4. When finished, choose the **V**iew **S**lides command. The changes appear in the slides.

See also **Colors**, **Font**, and **Borders**.

Slide Setup

See **Set Up Slides.**

Slide Sorter

Use the Slide Sorter to change the order of your slides and to get an overall view of the slide show. The Slide Sorter view reduces the slides and enables you to see up to six slides at a time on-screen. Additionally, PowerPoint displays the Slide Sorter toolbar, so that you can easily add transitions and builds.

To change to Slide Sorter view

Choose the **V**iew Sli**d**e Sorter command. The view changes to Slide Sorter, displaying thumbnails of the slides and the Slide Sorter toolbar.

To use the Slide Sorter toolbar

1. Select the first slide.

2. Click the down arrow to the right of the Transition Effects drop-down list. Choose a transition from the list. PowerPoint applies that transition to the selected slide; continue to apply transitions to each slide. PowerPoint marks each slide with a transition icon; by clicking on the icon, you can view the transition.

Tip

Click the Transition button on the Slide Sorter toolbar to display the Transition dialog box.

3. Select a slide with a bulleted list.
4. Click the down arrow to the right of the Build Effects drop-down list and choose a build effect to apply.

Tip

Click the Build button to display the Build dialog box.

To move slides in Slide Sorter view

Select and drag a slide to a new position. The mouse pointer changes to a small slide icon. As you drag the slide, a vertical dotted line follows the mouse pointer to indicate the position of the slide. Release the mouse button when the dotted line is in the proper position.

Shortcut

Click the Slide Sorter View button on the horizontal scroll bar to switch views.

Click the Hide Slide button on the Slide Sorter toolbar to hide a slide when you show the presentation.

Click the Rehearse Timing button on the Slide Sorter toolbar to run the slide show and set the timing for each slide.

Click the Show Formatting button on the Slide Sorter toolbar to hide slide formatting and backgrounds.

Speaker's Notes

PowerPoint enables you to create and print speaker's notes you can use when presenting your slide show. In speaker's notes pages, the notes you enter appear along with small images of the slides, so you know which notes go with each slide.

To create a notes page

1. Choose the **V**iew **N**otes Pages command. A notes page appears.

> **Note**
>
> The notes page is attached to the current slide; the next slide has its own notes page.

2. Click the mouse in the place holder, "Click to add text." Enter any notes you want to go along with the slide.
3. Select and format the text as you like.
4. To change the view back to slides, choose the **V**iew **S**lides command.

To print notes pages

1. Choose the **F**ile **P**rint command. The Print dialog box appears.
2. In Print **W**hat, choose Notes Pages.
3. Click OK to print.

Spelling

See the Integration section.

Starting PowerPoint

See the Common Features section.

Table

See **Tables** in the Word section.

Templates

A template provides you with a color scheme, background designs, and text formatting—all fitted together to provide a specific look to your presentation. PowerPoint contains more than one hundred templates on which you can base your presentation.

You can apply a template to an existing presentation; the new template replaces the current template. Fonts, designs, colors, and text arrangement change to suit the new template.

To apply a template

1. Choose the F**o**rmat **P**resentation Template command. The Presentation Template dialog box appears.
2. In the File **N**ame text box, enter a name or choose one from the list of template files. A sample of the template appears in the sample box in the lower right corner of the dialog box.
3. Choose **A**pply to apply the template.

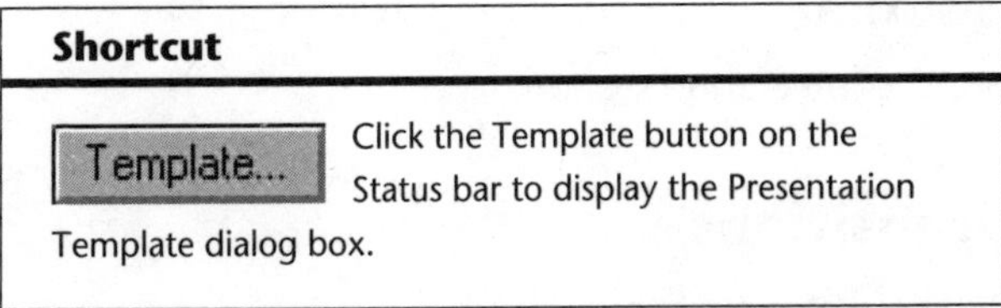

Shortcut

Click the Template button on the Status bar to display the Presentation Template dialog box.

See also **New Presentation**.

Timings

You can set an amount of time for each slide to show; after the designated time, PowerPoint automatically advances to the next slide. You can set the timing using the Rehearse Presentation method, or by the following method:

To set timing

1. Choose the **V**iew Sli**d**e Sorter command. The view changes to Slide Sorter.
2. Choose the **T**ools **T**ransition command. The Transition dialog box appears.
3. In Advance, choose **A**utomatically After button.
4. In the Seconds text box, enter the number of seconds you want the slide to remain on-screen.
5. Click OK. The timing is applied only to the current slide; you must select each slide and set the timing for each.

Shortcut

Click the Transition button on the Slide Sorter toolbar to open the Transition dialog box. In Advance, choose the timing you want to use.

See also **Rehearse Presentation**.

Toolbars

See the Integration section.

Transitions

See **Builds and Transitions**.

Undo

See the Common Features section.

Views

PowerPoint enables you to view your slides in a variety of ways; you can also view other, related documents, including notes and outlines. Additionally, you can magnify or reduce the view on the screen to better help you work on your presentation.

To use the views

Choose the **V**iew menu and choose from one of the following views:

View	Description
Slides	View and work on one slide at a time; enter text, change slide layout, add graphics, pictures, graphs, shapes, and so on.
Outline	View slide titles and text, instead of actual slides, in outline form; graphics are represented by icons. Use to organize your presentation.
Sli**d**e Sorter	View thumbnails of each slide, up to six at a time; move slides around, delete slides, set timing and transitions.
Notes Page	View a small image of the slide on the upper half of a page and enter speaker's notes on the bottom half. Type and format the notes, and then print them.
Slide Sho**w**	View the presentation as it will look in your slide show; the slide fills the screen. Transitions, builds, and timings are also active.

To magnify or reduce a view

1. Choose the **V**iew **Z**oom command. The Zoom dialog box appears.

2. In **Z**oom To, choose the magnification in which you want to view the screen. Alternatively, enter or select a percentage value in **P**ercent to set your own custom view.

3. Choose OK to close the dialog box.

Shortcut

Click the Slide View button on the horizontal scroll bar to change to the Slide view.

Click the Outline View button on the horizontal scroll bar to change to the Outline view.

Click the Slide Sorter View button on the horizontal scroll bar to change to the Slide Sorter view.

Click the Notes Pages View button on the horizontal scroll bar to change to the Notes Pages view.

Click the Slide Show button on the horizontal scroll bar to change to the Slide Show view.

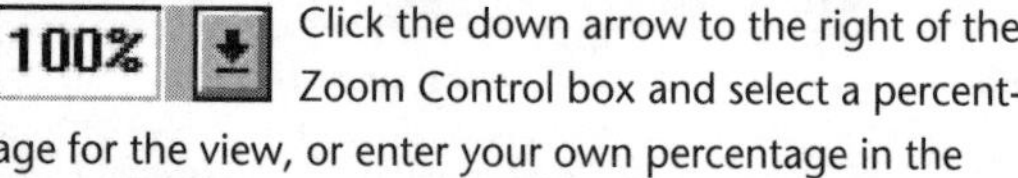

Click the down arrow to the right of the Zoom Control box and select a percentage for the view, or enter your own percentage in the Zoom Control box.

Wizards

See **AutoContent Wizard**, **New Presentation**, as well as the Common Features section.

Word Art

See the Integration section.

Common Features

The commands and features discussed in this section are common to Word, Excel, and PowerPoint. Microsoft makes it easy for you to learn these programs and work efficiently in all three; many of the commands and procedures in Word, Excel, and PowerPoint are identical.

Closing Files

When you are finished working with a file, such as a worksheet, presentation, or document, you close the file. Closing a file releases more memory to the computer for working on other programs and files, and it prevents you from accidentally making changes to the file.

To close a file

1. Choose the **F**ile **C**lose command. The program closes the file.
2. If you have not saved the file recently, the program displays a message box asking if you want to save. Choose **Y**es to save and then close the file, **N**o to close the file without saving, or Cancel to return to the document, presentation, or worksheet.

Shortcut
Double-click the Control menu for the document window (to the left of the File menu or title bar).

Cue Cards and Examples and Demos

Cue Cards are help features that contain step-by-step instructions for procedures. Cue Cards remain on-screen while you work to help you complete common and practical tasks. Microsoft Office also offers Cue Cards (found on the Office menu) that help you use the Office applications together.

Word and Excel use a different type of Help called Examples and Demos. When you choose this help feature, the program displays a help screen containing many topics. Choose a topic and Help takes you through the procedure step by step. Some Examples also include practice and demos.

To use Cue Cards

1. Choose the **H**elp C**u**e Cards command in PowerPoint, or choose the Office menu and the C**u**e Cards command. The Cue Cards screen appears.

2. Select the topic for which you want help. Cue Cards guide you through the procedure step by step.

3. Choose any of the following buttons to help you:

Menu	Displays topics for which you can receive help
Search	Displays Help's Search dialog box; enter a topic and the program searches Help for that topic
Back	Displays the previous Cue Card screen

4. Cue Cards remain on-screen until you close the dialog box. Choose the Cue Card Control menu and select **C**lose, or press Alt+F4 while the Cue Card window is active.

Shortcut

Double-click the Cue Card Control menu to close the Cue Card window.

To use Examples and Demos

1. Choose the **H**elp **E**xamples and Demos command. The Examples and Demos help window appears.

2. Choose a topic from the contents list, and a secondary list appears containing related topics for help.

3. Select any topic and the help screen appears. Samples appear on-screen with instructions for performing the task.

> **Note**
>
> Often, buttons or topics in callout boxes display on-screen. If you click a button or topic, further explanations appear. Click anywhere on-screen to hide the boxes when you're finished reading them.

4. When finished reading the screen, choose one of the following options:

Close	Closes the help window and returns to the document or worksheet
Demo	Demonstrates the procedure step by step; a small Demonstration box appears with two buttons: **C**lose and **S**tart. The Start button is replaced with the **N**ext button so you can proceed through the demonstration at your own speed
Practice	Displays a practice worksheet or document in which you are given instructions to practice the task. The Practice box includes two buttons: **C**lose and **H**int. If you choose Hint, a hint to help you along appears in another box, along with a **S**how Me button. Choose **S**how Me and the program performs the task for you

5. Choose **C**lose to quit the help feature.

See also **Help**.

Demos

See **Cue Cards and Examples and Demos**.

Dialog Boxes

Dialog boxes are extensions of a command. If, for example, you choose to format a font, the Font dialog box appears with several options you can choose to format the font. The dialog boxes in the Microsoft Office programs work similarly, as do dialog boxes in all Windows programs.

Dialog boxes consist of several types of boxes and choices. Following is a summary of those elements; however, not all boxes may include all elements.

Element	Description
Tabs	Similar to file folders, the tabs contain specific options pertaining to components of the dialog box subject.
Area	A boxed area containing related options; areas are often given titles that describe the contents.
Text box	Type a selection in the text box. Some text boxes are connected to a list; when you choose an item from the list, it automatically displays in the text box. Other text boxes, such as those containing measurements, use arrows to change the value in the text box. You can also type a measurement in these boxes.
List	A list displays options from which you can choose; use the scroll bar to view hidden parts of the list.

Element	Description
Drop-down list	A text box with a down arrow to its right. Click the down arrow and a list drops down; choose from the list.
Check boxes	Options preceded by square boxes that can be turned on or off. If an X is displayed in the check box, the option is on; if no X appears in the box, the option is off. Clicking the option turns it on or off. More than one check box in an area can be turned on at a time.
Preview or Sample	A box that displays changes as you make them so you can decide if you want to accept the changes or not.
Option buttons	Options preceded by a round check box that is white if turned off and contains a black dot if turned on. Only one option button in an area can be turned on at a time. Also called a radio button.

Command buttons are rectangular buttons that contain commands pertaining to the dialog box. Following are common command buttons:

Button	Description
OK	Accepts changes and closes the dialog box
Cancel	Abandons any changes and closes the dialog box
Close	Closes the dialog box
Apply/Apply to All	Accepts any changes and closes the dialog box
Help	Gets help on using the dialog box and its options
Find File	Displays the file management program to help you find specific files
Options	Displays the Option dialog box in which you can set preferences related to the dialog box options

Note

To display a dialog box, choose a menu and then a command, such as the F**o**rmat menu and the **F**ont command. The Font dialog box appears, as shown in the following figure.

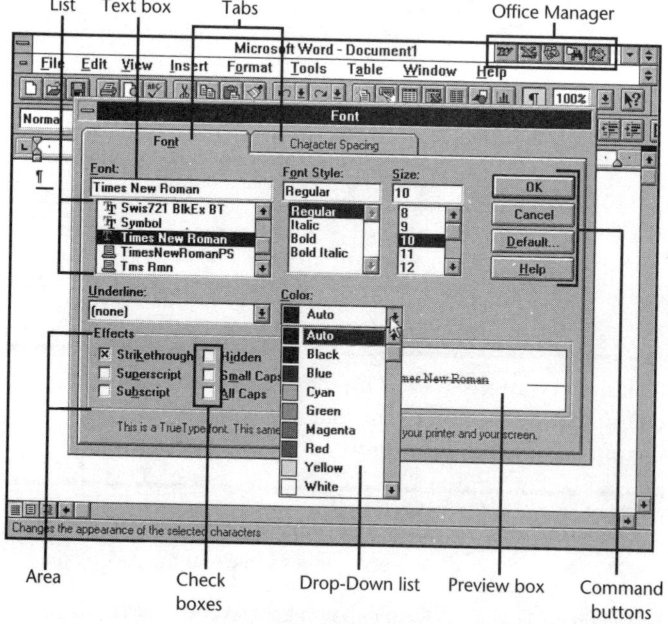

Note

All dialog boxes have the OK command button or a similar button that accepts the changes or proceeds with the action, such as Print or Apply. Additionally, all dialog boxes contain either a Close or Cancel button so you can get out of the dialog box. All dialog boxes contain the Help command button.

Tip

Since a dialog box is a window, it also contains a control menu and a title bar. You can drag the title bar of the dialog box and move the box around on the screen.

To get around in a dialog box

Use the mouse to select items, display drop-down lists, enter text in a text box, select and delete text in a text box, and click command buttons.

Press the Tab key to move from item to item in a dialog box; use Shift+Tab to move to the previous item. You can also press Alt plus the hot key, as you would in menus and commands.

Shortcut

Press Esc to cancel a dialog box; press Enter to accept the changes and close the dialog box.

Examples and Demos

See **Cue Cards and Examples and Demos.**

Exiting Applications

You can exit an application to close the program. You should always exit an application before exiting Windows so you do not lose data or files you have not saved.

To exit an application

Choose the **F**ile E**x**it command. The program either shuts down or displays a message dialog box reminding you to save. If you have not saved a file, the application displays the message dialog box asking if you want to save. Choose **Y**es to save, **N**o to close without saving changes, or Cancel to return to the program.

Shortcut

To exit the program double-click the Control menu, located on the left corner of the title bar.

Find File

Find File is a file management feature common to all three applications in Microsoft Office. Use Find File to preview files, search directories for specific files, copy or delete files, and more. You can set specific criteria—such as the title or keywords in a document or the date a file was created—and search through one or all directories to find any files meeting those criteria.

To open Find File

Choose the **F**ile **F**ind File command. The Find File window appears.

Alternatively, click the Find File button on the Microsoft Office toolbar.

Tip

The first time you use Find File, the **S**earch dialog box appears. You must first enter a search range before you can open Find File. After the first time you open Find File, it uses the search criteria specified in your last search.

To search for specific files

1. Choose the **S**earch button to display the Search dialog box.

2. In the Search For area, File **N**ame text box, enter an asterisk, period, and the extension of the documents you are searching for; *.DOC is used to search for all files with a DOC extension. Alternatively, click the down arrow and choose from the list of extensions.

Tip

The * (asterisk) is a wildcard character meaning all. You could, for example, enter *.* to search for all files. You can also use the ? (question mark) wildcard character to represent one character of a file name; for example, DOC??.TXT means all files beginning with DOC and ending with the TXT extension. The two question mark characters can be numbers, letters, or any other acceptable characters.

3. In the **L**ocation text box, enter the drive and directory in which you want to search. You can click the down arrow to choose a drive.

Note

You can enter the drive, colon, backslash (c:\, for example) in the **L**ocation text box to specify a drive to search in; then enter the directory. Alternatively, choose the Include Su**b**directories option to include all subdirectories in the specified directory in the search.

4. Choose OK to search for the specific file types. Find File searches and then displays the files in the Find File window.

To perform an advanced search

1. In the Search dialog box, choose the **A**dvanced Search button. The Advanced Search dialog box appears.

2. Choose one of the three tabs: **L**ocation, **S**ummary, or Timestam**p** as a way of setting search criteria.

Tip

You can set criteria on one tab, two tabs, or all three tabs; however, the more criteria, the longer the search will take.

Option	Description
Location	Enter the extension, drive, and directories where you want to search. Additionally, you can add other various directories by selecting them in the **D**irectories list and choosing the **A**dd button. For example, you can search the WINWORD and MSOFFICE directories for a specific file.
Summary	Enter information, such as Title, Author, and so on, as it is found in the Summary Info dialog box for the document you are searching. For example, you can search for all files created by a particular person or with certain keywords or specific words within the file itself.
Timestam**p**	Enter the date the file was last saved or created. You can enter one date or give a date range, such as **F**rom 1/12/94 **T**o 1/28/9**4**.

3. When you complete the advanced search criteria, choose OK to close the Advanced Search dialog box. Choose OK in the Search dialog box to search for the specified files.

To save a search

Note

You can save often-used search criteria, so the next time you search, you can choose it from a list.

1. In the Search dialog box, choose the **S**ave Search As button in the Saved S**e**arches area. The Save Search As dialog box appears.

2. In the **S**earch Name text box, enter a name for the search and choose OK. The saved name appears in the Saved S**e**arches drop-down list.

> **Tip**
>
> You can use spaces and other characters in the name, if you want.

To use a saved search, click the down arrow in the Saved Searches drop-down list and select the search from the list. Choose OK.

To change views in Find File

The Find File window provides three views: File Info, Preview, and Summary. Each view provides a different look at the files. To change views, choose the down arrow in the View box and select the view. When in a particular view, you can select a file and then view information about that file; for example, the date created, author of the file, file size, and so on.

The File Info view lists the drives, directories, and files in the File Name list. To the right of each file are the Title, Size, Author, and the Last Saved date of the file. The Title is specified in the Summary Info dialog box; if you did not specify a title, Find File uses the first characters in the file as a title. The Author is the person specified in the Options dialog box, User Info tab, unless a different author was specified.

In the Preview view, drives, directories, and files are displayed in the Listed Files window. In the Preview of window is a preview of the file's contents, formatted, if a preview is available. You cannot edit the file, but you can scroll the window to view all of the file.

In the Summary view, Drives, directories, and files are displayed in the Listed Files window. In the Summary of window is the information entered in the Summary Info dialog box, if any, including the title, subject, keywords, and so on. Also in the Summary of window are the created, last saved, and last printed dates, document size, number of words and pages, and other file information.

To select files in Find File

To select one file, click on it. The file appears highlighted.

To select more than one file in succession, click the first file, hold the Shift key, and click the last file. All files between the first and last are selected.

To select any number of non-sequential files, click the first file, hold the Ctrl key, click the other files you want to select.

To manipulate files

You can use various Find File commands to copy, delete, sort, print, and to perform other tasks to the selected files.

1. Select the file or files, in any view.

> **Tip**
>
> Some commands can only be performed on one file, whereas other commands can be performed on several selected files.

2. Choose the **C**ommands button. A menu appears with the following commands:

Commands	Description
Open **R**ead Only	Opens the selected file as read only: no changes or edits can be made to the file; use on one file at a time
Print	Displays the Print dialog box and closes Find File; print one or several files using this command
Summary	Displays the Summary Info dialog box for the selected file; enter summary information and then choose OK to return to Find File. Use on only one file at a time.

Commands	Description
Delete	Displays a confirmation message box: choose **Y**es to delete selected file or files, **N**o to cancel the command. Use on one or several files at a time.
Copy	Displays the Copy dialog box in which you can enter or choose a drive and directory to copy the selected files to; choose OK to complete the copy. Use on one or several files.
Sor**t**ing	Displays the Options dialog box in which you choose how to sort the files in the Find File View window. You can sort files by author, creation date, name, size, and so on. Additionally, you can list the files by Filename or Title. Choose OK when finished with the dialog box. Sorts all files in the window.

3. Choose from the following command buttons to complete the Find File task:

Open	Opens the selected file and closes Find File
Close	Closes Find File

Shortcut

Click the Find File button on the Office tool bar to open the Find File window.

Help

Each application in Microsoft Office provides an excellent Help feature. You can search for specific topics, view help contents, read the Tip of the Day, use Cue Cards and Examples, and more. Additionally, all three programs include a Help button you use to point to a feature or area of the screen and the program displays help on that feature. Finally, most dialog boxes contain help buttons that, when selected, display specific help on the options in the dialog box.

To use Help

Note

In any Help window, clicking an underlined (and colored, if you have a color monitor) command, word, or phrase displays more information. Sometimes the information is another help screen, a definition, an example, or another list of underlined items. When you place the mouse pointer over an underlined item, the pointer changes to a hand with a pointing finger.

1. Choose the **H**elp menu. From the menu, choose one of the following commands:

Note

Each command appears on the Help menu of Word, Excel, and PowerPoint unless otherwise specified.

Command	Description
Contents	Displays the Help dialog box with the contents of Help displayed. Choose a general topic that is underlined, and a window containing related underlined topics appears. Choose the related topic and view information about it.
Search for Help on	Displays the Help dialog box and the Search dialog box. In the text box, type a topic; as you type, the list moves to the topic. Select a topic and then choose the **S**how Topics button. More detailed topics appear in the lower list box; select one and choose **G**o To.

Command	Description
	Help displays the How To window with instructions or information about the specified topic.
Index	The Help dialog box appears with the index of commands, characters, features, and other topics. You can scroll through the topics or choose one of the letter buttons to move to that letter in the topic list. Select a topic and Help displays the How To window with specific information on the topic.
Quick Preview	Displays a preview of the program, tips for using it, what's new in the program, and so on. View demonstrations and examples as well as other information by following directions on-screen. Choose the **R**eturn button when done.
Examples and Demos	In Word and Excel, displays a contents list and then an example of the selected feature. For more information, see **Cue Cards and Examples and Demos**.
Cue Cards	In PowerPoint, displays step-by-step instructions that remain on-screen while you perform specific tasks. For more information, see **Cue Cards and Examples and Demos**.
Ti**p** of the Day	In Word and PowerPoint, displays the Tip of the Day dialog box in which you can view tips and shortcuts for running the application.

(continues)

Command	Description
WordPerfect Help	In Word, displays specific help and demonstrations for changing from WordPerfect to Word.
Lotus 1-2-3 and **M**ultiplan	In Excel, displays Help screens to show how to transfer your knowledge from these programs to Excel.
Technical Support	Displays information about common questions and answers, what to have ready when you call for support, types of support, and so on.
About Microsoft Word, Excel, or PowerPoint.	Displays information about the version, copyrights, and owner of the program. Additionally, choose the **S**ystem Info button to view information about your system, including DOS and Windows version, processor speed, memory, and so on.

Tip

Microsoft Office also includes a Help command, located on the Office menu. You can view contents, reference information, search for topics, and so on, related to Microsoft Office.

2. To close the Help dialog box, double-click the Help Control menu or choose the **F**ile E**x**it command from the Help window's menu.

Shortcut

Click the Help button on the Standard toolbar. The pointer changes to a pointer with a question mark. Point the mouse at any feature, menu, or screen element, and a Help dialog box about that item appears.

Press F1 to display the Help Contents window or a Help screen relating to any open dialog box.

Keyboard Shortcuts

Many of the same keyboard shortcuts can be used in any of the three programs. They include shortcuts for opening dialog boxes, assigning formatting, and moving around in the programs. For more information about getting around in a program using the keyboard, see the specific program.

To use the keyboard shortcuts

To	Press
Start a new file	Ctrl+N
Open a file	Crtl+O
Save a file	Ctrl+S
Print a file	Ctrl+P
Undo	Ctrl+Z
Cut	Ctrl+X
Copy	Ctrl+C
Paste	Ctrl+V
Delete or Clear	Delete key
Select All	Ctrl+A
Find	Ctrl+F

(continues)

To	Press
Replace	Ctrl+H
Check spelling	F7
Help	F1
Boldface	Ctrl+B
Italicize	Ctrl+I
Underline	Ctrl+U
Alt+Hot key	Select a command, menu, or option in dialog box
Enter	Selects the default command button, generally OK
Esc	Cancels a command, object selection, or dialog box
Spacebar	Displays the program's Control menu

Tip

Word and PowerPoint share many shortcut keys for formatting text. Choose the **H**elp **S**earch for Help on command and look for help on "Shortcuts, formatting."

See also **Dialog Boxes**.

Macros

See the Integration section.

Menus

The menu bar contains menus that enable you to perform tasks in the program. The three programs use similar menus and commands so you do not waste your time learning more than you need to get your work done. Following is a list of the menus and commands that behave similarly in the three programs:

Menu	Commands
File	New, Open, Close, Save, Save As, Find File, Summary Info, Page Setup or Slide Setup, Print, Exit
Edit	Undo, Cut, Copy, Paste, Paste Special, Clear, Select All, Find, Replace, Links, Object
View	Zoom
Insert	Picture, Object
Format	Style or Apply Style
Tools	Spelling, Options
Window	Arrange All
Help	Contents, Search for Help on, Index, Quick Preview, Technical Support, About Microsoft Word, Excel, or PowerPoint

Note

Additionally, Word and Excel share many commands, such as Insert Break, and Print Preview; Word and PowerPoint share many commands, such as View Ruler and View Toolbars.

To use a menu

1. Select a menu by clicking the menu name with the mouse, or by pressing Alt and the hot key; in File, the underlined F is the hot key.

2. The menu opens to display a list of commands. If you are using a mouse, click the command you want. You can instead move to the command using the down-arrow key, and then press Enter. You can also select a

command by pressing the hot key letter for the command you want.

> **Tip**
>
> If the selected command displays a secondary menu, choose the command you want from that menu.

Depending on the command, a variety of actions can take place:

- A command with an ellipsis (...) after it displays a dialog box with related options.
- A command with no ellipsis performs the command and returns to the document. Some commands display new elements on-screen, such as the **I**nsert **A**nnotation command in Word; this command inserts an annotation pane in which you enter text and close when done.
- A command with a check mark is a toggle command; when you select the command, a check mark appears indicating the command is active. Select the command again and the check mark disappears—the command is inactive. Some commands may display a bullet instead of a check mark.

Objects

An object—such as a worksheet, table, or chart from another application—is treated similarly in all three programs. When you insert an object, Microsoft attaches that object to the application in which it was created using OLE (Object Linking and Embedding). Most Windows applications support OLE, including the Microsoft Office programs.

OLE represents linking objects and embedding objects. When you insert an object, you embed it into the currently opened file. An embedded object can be a graph, spreadsheet, art work, or other file created in one application but stored in another.

You can insert the object using the **I**nsert **O**bject command. In the Object dialog box, a variety of objects are listed, depending on which programs are installed to your machine; the same objects are listed in all three programs. If, for example, you performed a complete install of Microsoft Office, some objects you can insert come from the following applications and applets: MS ClipArt Gallery, MS Equation, Excel, MS Graph, MS Organization Chart, Word, WordArt, and PowerPoint.

To insert a new object

1. Choose the **I**nsert **O**bject command. The Object dialog box appears.
2. Choose Create **N**ew. A list of Object **T**ypes appears.
3. From the list, choose the application you want to use to create the new object; for example, MS Excel 5.0 Chart or MS Graph 5.0.

> **Note**
>
> The program in which you create the object is called the source, and the program in which you insert the object is called the destination.

4. Choose OK and the specified program opens. Create the object in the application.
5. Close the program and the object is inserted into your current document.

> **Tip**
>
> If the program is an applet, such as WordArt or MS Graph, you can double-click the Control menu to close it. If the program is Excel, Word, or other program, choose the **F**ile **U**pdate command and then the **F**ile E**x**it command.

To insert an object created from a file

1. Choose the **I**nsert **O**bject command. The Insert Object dialog box appears.
2. Choose the Create from **F**ile option.
3. In the Fil**e** text box, enter the drive, directory, and the file name you want to use as an object.
4. Choose OK to close the dialog box and create the object.

To edit an object

1. Double-click the object in the destination program and the source application opens.
2. Edit the object.
3. If applicable, update the object to the destination program and then exit the source application.

See also the Integration section.

Open

You open documents in Word, presentations in PowerPoint, and workbooks in Excel in the same way. Additionally, you can open such documents as outlines in PowerPoint, templates and text files in Word, and Lotus or Quattro Pro files in Excel.

To open a file

1. Choose the **F**ile **O**pen command. The Open dialog box appears.
2. In Dri**v**es, choose the drive, and in **D**irectories, choose the directory containing the file.
3. In File **N**ame, type the name of the file or select the file name from the list.

Tip

You can choose List Files of **T**ype and select a different file type—such as a template, text file, or outline—to display and open.

4. Choose OK to close the dialog box and open the file.

Shortcut

 Click the Open button on the Standard toolbar to display the Open dialog box, or press Ctrl+O to display the Open dialog box.

Printing

Printing is similar in each of the three programs. You can print, using default settings, by choosing the Print button on the Standard toolbar. You can also choose specific settings in the Print dialog box.

Note

For specific printing information for each program, see **Printing** in the program's task reference section in this book.

To print

1. Choose the **F**ile **P**rint command. The Print dialog box appears.
2. In the Print What area, choose what it is you want to print.
3. In **C**opies, enter or select a number of copies.
4. In Page Range, identify the range of pages or slides you want to print.

Note

You can change settings by choosing the Printer or Printer Setup button to specify the printer and setup. Furthermore, each application's Print dialog box offers additional command buttons for viewing or changing options before printing.

5. Choose any other options offered in the specific Print dialog box.

6. Choose OK to print and close the dialog box.

Shortcut

Click the Print button on the Standard toolbar to print using the default settings.

Alternatively, press Ctrl+P to display the Print dialog box.

Save/Save As

When you are finished working on a file in any of the programs, you will want to save that file so you can later open it and view it, edit it, or print it. Save and Save As work the same in the Microsoft Office applications.

The Save As command is used when you first save a file. In the Save As dialog box, you enter a name and location in which to store the file. The Save command is used after a file has been named and you have made changes you want to add. The Save command does not display a dialog box; it just saves the file with the current name.

Tip

After you have saved a file using the Save As command, you can save the file again using the same command for various reasons: to save a copy of the same file under a different name, to save a copy of the file to a disk or tape drive, or to save a copy of the file to a different file format.

To Save As

1. Choose the **F**ile Save **A**s command. The Save As dialog box appears.

> **Tip**
>
> If you forget and choose the **F**ile **S**ave command for a new document, workbook, or presentation instead of the Save **A**s command, the Save As dialog box appears so you can name the file.

2. In Dri**v**es, select a drive to save the file to.
3. In **D**irectories, choose a directory.
4. In File **N**ame, enter the name of the file.

> **Tip**
>
> You can leave off the extension (DOC, PPT, XLS); the program automatically fills it in for you.

5. Choose OK to save the file.

> **Note**
>
> If you want to save a file as something other than a document in Word, a presentation in PowerPoint, or a worksheet in Excel, choose Save File as **T**ype and select the file type you want to save. Use this option when saving a file to use in another application, such as WordPerfect or 1-2-3, or when saving templates, outlines, and so on.

To Save

Choose the **F**ile **S**ave command. The application saves the changes to the named document.

Shortcut

 Click the Save button on the Standard toolbar to save changes to a file, or press Ctrl+S.

Shortcut Menus

Shortcut menus enable you to quickly access common and often-used commands. Some shortcuts include editing commands, while others apply only to objects.

All three programs offer shortcut menus for the following elements, although the menus in each application vary:

Element	Shortcut menu items
Toolbars	Shortcut menu displays the names of the toolbars; display or hide a toolbar by selecting it from the menu. Additionally, the Toolbars and Customize commands appear on the shortcut menus; select one of these commands to display a related dialog box.
Work Area	Shortcut menu displays various common commands used in the work area, such as Cut, Copy, and Paste plus other commands individual to each program.
Objects	Shortcut menu displays editing commands, and various commands relating to the selected object, individual to each application.
Text	Shortcut menu displays editing commands, font, bullet, and alignment commands, plus commands individual to each application.

To use a shortcut menu

1. Point to the area, selected object, or element you want to use.

2. Click the right mouse button. The shortcut menu appears.

3. Select the command and click the left mouse button.

> **Tip**
>
> To cancel the shortcut menu, click elsewhere on the screen, or press the Esc key.

Starting Applications

You can start applications by double-clicking the program icon in the Program Manager, as you would any Windows program. However, with Microsoft Office, you can start an application faster and easier using the Office Manager (the Microsoft Office toolbar).

When Office starts, it displays the Office Manager containing icons, or buttons, representing Excel, Word, and PowerPoint. Not only can you use these buttons to start the applications, you can use the buttons to switch quickly from one application to another.

To start an application

Click the button on the Office Manager that represents the application you want to open.

> **Tip**
>
> 
> 
> 
>
> You can open any of the applications from any other application. If, for example, you are in Word and want to open Excel, simply click the Excel button. This saves time, since you do not have to use the Windows Task List to switch to Program Manager and then open the program.

To switch to an application

Click the button on the Office Manager that represents the application you want to open.

Toolbars

Each application has its own toolbars that help you create charts, drawings, forms, documents, databases, borders, shapes, and so on; you can display one, two, or all of the toolbars on-screen at the same time. Two toolbars, however, are common to all the Microsoft Office applications: the Standard and Formatting toolbars (though some buttons differ from application to application).

To display a toolbar

1. Choose the **V**iew **T**oolbars command. The Toolbars dialog box appears.
2. In **T**oolbars, choose the toolbars you want to display.
3. Choose OK.

> **Tip**
>
> You can point the mouse at any toolbar on-screen and press the right mouse button to display a list of toolbars. Select the toolbar you want to show or hide. Toolbars with a check mark are already on-screen.

To use a toolbar

To use a tool on a toolbar, click the tool button with the mouse. Some tools require you to select an object or text first, such as the Bold button.

To use like buttons on the Standard Toolbar

Each application has buttons on the Standard toolbar that are not on the Standard toolbars of other applications; however, following are the tool buttons that are the same for all three programs on the Standard toolbar:

Button	Name	Description
	New	Click to start a new file in the application; the button displays the New Presentation dialog box in PowerPoint or starts a new workbook or document using the defaults in Excel and Word.
	Open	Click to display the Open dialog box.
	Save	Click to save changes to the file; if you have not yet saved the file as a name, this button displays the Save As dialog box.
	Print	Click to print the current file using default settings, such as one copy, all pages, and so on.
ABC	Spelling	Click to begin the spell check and display the Spelling dialog box if any questionable words are found.
	Cut	Click to cut selected item.
	Copy	Click to copy selected item.
	Paste	Click to paste cut or copied item to insertion point.
	Format Painter	Click to use Format Painter to copy a text or object format and apply it to another text or object.
	Undo	Click to Undo the previous command or procedure.
100%	Zoom	Enter or select the percentage of magnification you want to view.
	Help	Click and then click on an item, command, feature, or other item to display a context-sensitive help screen.

To use the Formatting toolbar

The Formatting toolbar can be used to format selected text. With the buttons on the toolbar, you can change font, size, alignment, and other formatting. Following are the common buttons on the Formatting toolbars of the three applications:

Button	Name	How to Use It
Times New Roman	Font	Click the down arrow to the right of the Font box to display a drop-down list of available fonts. Choose one to apply.
24	Size	Click the down arrow to the right of the Size box to display a drop-down list of available font sizes; alternatively, type a size in the text box.
B	Bold	Click to apply bold; click again to turn it off.
I	Italic	Click the Italic button to apply it; click again to turn it off.
U	Underline	Click the Underline button to apply it; click again to turn it off.
	Align Left	Click the Align Left button to apply left alignment.
	Center	Click the Center button to apply center alignment.

To customize a toolbar

1. Choose the **V**iew **T**oolbars command. The Toolbars dialog box appears.

2. Choose the **C**ustomize button. The Customize dialog box appears.

3. In **C**ategory, choose the category for which you want to display buttons. To view a description of a button, click

it and a description appears in the area near the bottom of the dialog box.

4. To remove a button from a toolbar, drag the button down and off of the toolbar toward the Customize dialog box.

   To add a button to a toolbar, drag the button from the Customize dialog box to the toolbar. The new button bumps the other buttons to the right.

5. Choose Close when finished.

> **Tip**
>
> You can add space between buttons to help separate and organize your toolbar, by dragging the button so that it overlaps about half of the next button. The buttons then adjust to add the extra space. The Customize dialog box must be open for this to work.

ToolTips

ToolTips are yellow boxes containing the name of a toolbar button. A ToolTip appears when you hold the mouse pointer over a tool button. When you display a ToolTip, a description of the function of the button displays in the Status bar, as well. ToolTips are especially useful when you are learning to use the programs.

You can choose to show or hide ToolTips.

To show or hide ToolTips

1. Choose the **V**iew **T**oolbars command. The Toolbars dialog box appears.

2. Choose the **S**how ToolTips check box. If an X appears in the box, choosing it turns the ToolTips off; if no X appears, choosing the option turns the ToolTips on.

3. Choose OK to close the dialog box.

Undo

Undo is a useful command; it enables you to reverse a previous action. Some actions, however, cannot be reversed. If the program cannot undo an action, the Undo command is dimmed on the menu.

To undo

Choose the **E**dit **U**ndo command; alternatively, press Ctrl+Z.

Shortcut

Click the Undo button from the Standard toolbar to undo the previous action.

Windows

Word, Excel, and PowerPoint all have the same properties as other Windows programs. Each program is made up of windows: the document window, Find File window, Help windows, and so on. All windows consist of the same elements and all windows have the same parts and properties.

To enlarge or reduce windows

1. Position the mouse pointer over the window border; the mouse cursor changes to a double-headed arrow.

Tip

Position the mouse over a corner of the window and you can drag two borders at the same time.

2. Drag a border in any direction to resize a window, and then release the mouse button.

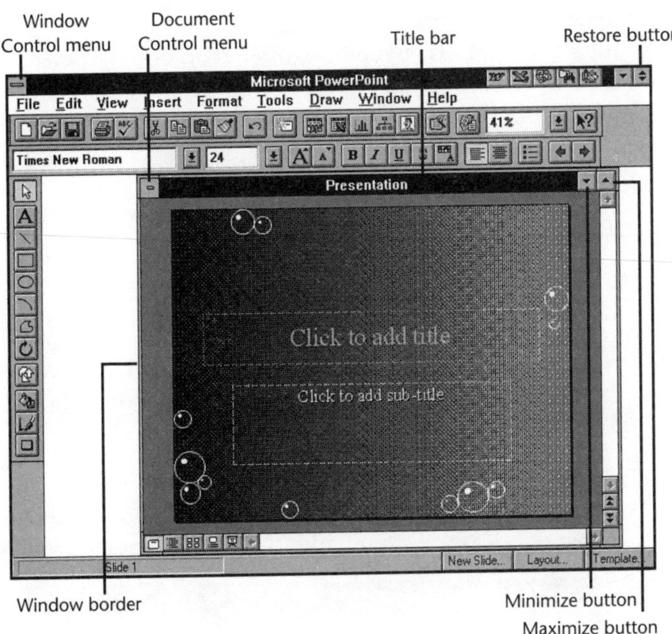

To move windows

1. Position the mouse pointer in the title bar of the window.
2. Drag the window to a new location.

To close windows

1. Click the Control menu of the window and the menu drops down.
2. Choose **C**lose.

> **Tip**
>
> You can press Alt+F4 or double-click the control menu to close a window.

To arrange windows

Arrange windows when you have more than one document, worksheet, or presentation open within the program. For example, arranging the windows enables you to display all open Word documents on-screen together, so you can work on several documents at a time.

Choose the **W**indow **A**rrange All command.

- Word tiles the windows automatically; you cannot choose either tiling or cascading.
- Excel displays the Arrange dialog box from which you can choose to arrange the windows as tiled or cascaded. Choose OK to close the box.
- PowerPoint tiles the windows when you choose the Arrange All command. You can, however, choose the **W**indow **C**ascade command to cascade the windows.

Note

Each tiled or cascaded window contains the same elements of any other window: border, Control menu, scroll bars, and so on.

To switch between windows

When there are several windows on-screen, the active window is the one with the different color in the title bar; the title bar may appear highlighted. Switch to another window by clicking anywhere in the window that you want to work in. If the windows are cascaded, click the title bar of the window.

Wizards

Each program includes several wizards that can help you create a specific document quickly and efficiently. Wizards guide you step by step, by displaying dialog boxes with questions and choices about layout, design, and text you will use in the project.

Word, for example, includes many document wizards: agenda, calendar, fax cover, newsletter, memo, and so on. Excel, on the other hand, contains wizards that help you create elements, such as the ChartWizard, Convert Text to Columns Wizard, and so on. PowerPoint contains the AutoContent and Pick a Look wizards that help you design your presentation. For more information about an individual application's wizards, see that application's task reference section in this book.

All wizards are set up about the same. When you choose to run the wizard, the first step dialog box appears. You answer questions, fill in text boxes, and follow the directions for creating the document, table, presentation, chart, or other element.

All wizards contain the following command buttons:

Cancel	Stops the wizard, cancels it, and returns to the program screen.
Back	Displays the previous wizard dialog box. You can review or change your choices.
Next	Displays the next wizard dialog box.
Finish	Stops the wizard and creates the document, presentation, or other element using the information you entered in the wizard dialog boxes. If you choose the **F**inish button before you reach the end of the wizard, the program works with what you have so far.

Note

Anything you create with a wizard can be modified or edited.

Integration

Microsoft Office offers the user a strong group of excellent applications, and also enables data, documents, and other information to be quickly and easily shared among them. Integrating the programs means you can produce a report in Word with up-to-date figures from your Excel worksheet. You can create a presentation from an outline produced in Word and charts created in Excel. Office enables you to produce professional-looking, effective documents to represent you and your business.

Chart

See **Chart** in the PowerPoint or Excel section.

Clip Art

Office includes a Clip Art Gallery where you can choose a clip art file to insert into a document, presentation, or worksheet. The Clip Art Gallery contains all clip art in the Office programs, and you can add other art files, as well. Any picture in the Gallery can be used in any of the Office programs.

Note

The first time you insert clip art into one of the programs, Office displays a message box asking if you want to compile the Gallery. Choose **Y**es. The Gallery opens normally from that point on.

To open and view the Clip Art Gallery

1. Choose the **I**nsert **O**bject command. The Object dialog box appears.
2. In the **O**bject Type list, choose Microsoft ClipArt Gallery and choose OK. The Microsoft ClipArt Gallery window opens.
3. In Choose a **C**ategory to View Below, select a category. Alternatively, the option All Categories is selected by default and displays all clip art in the Gallery.
4. Scroll through the clip art pictures and choose the one you want.
5. Choose OK to accept the clip art file and insert it.

To customize the Gallery

1. Choose the **I**nsert **O**bject command. The Object dialog box appears.
2. In the **O**bject Type list, choose Microsoft ClipArt Gallery and choose OK. The Microsoft ClipArt Gallery window opens.
3. Choose the **O**ptions button. The Options dialog box appears. Choose from the following options:

Option	Description
Refresh	Scans the drive and adds any pictures to the Gallery that are not already in it, and removes any unavailable pictures. Depending on the drive size and amount of pictures, this could take several minutes. Follow directions presented in the Refresh dialog boxes.
Add	Adds specific files by displaying the Add Clipart dialog box. Select a file or files and add them to the Gallery.
Change a Category	Enables you to delete or rename a category in the list of categories.

Option	Description
Edit Picture Information	Enables you to move clip art files to new categories or give them new names or descriptions.

To find a clip art file

1. In the Microsoft ClipArt Gallery dialog box, choose the **F**ind button. The Find Picture dialog box appears.
2. Choose from one of the following options:

Option	Description
With the **C**ategory	Select a category from the drop-down list
With a **D**escription containing	Enter a description as you described in the Options dialog box (as described in the previous section)
With a **F**ilename containing	Enter all or part of the file name
Of this **T**ype of file	Select a specific file type—such as bitmap, Encapsulated PostScript, and so on—from the drop-down list

3. Choose OK and the Gallery displays all files it finds.

Clipboard

The Clipboard is a Windows feature common to all of the Office programs. The Clipboard is a temporary storage area for cut or copied items. When you cut or copy text or objects in one of the programs, Windows places that item on the Clipboard. You can paste that item to the same document, a different document, or a different program; you can continue to paste the same item over and over again until you cut or copy another item.

To use the Clipboard

1. Select the text or object to be cut or copied.

2. To cut the item, choose the **E**dit Cu**t** command, or press Ctrl+X.

   To copy the item, choose the **E**dit **C**opy command, or press Ctrl+C.

3. Position the insertion point in the location you want to paste the object; you can paste it in the same file, in another file within the same program, or in a different program.

4. Choose the **E**dit **P**aste command, or press Ctrl+V.

Shortcuts

  Select the text or object, then click the Cut or Copy button on the Standard toolbar,  reposition the insertion point, and click the Paste button.

To view the Clipboard

1. Switch to the Program Manager by pressing Ctrl+Esc to display the Task List. Double-click the Program Manager.

2. In the Main window, double-click the Clipboard Viewer icon. The Clipboard Viewer window appears.

Tip

You can save the contents of the Clipboard viewer by choosing the **F**ile Save **A**s command and naming the contents. Then you can open that file in the Clipboard at any time and paste it into other files.

3. To close the Clipboard Viewer, choose the **F**ile E**x**it command.

Closing Office

Closing the Office removes the Office Manager toolbar from the screen, but does not close the Office programs that were already open. If you want to switch from program to program, you must use the Windows Task List (press Ctrl+Esc to display the task list).

To close the Office Manager

1. 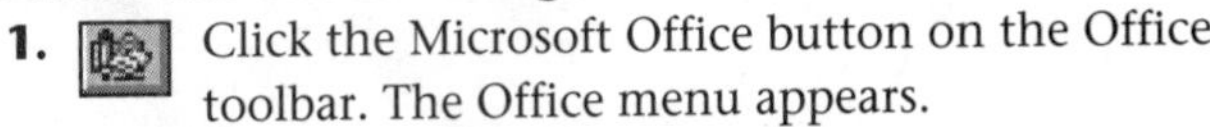 Click the Microsoft Office button on the Office toolbar. The Office menu appears.
2. Choose the E**x**it command and the toolbar disappears.

See also **Starting Office**.

Copy

See **Clipboard**.

Customizing Microsoft Office

Use the Office Manager toolbar to switch between programs, and to control which programs you view on-screen. You can customize the Office toolbar, menu, and view to better suit the program to your needs and preferences. You can change the position of the toolbar buttons and add or delete buttons from the toolbar. Additionally, you can add or delete commands from the Office menu. Finally, you can customize the toolbar buttons so you can better see them, move them around on-screen, and so on.

To customize the Office toolbar

1. Click the Microsoft Office button on the Office toolbar. The menu appears.
2. Choose the **C**ustomize command. The Customize dialog box appears.

3. Choose the **T**oolbar tab.

4. In the list of programs, select any of the applications you want to add as a button to the toolbar and click the check box. Those applications with an X in the check box are currently displaying on the toolbar. You can remove those buttons from the toolbar by clicking the check box and removing the X.

> **Tip**
>
> In the Toolbar tab, select an application that is showing on the toolbar; then click the up or down Move arrows to move the application's position on the toolbar.

5. Choose OK.

> **Note**
>
> Choose the **A**dd button in the **T**oolbar tab to add a program not in the list. To add a program, you must know the command line that starts it, as well as its working directory.

To customize the Office menu

1. Click the Microsoft Office button on the Office toolbar. The menu appears.

2. Choose **C**ustomize. The Customize dialog box appears.

3. Choose the **M**enu tab.

4. In the list of applications, choose any application you want to add to the Office menu by clicking the check box. Click a check box with an X in it to remove that item from the menu.

> **Tip**
>
> Click the up or down Move arrows to move the selected item on the Microsoft Office menu.

5. Choose OK.

To customize the view

1. Click the Microsoft Office button on the Office toolbar. The menu appears.
2. Choose **C**ustomize. The Customize dialog box appears.
3. Choose the **V**iew tab.
4. In the Toolbar Button Size area, choose from one of the following options:

Option	Description
Small Buttons	Displays the small toolbar buttons automatically positioned at the top of the screen in the title bar of the programs
Regular **B**uttons	Displays the toolbar buttons in a medium size on a movable toolbar
Large Buttons	Displays the toolbar buttons in a large size on a movable toolbar

5. You can also choose any or all of the following options; an X indicates the option is activated.

Option	Description
Toolbar is Always Visible	Shows the Office toolbar so it always remains on top of the program windows
Show ToolTips	Displays ToolTips for the toolbar
Show Title Screen at Startup	By default, Office is in your Windows Startup group so it automatically opens when you open Windows; this option displays the Office startup screen

6. Choose OK to close the dialog box.

Customizing Applications

See **Toolbars** in the Common Features section.

Cut

See **Clipboard**.

Drag and Drop

You can move text within a document or between two applications using the Drag and Drop editing feature of the Microsoft Office applications. You can, for example, display Word and PowerPoint on-screen at the same time, and drag and drop text from one program to the other.

To drag and drop text

1. Select the text you want to move.
2. Drag the text to its new position. As you drag, a box is added to the mouse pointer as well as a vertical line that shows where the text will be placed.

Tip

You can drag the text across the window borders of two programs, or within the area of just one program. It is suggested, however, that drag and drop editing be used over short distances; if you want to move text over a long distance, use the Cut and Paste commands.

3. When the vertical line is positioned where you want the text to go, release the mouse button and the selected text moves.

See also **Windows** in the Common Features section.

Drawing

The three programs—Excel, Word, and PowerPoint—all enable you to draw shapes and lines to add to your documents, worksheets, charts, presentations, and so on. You use the tools on the Drawing toolbar to create drawings in any of the programs. Many of the tool buttons on the toolbars are the same, as well as the basic procedures for drawing. You can also copy or cut and paste your drawings from application to application.

To create a drawing

1. Display the drawing toolbar by pointing to a current toolbar, clicking the right mouse button, and selecting the Drawing toolbar.

Note

PowerPoint offers two drawing toolbars: Drawing and Drawing+.

2. To use a drawing tool—such as the Line or Rectangle tool—click the tool and drag it across the work area.

> **Note**
>
> Word requires you be in Page Layout view to use the drawing tools.

To use the drawing tools

Click a drawing tool to use it. After you draw with the tool, the mouse changes back to a pointer. The line or shape you draw has handles on it indicating the object is selected. You can move, resize, delete, or perform other actions on a selected line or shape.

You must click the button of a line, arc, or shape each time you want to draw that particular element. When you release the mouse button, the tool changes back to the selection tool. However, if you double-click the drawing tool, the mouse remains the tool until you click the button again. This way, you can draw many lines or shapes without clicking the tool button after each drawing.

Following is a list and descriptions of the tools that are the same on the drawing toolbars of the Microsoft applications:

Button	Name	Description
	Line	Draws straight lines
	Rectangle	Draws rectangles and squares
	Ellipse	Draws ovals and circles
	Arc	Draws arcs or curves
	Freeform	Draws freeform lines and shapes

Button	Name	Description
	Text Box	Draws a box in which you can enter text
	Selection	Selects objects or lines
	Bring to Front	Brings the selected object to the top of the stack of objects
	Send to Back	Sends the selected object to the bottom of a stack of objects
	Group	Arranges several selected objects into a group to which you can copy, delete, change line styles, and add color
	Ungroup	Ungroups selected objects

See also **Drawing** in the PowerPoint section.

To draw shapes

1. Click the rectangle or ellipse tool on the Drawing toolbar. The mouse pointer changes to a cross.

2. Drag the tool in the work area to create the shape, and release the mouse button. The cursor changes back to the normal mouse pointer.

Tip

Hold the Shift key while dragging to constrain the shape to a perfect square or perfect circle.

Note

Resize a shape by selecting it, and then dragging its handles. You can also move the shape by selecting it and dragging the border to a new location.

To draw lines and arcs

1. Click the Line or Arc tool on the Drawing toolbar. The mouse pointer changes to a cross.

2. Drag the Line or Arc tool to draw the object, and then release the mouse button.

Tip

After drawing an arc, you can select it and drag any of the handles to change its shape.

To draw a freeform line or shape

1. Click the Freeform button. The mouse pointer changes to a pencil.

2. Drag the pencil around the work area to create a freeform line or a shape.

3. To complete the line, double-click the mouse.

See also **Drawing**, **Borders**, and **Colors** in each application's task reference.

E-mail

See **Mail**.

Embedding

See **Object Linking and Embedding (OLE)**.

Equation Editor

Word includes an applet called the Equation Editor that creates an object you can insert into Word, Excel, or PowerPoint. When you insert the equation, you embed it. See **Object Linking and Embedding (OLE)** for more information.

The Equation Editor enables you to add fractions, exponents, integrals, and other mathematical elements to your document. Equation Editor applies the formatting—such as superscripting or the font size of exponents—for you.

To create an equation

1. Position the insertion point at the location you want to place the equation.

2. Choose the **I**nsert **O**bject command. The Object dialog box appears.

3. Choose to Create New.

4. In **O**bject Type, choose Microsoft Equation 2.0 and choose OK. The Equation Editor toolbar and menu appear, as well as a box in which you type your equation.

5. Create the equation by entering the data, choosing symbols, operators, and so on from the toolbar and menu.

> **Tip**
>
> Press F1 for context-sensitive help while working in the Editor.

6. When finished, click outside of the equation box and in the work area. The toolbar and menu disappear, and the equation appears at the insertion point.

To edit an equation

In any program, edit the equation by double-clicking it. The Equation toolbar and menu appear.

Exporting

See **Importing and Exporting.**

Graphs (Microsoft Graph)

Word includes an applet called Microsoft Graph that creates a graph as an object you can insert into Word, Excel, or PowerPoint. When you insert the graph, you embed it.

With Graph, you can create area, bar, column, line, pie, and other types of charts to insert into your documents. You can type the data directly into the Graph datasheet, or you can copy data from a Word table or Excel worksheet and insert it into Graph's datasheet.

See also **Object Linking and Embedding (OLE)**.

To create a graph

1. Choose the **I**nsert **O**bject command. The Object dialog box appears.

2. Choose Create New.

3. In the **O**bject Type list, choose Microsoft Graph 5.0 and choose OK. The Microsoft Graph Datasheet dialog box appears with sample data in the box.

4. Delete the sample data and enter your own. Double-click the Control menu to close the Datasheet, or click outside of the dialog box. The chart displays in a selected box. A Graph menu and toolbar are also displayed.

To change the chart type

1. Select the chart box.
2. Choose the F**o**rmat **C**hart Type command. The Chart Type dialog box appears.
3. In Chart Dimension, choose either **2**-D or **3**-D.
4. Below Chart Dimension, choose a chart type.
5. Choose OK to close the dialog box.

To display the datasheet

Choose the **V**iew **D**atasheet command. The datasheet appears; you can edit it as you want.

To save the changes to the chart, close the datasheet.

To display and remove gridlines

1. Select the graph.
2. Choose the **I**nsert **G**ridlines command. The Gridlines dialog box appears.
3. In each Category area—X, Y, and Z axis—choose to show **M**ajor and/or Mi**n**or Gridlines.
4. Choose OK to close the dialog box.

Note

To remove the gridlines, open the Gridlines dialog box by choosing the **I**nsert **G**ridlines command; deselect the options so no X's appear in the check boxes.

To remove a legend

Click the Legend button on the MS Graph toolbar to remove or to add a legend.

To add elements to a chart

You can add labels and titles to your chart.

To add a title

1. Choose the **I**nsert **T**itles command. The Titles dialog box appears.

2. Choose to Attach Text to a Chart **T**itle, **V**alue (z) Axis, or **C**ategory (x) Axis, and choose OK. The dialog box closes and adds a text box in the specified position. Enter the text and format it, if you want.

To add data labels

1. Choose the **I**nsert **D**ata Labels command. The Data Labels dialog box appears.

2. In Data Labels, choose Show **L**abel and choose OK. The data labels appear in the chart.

To add explanatory text

1. Click the Text Box tool on the MS Graph toolbar. The pointer changes to a cross when you position it in the graph box.

2. Drag the tool to create a text box and enter the text.

Shortcuts

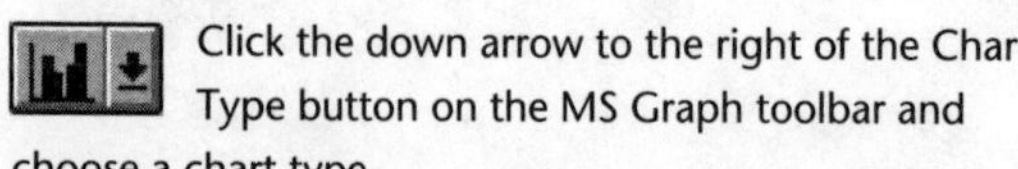

Click the down arrow to the right of the Chart Type button on the MS Graph toolbar and choose a chart type.

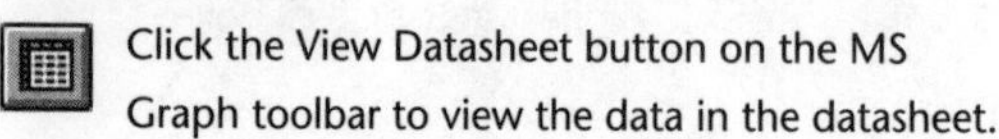

Click the View Datasheet button on the MS Graph toolbar to view the data in the datasheet.

Click the Vertical Gridlines button on the MS Graph toolbar to add lines; click the button again to remove them.

Click the Horizontal Gridlines button on the MS Graph toolbar to add lines; click the button again to remove them.

Importing and Exporting

When you import and export text from any of the three programs, you are provided with various file formats you can use to translate the text into a file type the application can read. A file format determines the way data or text is stored in a file; different programs use different file formats.

Each application has a list of file formats to which it can import (Open) and export (Save As). When you want to export a file to another program, you must first find out what file formats the other program supports. Then save the file in that format so you can easily export it (or open it) in the other program.

Following are the compatible file formats you can import and export in Excel, PowerPoint, and Word:

Program	Import	Export
Excel	Text files (TXT)	Text files (TXT), Excel files (XLS, XL5)
Word	Text files (TXT), Rich Text Format (RTF)	Text files (TXT), Word files (DOC)
PowerPoint	Word files (DOC), Excel files (XLS, XL5)	Rich Text Format (RTF)

To export a file

1. Choose the **F**ile Save **A**s command. The Save As dialog box appears.
2. In Save File as **T**ype, choose the file format you want to use.
3. Choose the Dri**v**e and **D**irectory, and enter a File **N**ame for the file.

> **Tip**
>
> Use the File Format table to check the file format the receiving program can import.

4. Choose OK.

To import a file

1. Choose the **F**ile **O**pen command. The Open dialog box appears.
2. In List Files of **T**ype, choose the file format of the file you are importing.
3. Choose the Dri**v**e and **D**irectory in which the file is located.
4. Enter or select the File **N**ame.
5. Choose OK.

Inserting a Picture

You can insert a picture from another program or the same program into your document, worksheet, or presentation as long as the appropriate graphic, or file, filter is installed on your computer. A graphic filter enables an application to interpret and display a file created in another application. The following is a list of file formats and their extensions that you can import:

File Format	Extension
Windows Bitmaps	DIB, BMP
HP Graphic Language	HGL
Encapsulated PostScript	EPS
Tagged Image Format	TIF
Windows Metafile	WMF

File Format	Extension
DrawPerfect	WPG
Micrografx Designer/Draw	DRW
Computer Graphics Metafile	CGM
PC Paintbrush	PCX
CompuServe GIF	GIF
Macintosh PICT	PCT
AutoCAD Plot File	ADI
HP Plotter Print File	PLT
Lotus 1-2-3 Graphics	PIC
Windows DIB	DIB

To insert a picture

1. Choose the **I**nsert **P**icture command. The Insert Picture dialog box appears.
2. In List Files of **T**ype, choose the file format of the picture.
3. Choose the Dri**v**e and **D**irectory in which the picture is located.
4. In File **N**ame, enter or select the picture file.
5. Choose OK.

Installing Office

Before installing Office, make sure you have the following:

- Windows 3.1 or later
- DOS 3.1 or later
- 80386 or higher personal computer with a hard disk and a high-density floppy disk drive

- At least 15.5M of free disk space for the minimum installation; 48M for complete installation
- EGA or higher resolution video adapter
- At least 4M RAM; 6M recommended

Note

It is always a good idea to copy all of the Office disks before installing it; install Office from the copies to keep your originals as a backup.

When installing, you are asked to choose from one of the following three installations:

- **T**ypical. Installs the most common files you need to use the application.
- **C**omplete/Custom. Displays a list of options and features, of each application, from which you choose to install.
- **L**aptop (Minimum). Installs only the minimum files required to run the applications. Use when disk space is limited.

To install Office

1. Start Windows by typing **WIN** at the DOS prompt if Windows is not already open.
2. Insert the Office Setup disk in the appropriate floppy disk drive.
3. In Program Manager, choose the **F**ile **R**un command. The Run dialog box appears.
4. In the **C**ommand Line text box, enter the letter for the drive holding the Setup disk, a colon, and then **setup**. For example, type **a:setup**.
5. Choose OK.

6. Setup starts. Follow all directions in the Setup screens, answer all questions, and insert the disks as required.

7. When Setup is finished, it displays a message box. Choose OK, and Setup returns to the Program Manager. The Office group and program icons are displayed.

Linking Dynamically

DDE (Dynamic Data Exchange) is a Windows feature that enables you to share data between applications. The shared data is linked so that when data is updated in the source application, the data in the destination application is automatically updated. DDE is not available with all Windows applications; check the reference manual for specific programs for more information.

To link dynamically

1. Make sure that both the source and the destination applications are running within Windows.

2. Open the source document and the destination document.

> **Tip**
>
> Make sure both documents are saved before you link them.

3. Select and copy the data from the source application.

4. Switch to the destination application and document.

5. Position the insertion point.

6. Choose the **E**dit Paste **S**pecial command. The Paste Special dialog box appears with the Source listed for the data.

7. Choose the Paste **L**ink option button.

> **Tip**
>
> If the Paste Link option button is dimmed or not available, the application does not support linking, or cannot supply the data in the correct format.

8. In the **A**s list box, select the type of object you are linking; for example, Formatted text, Unformatted text, Picture, Bitmap, or Excel Worksheet.

9. Choose OK. The data is inserted, and the program creates the link.

To update links automatically

> **Tip**
>
> All Excel links are automatically updated unless you change them in the Links dialog box.

1. In either of the linked documents, choose the **E**dit Lin**k**s command. The Links dialog box appears.

2. In the Update area, choose **A**utomatic.

To break a link

1. In the source document, choose the **E**dit Lin**k**s command. The Links dialog box appears.

2. Choose **B**reak Link. A confirmation message box appears.

3. Choose **Y**es to break the link or **N**o to cancel the command.

See also **Object Linking and Embedding (OLE)**.

Macros

Macros are mini-programs you can use to automate repetitive tasks, such as formatting, moving from one document or worksheet to another, inserting specific data or text, saving, printing, and so on. You can record a macro in either Word or Excel using any commands and features available to you from the programs and from Office. Run the macros to save time and energy when working with the Office and its programs.

To record a macro in Word

1. Choose the **T**ools **M**acro command. The Macro dialog box appears.
2. Choose Rec**o**rd. The Record Macro dialog box appears.
3. In the **R**ecord Macro Name, enter a name for the macro.
4. Choose OK. The dialog box closes and the Macro Recorder toolbar appears on-screen. Additionally, the mouse pointer changes to a pointer with an icon of a cassette tape attached. All mouse and keyboard actions will be recorded.

Note

The Macro Recorder toolbar includes two buttons: Stop and Pause. Click Stop to stop recording the macro; click Pause to stop recording temporarily, and click the Pause button again to continue.

Tip

You can also start or stop recording a macro by double-clicking the REC indicator on the status bar.

5. Record the actions you want and then click the Stop button on the Macro Recorder toolbar.

To record a macro in Excel

1. In Excel, choose the **T**ools **R**ecord Macro command. A secondary menu appears.

2. Choose **R**ecord New Macro. The Record New Macro dialog box appears.
3. In the **M**acro Name text box, enter a name for the macro.
4. Choose OK. The Stop toolbar appears containing a Stop button.
5. Any actions you take with either the keyboard or the mouse are recorded. Click the Stop button on the Stop toolbar when finished recording.

To run a macro

1. Choose the **T**ools **M**acro command. The Macro dialog box appears.
2. In the list of **M**acro Names, select the macro you want to run.
3. Choose the **R**un button. The dialog box closes and the macro runs.

> **Tip**
>
> You can also select a macro in the Macro dialog box, and choose the **D**elete button to remove it from the list.

Mail

If you have Microsoft Mail, you can send electronic mail, including messages and files, to other users on your network who have Mail. The **F**ile Sen**d** command enables you to mail a copy of the open file to another person or persons from within Word, Excel, or PowerPoint. The Routing Slip feature enables you to route the document to several users, in whatever order you wish, for their approval or revision.

Note

A license to use Microsoft Mail (MS Mail) is included with your copy of Office; the MS Mail software, however, is not. The license enables you to use mail and install the necessary files on your workstation, provided you have the necessary software on the network.

Starting Mail

See **Starting Applications** in the Common Features section.

Sending Mail

You can send mail directly from Microsoft Mail or from inside an open Office application. To send mail to another user, you need to address and prepare the message and attach any files you want to send with the message. If you are already in an Office application such as Word or Excel, you can route a message or a document from within that application.

To send mail from Microsoft Mail

1. Choose the **M**ail Compose **N**ote command, or press Ctrl+N. The Send Note window appears.

Shortcut

You can quickly open the Send Note window by clicking the Compose Note button.

2. To address the message, click in the **T**o text box and do one of the following:
   - Type the name of the person or the group you want to receive the message. (See "Creating a personal mailing group.")
   - Choose **M**ail A**d**dress Book, select the name in the Address text box, and click the **T**o button.

Shortcut

Double-clicking a name adds it to the To list.

3. Repeat step 2 for each name you want to add to the list.

4. If necessary, move to the **C**c text box and repeat step 2 for other recipients.

5. If you want to check the names to see whether they are spelled correctly or are part of the current address list, press Alt+K.

6. When you are done addressing the mail, click OK.

7. Enter a subject for the message in the Sub**j**ect box.

8. Type the text of the message in the message area below the address and subject information.

Tip

Use the **E**dit Spe**l**ling command to check the spelling in your message.

9. If you want to attach a file, attach it now. (See "To attach a file or a document to the message.")

10. When the message is complete, click the **S**end button or press Alt+S to send it to all recipients on the To and Cc lists.

To attach a file or a document to the message

1. In the Mail - Send Note window, move to the point in the message where you want to attach the document.

2. Click the **A**ttach command button or press Alt+A. The Attach dialog box appears.

3. Select the location and file name of the file to attach. Choose the **A**ttach command button. A document icon

appears in your message, showing the file name and icon of the application that created the file.

4. Repeat step 3 for each file you want to attach.

5. When you finish attaching files, click Cl**o**se, or press Esc.

6. Finish the message, and click **S**end.

To send mail from within an Office application

1. Open the application and the file you want to send.

2. Choose the **F**ile Sen**d** command. Mail automatically attaches the open document to the message and includes the file name as the subject.

3. In the Send Note dialog box, fill in the **T**o and **C**c text boxes. You can modify the subject box and type a message, if desired.

4. Choose the **S**end button or press Alt+S to send the current document. After sending the file, you return to the source application.

To attach a routing slip to a file

1. From an Office application, choose the **F**ile Add **R**outing Slip command. The Routing Slip dialog box appears. Microsoft Mail automatically enters the subject as "Routing" and the name of the file you are routing.

> **Note**
>
> You can only use the Routing Slip feature from within another Office application, not from Mail directly.

2. Click the A**d**dress button. This opens the Address dialog box.

3. Select each recipient in the order you want them to receive the mail. Click the **A**dd button to add each recipient to the list. When you are done adding names to the list, choose OK.

Tip

You can change the order of the names on the recipient list by selecting a name in the **T**o box in the Routing Slip dialog box and clicking the up or down Move arrows.

4. To send the mail to each recipient in the order they are listed in the To box, select **O**ne After Another. To send the mail to everyone on the list at once, select A**l**l at once.

5. To have the mail returned to you when all recipients are done, select Return when done.

6. To track the status of the mail as each recipient sends it to the next person on the list, select Trac**k** Status.

7. If you have a message to send with the document you are routing, type the message in the **M**essage Text box.

Note

A brief message is automatically added, telling recipients that this mail is routed and that they need to forward it .

8. When you are done, click Route to send the mail.

Creating a personal mail group

If you often send mail to a certain group of co-workers, such as all managers or project team members, you can create a personal mail group. Then when you address your mail, you can simply select the group name rather than individual users. Microsoft Mail automatically sends the mail to everyone in the selected group.

1. Choose the **M**ail Personal **G**roups command. The Personal Groups dialog box appears, showing a list of the current groups.

2. To create a new group, click **N**ew.

3. In the New Group Name text box, type the group name and click the **C**reate command button. The Personal Groups dialog box appears.
4. Select the name you want to add. Hold down the Shift key and click to select adjacent names, or hold down the Ctrl key and click to select nonadjacent names.
5. Click **A**dd, or double-click the name.
6. Repeat steps 4 and 5 for all the names you want to add to your group.
7. When you finish adding names, choose OK. You return to the Personal Groups dialog box.
8. Choose Cl**o**se.

Receiving mail

When you receive mail from someone, you will probably want to read it. You can print, delete, reply to, or forward the mail to someone else. If a file is attached, you can save the file for later use. You can also forward a routed message when you are finished with it.

To read mail

1. From within MS Mail, choose the **W**indow Inbox command. The window will display all mail you have received.

> **Note**
>
> If the Window menu doesn't contain an Inbox option, look for the name of one of your other private folders—such as Sent Mail or Wastebasket—on the menu. Choose one of those, and then double-click the Inbox folder icon in the Private Folders list.

2. Double-click the message you want to read.

> **Tip**
>
> Unread mail is indicated by a closed envelope next to the sender's name.
>
> Messages that have been read show a gray open envelope.

3. After you read the message, you can do any or all of the following:

    - Print the message by choosing **F**ile **P**rint.
    - Send a reply. See "Replying to a Message."
    - Open or save a copy of the attached document (if applicable). See "To view an attached file."
    - Forward the message to another user. Choose **M**ail **F**orward and proceed as you would to send an original message.
    - Choose the **F**ile **D**elete command (or press Ctrl+D) to delete the mail message from your inbox.

> **Tip**
>
> Delete You can delete a message from the inbox without opening or reading it by selecting the message in the inbox and choosing the **F**ile **D**elete command.

To view an attached file

1. From within MS Mail, choose the **W**indow Inbox command. Mail with attached documents will have an icon that looks like a paper clip next to the envelope.
2. Double-click the file icon to open the application that is associated with the file type. When you double-click the file icon within Mail, the application opens, and then the file opens.
3. Read or edit the document. Close the document when you finish.

4. To save the attached document to disk, choose **F**ile Save **A**ttachment. The Save Attachment dialog will appear, enabling you to specify the path and filename to use in saving the document.

5. When you have specified a path and file name, choose **S**ave.

6. To return to the Mail message, click the Microsoft Mail button in the Microsoft Office toolbar.

Replying to a message

Shortcut

You can quickly reply to an open message by clicking the Reply button.

1. With the message open, choose **M**ail **R**eply, or press Ctrl+R. The message and address change.

2. Compose your reply at the insertion point before the message.

3. Click the **S**end button or press Alt+S.

Forwarding a routed document

1. From within MS Mail, choose the **W**indow Inbox command. Routed mail will have the word "Routed" in the subject.

2. Double-click the message you want read.

3. Read any message included with the routed document, including the routing directions.

4. Double-click the document icon in the message to open any attached file or document.

5. Edit the document if needed.

6. Choose the **F**ile Sen**d** command. The Routing Slip dialog box appears, enabling you to continue the routing,

or to send the document in a new message to another recipient.

7. Choose **O**K to continue the routing.

Managing Files

See **Find File** in the Common Features section.

Microsoft Office Manager

The Microsoft Office Manager is the Office toolbar you use to switch from one Office application to another. When you install Office, the Office Manager is automatically placed in your StartUp group so each time you open Windows, MS Office opens too.

Following is a list of things you can do with the Manager:

- Launch any of the applications by clicking the button on the Manager toolbar.
- Switch between applications by clicking the button on the toolbar.
- Get help using Office as well as access each application's help files.
- Customize the Office toolbar, buttons, and menu.
- Run Office Setup.

Button	Application
	Microsoft Word
	Microsoft Excel
	Microsoft PowerPoint

Button	Application
	Find File
	Microsoft Office

See also **Customizing Microsoft Office**.

Note

If you have installed other Microsoft Applications on your computer, buttons for these programs may also appear on the Office toolbar.

Object Linking and Embedding (OLE)

OLE enables you to link and embed objects or data from one application to another, thus providing your documents with up-to-date data and making your work easier. *Linking* is to insert a copy of information created in a source file into another file, whether in the same application or another Windows application. When a file is linked between two documents, changes to the source can easily and quickly be updated to the destination, either automatically or manually.

Embedding is to insert an object—such as a chart, graph, or picture—created in one application into a file in another application. An embedded object becomes part of the destination file, with one very important advantage. You can edit the object while in the destination document by double-clicking the object. When you double-click it, the source application opens to enable editing; when you're finished, you close the source application and the object is updated in the destination file.

To link an object

1. Choose the **I**nsert **O**bject command. The Object dialog box appears.

2. Choose the Create From File tab.

3. In the File **N**ame text box, enter or select the name of the file you want to link.

4. Choose the **L**ink To File check box and choose OK.

To choose automatic or manual linking

1. Choose the **E**dit Lin**k**s command. The Links dialog box appears.

2. In the list of links, select the link.

3. In the Update area, choose **A**utomatic or **M**anual.

4. Choose OK.

To update manually

1. Choose the **E**dit Lin**k**s command. The Links dialog box appears.

2. In the list of links, choose the link you want to update.

3. Choose the **U**pdate Now button.

4. Choose OK.

> **Shortcut**
>
> To quickly update links in Word, select the link in the document and press F9.

To edit linked data

1. Choose the **E**dit Lin**k**s command. The Links dialog box appears.

2. In the list of links, choose the link you want to update.

3. Choose the **O**pen Source button.

4. Edit the file and save it in the source application.

5. Choose the **F**ile E**x**it command to exit the source application.

To break a link

1. Choose the **E**dit Lin**k**s command. The Links dialog box appears.
2. In the list of links, select the link you want to break.
3. Choose the Break Link button. If a confirmation message box appears, choose **Y**es.
4. Choose the Close button.

Note

In Excel, you cannot break a link using the previously described method. To break a link in Excel, you must choose the Update **M**anual option in the Links dialog box when you choose to link. Then, you manually update the link each time until you want to break it. By not manually updating the link, you break it.

Shortcut

Quickly break a link by selecting the link and pressing Ctrl+Shift+F9.

Note

When you open a file that contains links, the program may display a message box asking if you want to re-establish links. Choose **Y**es.

To embed an object

1. Position the insertion point where you want to embed the object.
2. Choose the **I**nsert **O**bject menu. The Object dialog box appears.
3. Choose one of the following options or tabs:

Create from File	To embed an existing file as an object in another application
Create New	To create a new object

4. If you choose to create from a file, enter the name of the file in the File **N**ame box or select the file from the list and choose OK. The object is inserted.

   Alternatively, if you choose to create a new object, select the type of object you want to create in the Object Type list box. Choose OK.

5. If creating a new object, the application opens and you create the object. When finished, choose the **F**ile E**x**it command. A message box asks if you want to update the object in the destination application. Choose **Y**es. The object is inserted into the destination.

To edit an embedded object

1. Double-click the object. The application in which the object was created appears.
2. Edit the object.
3. Choose the **F**ile E**x**it command. If asked to update, choose **Y**es.

To convert an embedded object to a graphic

Select the embedded object and press Ctrl+Shift+F9.

See also **Linking Dynamically** and **Objects** in the Common Features section.

Opening Office

See **Starting Office.**

Organization Chart

See **Chart** in the PowerPoint section.

Paste

See **Clipboard**.

Spelling Checker

The spelling checkers in the three programs are similar in the way they look and act. The spelling checker examines the text in a document, presentation, or worksheet, and queries you if it finds a word that is not in the Custom dictionary (or other dictionary you may have installed for use with your Windows programs). You can choose to ignore, change, or add the questionable word to the dictionary and continue with the spelling check. The spelling checkers also query unusual capitalizations of words.

To check the spelling

1. Choose the **T**ools **S**pelling command, or press F7. The spell checker begins verifying the text; if it finds a questionable word, the Spelling dialog box appears.

2. The questionable word is highlighted in the text and appears in the Change **T**o text box.

3. The spell checker lists possible replacements for the questionable word in the Suggestio**n**s list box.

> **Note**
>
> If no suggestions are listed, choose the Suggest button in the Spelling dialog box.

4. Choose one of the following buttons:

Button	Description
Ignore	Skip this one instance of the word's spelling
I**g**nore All	Skip all instances of this spelling within this document
Change	Select one of the Suggestio**n**s or enter a correction in the Change **T**o box, and choose the **C**hange button to substitute the correction for this one instance
Change A**l**l	Select one of the Suggestio**n**s or enter a correction in the Change **T**o box, and choose the Change A**l**l button to change all occurrences of this misspelling in this document
Add	Add the word to the dictionary so the checker will not question it in any document

Tip

In Word and Excel, you can choose the **U**ndo Last button if you change your mind about the last change you made.

5. When you choose an option, the spell checker continues to check your spelling.

6. You can choose the Close button at any time to stop checking the spelling. Alternatively, if you let the spell checker finish the spell check, it displays a message dialog box saying it is finished. Choose OK.

Tip

Unless you only want to check a specific word or section of the document, move the insertion point to the beginning of the document, worksheet, or presentation before starting the spelling checker, for the most efficient use of the tool. To move to the beginning, press Ctrl+Home.

Starting Office

You start Office like any other Windows program. If Office is in your Windows StartUp group, it automatically starts when you start Windows. If you have closed Office, or if the program did not start up with Windows, you can open it from the Program Manager.

To start Office

1. Locate the Microsoft Office program icon. It may be in the StartUp program group, the Microsoft Office group, or another group in the Program Manager.
2. Select the Office program icon.
3. Choose the **F**ile **O**pen command; alternatively, press Enter. The program opens. You see a start-up screen and the Microsoft Office Manager, or toolbar, appears on-screen.

Shortcut

Double-click the program icon to start Office.

Switching Between Applications

One of the best features of Microsoft Office is that it enables you to quickly open and switch between the Office applications. Normally in Windows programs, you must switch to the Task List and then select the program; in Microsoft Office, however, you can switch between applications with just one click of the mouse button.

To switch between applications

1. Start Office if it is not already running. The Office Manager, or toolbar, appears on-screen.

2. Click the button for the program you want to switch to. If the program is not already open, Office opens it for you; if the program is open, Office switches you to the program.

> **Tip**
>
> You can add other program buttons to the Office toolbar, whether they are Microsoft programs or not. You can also add Windows applications such as the Control Panel, File Manager, and Notepad.

See also **Customizing Microsoft Office.**

WordArt

WordArt is an applet that comes with Microsoft Office that enables you to create attention-grabbing text effects. WordArt helps you create text that you can use for logos, display type, headlines, and other text elements. You can insert WordArt into a document, worksheet, or presentation using OLE.

To insert a WordArt object

1. Position the insertion point.

2. Choose the **I**nsert **O**bject command. The Object dialog box appears.

3. Choose the Create New tab or option.

4. In **O**bject Type list box, choose Microsoft WordArt 2.0 and choose OK. A scroll box appears in which you enter your text. Above the scroll box is the text in a frame as it appears when you close the WordArt applet. Additionally, the WordArt menu and toolbar appear.

5. Enter the text in the scroll box and choose the **U**pdate Display. The text appears in the text box.

To format the text

Note

Be careful not to click outside of the scroll box or the text box; if you do, the WordArt applet closes and returns to Word. Double-click the WordArt text box to start WordArt again.

1. Change font attributes, using the WordArt toolbar buttons:

   - To mold the text into a shape, click the down arrow to the right of the shape box (the first box on the left in the toolbar). A drop-down box displays a variety of shapes; select one to use for the text.

   - To change the font, click the down arrow to the right of the font box on the WordArt toolbar.

   - Change the size of the font by clicking the down arrow to the right of the size box on the toolbar.

   - Click the Bold, Italic, or Case button to change the text attributes of the WordArt text.

   - Click the Stretch to fit button to fill the text box with the text.

   - Click the alignment button to display a drop-down list of alignments from which to choose.

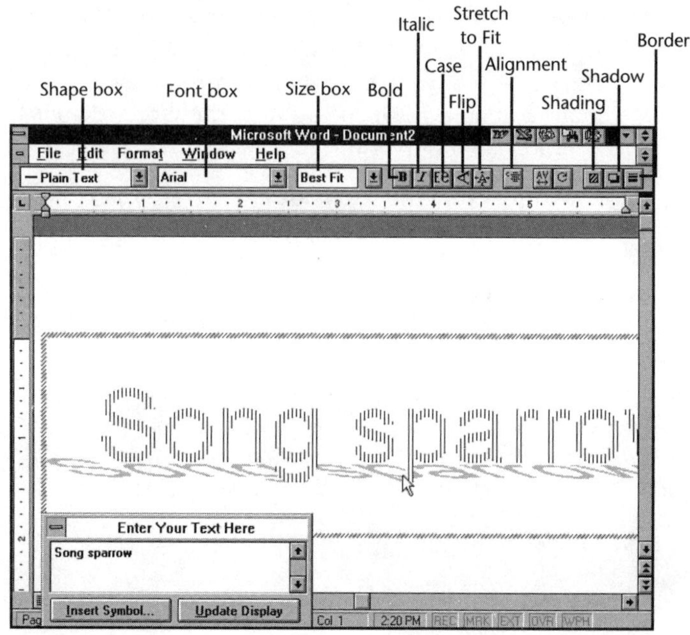

2. To add shading, shadows, and borders:

   - Click the Shading button to display the Shading dialog box. Choose any **S**tyle to apply to the text and choose OK. You can also choose colors other than black and white for the text shading in the Color area of the dialog box.

   - Click the Shadow button to display various shadows you can apply to the text. Choose a shadow or choose the More box to display the Shadow dialog box, where you can select a color for the shadow. Choose OK to accept.

   - Click the Border button to display the Border dialog box. In the Thickness area, choose a line thickness for the outline of the text. You can also choose a Color for the border. Choose OK to close the dialog box.

3. When finished designing the WordArt, click outside of the scroll box and text box. The object is inserted into the application.

> **Tip**
>
> To resize the text box, you must exit the WordArt program and use the sizing handles.

To edit the WordArt

Double-click the WordArt and the program opens.

See **Object Linking and Embedding (OLE)**.

Index

Symbols

*** (asterisk) wildcard, 295**
... (ellipsis) in commands, 306
= (equal sign), 173

A

addresses on envelopes (Word), 66
alignment
- Excel, 132-134
  - centering, 139-140
  - chart axes, 147
- PowerPoint
  - objects, 223-225
  - rulers, 224
  - text, 225-226
- *see also* formatting
- Word
  - page numbers, 80
  - tabs, 98
  - text 46

anchoring text (PowerPoint), 226-227
annotations
- PowerPoint slide shows, 227-228
- Word, 9-11

applications
- exiting, 293-294
- moving objects between, 186
- starting, 313-314
- switching between, 361-362

applying
- borders (Excel), 137-138
- styles
  - Excel, 213
  - Word, 108
- templates (PowerPoint), 284
- transitions (PowerPoint slides), 232

arcs (drawing), 334
arranging windows, 320
assigning passwords (Word), 86-87
assigning styles (Excel), 172
asterisk (*) wildcard, 295
attaching files to mail (Mail), 348-349
Auditing toolbar (Excel), 137
auditing worksheets (Excel), 134-137
AutoContent Wizard (PowerPoint), 228-229, 262
AutoCorrect (Word), 12-13
AutoFilter (Excel), 158-159
AutoFit (Excel columns), 152
AutoFormat (Word), 13-16
automatic linking (OLE), 356
AutoShapes (PowerPoint), 248
AutoSum button (Standard toolbar), 215
AutoText (Word), 16-17
axes (Excel charts), 147-150

B

BMP files (Word), 58
bold text
- Excel, 171
- PowerPoint, 254
- Word, 45

bookmarks (Word), 17-18
borders
- Excel, 137-138
- PowerPoint, 230-231
- Word, 18-19

Borders toolbar (Word), 19
breaking links
- DDE, 344
- OLE, 357

building slides (PowerPoint), 231
Bullet On/Off button (Formatting toolbar), 233
bullets
- PowerPoint, 232-233
- Word, 19-20

buttons (Standard toolbar), 314

C

calculating worksheets (Excel), 138-139
capitalization (Word)
- case, 21-22
- drop caps, 32-33

captions
- PowerPoint objects, 264
- Word, 20-21

cells (Excel)
- color, 151
- data entry, 164-165
- deleting, 162
- deleting contents, 163
- editing contents, 182
- inserting, 183
- locking, 203
- naming, 188
- text, 133

Center Alignment button (Formatting toolbar), 226
centering
- Excel, 139-140
- Word, 47

CGM files (Word), 58
Change Case (Word), 21-22
changing
- chart type (Excel), 144
- fonts
  - Excel, 169-172
  - Word, 42-43
- margins (Excel), 184
- passwords (Word), 88
- styles (Word), 108-109

character formatting (Word), 44-45
Chart toolbar (Excel), 142, 144
charts
- Excel
  - alignment, 147
  - axes, 147-150
  - color, 147, 151
  - creating, 140-142
  - editing data, 143-144
  - editing elements, 144-146
  - fonts, 147
  - formatting numbers, 148
  - frames, 146
  - locking, 203
  - scale, 148
- MS Graph, 336-337
- PowerPoint, 234-236

ChartWizard button (Standard toolbar, Excel), 150
Clip Art Gallery
- integrated, 323-325
- PowerPoint, 236-238

Clipboard, 22-23, 156, 325-326
closing
- annotations (Word), 10
- files, 287
- Office Manager, 327
- windows, 319

clusters (Excel charts), 144
collapsing outlines (Word), 83
color
- Excel, 150-151
  - cells, 151
  - charts, 147, 151
  - fonts, 150
- PowerPoint, 238-242

color scheme (PowerPoint), 241-242
columns
- Excel
  - deleting, 163
  - deleting contents, 163
  - hiding, 181

inserting, 182
printing headings, 201
viewing, 181
width, 152-153
Word, 23-24
tables, 119-120

combining documents (Word), 64-65

commands
... (ellipsis), 306
common
Edit Undo, 318
File Close, 287
File Exit, 293
File Find File, 294
File Open, 308
File Print, 309
File Save As, 311
Insert Object, 307
View Toolbars, 314
Window Arrange All, 320
Excel
Data Consolidate, 153
Data Filter, 158
Data Group and Outline, 191
Data Pivot Table, 197
Data Subtotals, 214
Edit Delete, 162
Edit Find, 167
File Print Report, 206
Format Cells, 132
Format Chart Type, 144
Format Column, 152
Format Selected Axis, 148
Insert Cells, 183
Insert Chart, 140
Insert Function, 177
Insert Name, 188
Insert Notes, 189
Insert Page Break, 192
Insert Remove Page Break, 192
Insert Worksheet, 183
Tools Auditing, 134
Tools Record Macro, 345
Window Freeze Panes, 175
Window Split, 212
Mail, 347
MS Graph, 337
PowerPoint
Draw Align, 225
Draw Snap to Grid, 256
File Print, 271
File Update Presentation, 235
Format Alignment, 226
Format Bullet, 233
Format Line Spacing, 259
Format Text Anchor, 226
Insert Clip Art, 237
Insert New Slide, 222, 259
Insert Object, 234
Tools Build, 231
Tools Transition, 232
View Ruler, 224
View Slide Show, 227
Word
Edit AutoText, 16
Edit Bookmark, 17
Edit Clear, 29
Edit Copy, 25
Edit Cut, 27
Edit Find, 37
Edit Go To, 55
Edit Paste, 89
Edit Replace, 40
File Print, 11, 90
File Summary Info, 30
Format AutoFormat, 14
Format Borders and Shading, 18
Format Bullets and Numbering, 20, 78
Format Change Case, 22
Format Columns, 23
Format Drop Cap, 32
Format Font, 42
Format Frame, 53
Format Style, 108
Format Tabs, 120
Insert Annotation, 9
Insert Break, 84, 99
Insert Caption, 21
Insert Cross-reference, 26
Insert Date and Time, 28
Insert File, 65
Insert Footnote, 33, 43-44
Insert Frame, 51
Insert Index and Tables, 62
Insert Page Numbers, 80
Insert Picture, 58
Insert Symbol, 104-105
Repeat, 93-94

Table Delete Rows/Columns, 119
Table Insert Table, 118
Table Sort Text, 103
Tools AutoCorrect, 12
Tools Envelopes and Labels, 35
Tools Grammar, 56
Tools Hyphenation, 61
Tools Macro, 345
Tools Mail Merge, 68
Tools Protect Document, 87
Tools Revisions, 24, 95
Tools Spelling, 106
Tools Thesaurus, 124
Tools Word Count, 128
View Annotations, 10
View Header and Footer, 59
View Outline, 82
View Ruler, 97
View Zoom, 128-129

comments (Word), 9-11
Compare Versions (Word), 24-25
compiling (Word)
indexes, 63-64
Table of Authorities, 112-113
Table of Contents, 115-116
Table of Figures, 117-118
Complete/Custom installation, 342
Computer Graphics Metafile (CGM) files (Word), 58
consolidation (Excel), 153-154
constraining objects (PowerPoint), 267
converting Excel elements
decimals, 174
files, 155
fractions, 174
copying
Excel, 155-156
PowerPoint
objects, 266
text, 242-243
to Clipboard, 156, 326
Word, 25-26
drag-and-drop technique, 32
styles, 110
correcting errors (Word), 12-13
counting words (Word), 128
creating
AutoCorrect entries (Word), 12
AutoText entries (Word), 16
bookmarks (Word), 17
charts
Excel, 140-142
PowerPoint, 234-235
columns (Word), 23-24
cross-references (Word), 26-27
drawings, 331-332
drop caps (Word), 32-33
endnotes (Word), 33-34
envelopes (Word), 35-36, 71
equations (Equation Editor), 335
footers
Excel, 179
Word, 60-61
footnotes (Word), 43-44
graphs (MS Graph), 336
handouts (PowerPoint), 257
headers
Excel, 179
Word, 59-60
labels (Word), 66-67, 72
mail groups (Mail), 350-351
mailing lists (Word), 68-70
notes pages (PowerPoint), 282-283
outlines
Excel, 191
PowerPoint, 269-270
pivot tables (Excel), 197-198
reports (Excel), 207
styles
Excel, 213
Word, 109-110
tables (Word), 118-120
templates
Excel, 215-216
Word, 122-123
text boxes (Excel), 216
cross-references (Word), 26-27
Cue Cards, 288-290
customizing
Clip Art Gallery, 324-325
Office, 327-330
toolbars, 316-317
views, 329-330

cutting
- to Clipboard, 326
- Word, 27

D

Data Consolidate command (Excel), 153
data entry (Excel), 164-165
Data Filter command (Excel), 158
Data Group and Outline command (Excel), 191
data labels (MS Graph charts), 338
Data Pivot Table command (Excel), 197
Data Subtotals command (Excel), 214
databases (Excel), 156-160
datasheets (MS Graph), 337
date and time (Word), 28
date math (Excel), 160-161
DDE (Dynamic Data Exchange), 343-344
decimal places (Excel), 161-162
deleting
- annotations (Word), 11
- borders
  - Excel, 138
  - PowerPoint, 230-231
  - Word, 19
- cells, (Excel)
- chart data (Excel), 143
- columns
  - Excel, 163
  - from tables (Word), 119
- database records (Excel), 160
- fills (PowerPoint), 252
- footers, (Excel), 179
- frames (Word), 54
- headers (Excel), 179
- line numbers (Word), 80
- notes (Excel), 190
- objects (PowerPoint), 243-244
- outlines (Excel), 192
- page breaks
  - Excel, 192
  - Word, 85
- passwords (Word), 88
- patterns (PowerPoint), 252
- rows, 163
  - Excel, 163
  - from tables (Word), 119
- shading (Word), 19
- slides (PowerPoint), 244
- subtotals (Excel), 214
- text
  - PowerPoint, 244-245
  - Word, 29
- text boxes (PowerPoint), 223

dialog boxes, 290-293
displaying
- datasheets (MS Graph), 337
- margin measurements (Word), 76
- rulers
  - PowerPoint, 273
  - Word, 97
- toolbars, 314

document navigation (Word), 76-77
drag-and-drop technique
- integrated, 330-331
- Word, 31-32

Draw Align command (PowerPoint), 225
Draw Snap to Grid command (PowerPoint), 256
drawing
- integrated, 331-334
- PowerPoint, 245-249

Drawing toolbar (PowerPoint), 245-246
- Line Color tool button, 231
- Line Style tool button, 231
- Text Tool, 223

drawing tools, 248, 332-333
Drawing+ toolbar (PowerPoint), 246
DrawPerfect (WPG) files (Word), 58
drop caps (Word), 32-33
DRW files (Word), 58
Dynamic Data Exchange (DDE), 343-344
dynamic linking, 343-344

E

Edit AutoText command (Word), 16
Edit Bookmark command (Word), 17
Edit Clear command (Word), 29
Edit Copy command (Word), 25
Edit Cut command (Word), 27
Edit Delete command (Excel), 162
Edit Find command (Excel), 167
Edit Find command (Word), 37
Edit Go To command (Word), 55
Edit Paste command (Word), 89
Edit Replace command (Word), 40
Edit Undo command, 318
editing
  annotations (Word), 10
  cells (Excel), 182
  chart data (Excel), 143-144
  chart elements (Excel), 144-146
  charts (PowerPoint), 235-236
  embedded objects (OLE), 358
  equations (Equation Editor), 336
  linked data (OLE), 356
  objects, 308
  pivot tables (Excel), 198
  slides (PowerPoint), 249-250
  styles (Excel), 213
  WordArt, 365
  worksheets (Excel), 164
  see also modifying
ellipsis (...) in commands, 306
e-mail, 346-354
embedding objects (OLE), 355, 358
Encapsulated PostScript (EPS) files (Word), 57
endnotes (Word), 33-34
enlarging windows, 318
entering Excel data
  formulas, 165, 173-174
  fractions, 174
  functions, 176-177
envelopes (Word), 35-36, 71
EPS files (Word), 57
equal sign (=), 173
Equation Editor, 335-336
error correction (Word), 12-13
error values (Excel), 135-136
Examples and Demos, 288-290
exiting applications, 293-294
expanding outlines (Word), 83
exporting, *see* importing/exporting

F

File Close command, 287
File Exit command, 293
file filters, 340-341
File Find File command, 294
File Open command, 308
File Print command, 309
  PowerPoint, 271
  Word, 11, 90
File Print Report command (Excel), 206
File Save As command, 311
File Summary Info command (Word), 30
File Update Presentation command (PowerPoint), 235
files
  attaching to mail (Mail), 348-349
  closing, 287
  converting, 155
  exporting, 339-340
  formats, 339
  importing, 340
  inserting (Word), 64-65
  listing (Word), 65
  opening, 308-309
  protecting (Excel), 203-206
  saving, 310-312
  selecting, 298
  see also Find File
fill color (PowerPoint), 240-241
filling ranges (Excel), 165-166
fills (PowerPoint), 250-252
filtering lists (Excel), 158-159
filters, 340-341
Find and Replace
  Excel, 166-169
  Word, 36-41
Find File, 294-299
finding
  clip art files, 325
  error values (Excel), 135-136

formatting (Word), 39-40
text (Word), 37-38
fonts, 252-253
charts (Excel), 147
color (Excel), 150, 169-170
PowerPoint, 253-255
Word, 41-43
footers
Excel, 178-180
Word, 59-61
footnotes (Word), 43-44
form letters (Word), 70-71
Format Alignment command (PowerPoint), 226
Format AutoFormat command (Word), 14
Format Borders and Shading command (Word), 18
Format Bullet command (PowerPoint), 233
Format Bullets and Numbering command (Word), 20, 78
Format Cells command (Excel), 132
Format Change Case command (Word), 22
Format Chart Type command (Excel), 144
Format Column command (Excel), 152
Format Columns command (Word), 23
Format Drop Cap command (Word), 32
Format Font command (Word), 42
Format Frame command (Word), 53
Format Line Spacing command (PowerPoint), 259
Format Painter (PowerPoint), 255-256
Format Painter button (Standard toolbar), 255
Format Selected Axis command (Excel), 148
Format Style command (Word), 108
Format Tabs command (Word), 120
Format Text Anchor command (PowerPoint), 226
formatting
Excel, 172-173
frames, 146
numbers in charts, 148
percentages, 196
pivot tables, 199
PowerPoint bulleted text, 233-234
Word
alignment, 46
AutoFormat, 13-16
finding, 39-40
frames, 52-55
page numbers, 81
paragraphs, 46-51
sections, 100-102
text, 14-15, 44,-45
WordArt text, 363
Formatting toolbar, 316
Excel, 134
Bold button, 172
Borders button, 138
Color button, 151
Decrease Decimal button, 162
Increase Decimal button, 162
Italic button, 172
numbering styles, 172
Percent Style button, 196
Underline button, 172
PowerPoint
Bullet On/Off button, 233
Center Alignment button, 226
Left Alignment button, 226
Word, 43
Bold button, 45
Bullet icon, 20
Italic button, 45
Numbering button, 78
Style box, 82
Underline, 45
Formula Bar (Excel), 176, 218
formulas (Excel), 165, 173-174
fractions (Excel), 174-175
frames
Excel charts, 146
Word, 51-54
freezing panes (Excel), 175
Function Wizard (Excel), 174
functions (Excel), 176-177

G

Glossary (Word), *see* AutoText
Go To (Word), 55
grammar checker (Word), 56-57
graphics (Word), 57-58
graphics filters, 340-341
graphs (MS Graph), 336-338
  see also charts
gridlines (charts)
  Excel, 177-178
  MS Graph, 337
grids (PowerPoint), 256-257
grouping
  objects (PowerPoint), 265
  worksheets (Excel), 164
guidelines (PowerPoint), 224, 256-257
gutters (margins), 75

H

handouts (PowerPoint), 257-258
hanging indents (Word), 49
Header and Footer toolbar (Word), 59
headers
  Excel, 178-180
  Word, 59-61
headings for columns/rows (Excel), 201
Help, 299-303
  Cue Cards, 288
  Examples and Demos, 289
HGL files (Word), 58
hiding
  Excel
    columns, 181
    gridlines, 177-178
    rows, 181
    sheets, 180
  guides (PowerPoint), 224
  rulers
    PowerPoint, 224, 273
    Word, 97
  ToolTips, 317
horizontal alignment (Excel), 132-133
hue (color), 239
hyphenation (Word), 61-62

I-J

importing/exporting, 339-340
indents
  PowerPoint rulers, 274
  Word, 48-49, 98
indexes (Word), 62
Insert Annotation command (Word), 9
Insert Break command (Word), 84, 99
Insert Caption command (Word), 21
Insert Cells command (Excel), 183
Insert Chart command (Excel), 140
Insert Clip Art command (PowerPoint), 237
Insert Cross-reference command (Word), 26
Insert Date and Time command (Word), 28
Insert File command (Word), 65
Insert Footnote command (Word), 33, 43-44
Insert Frame command (Word), 51
Insert Function command (Excel), 177
Insert Index and Tables command (Word), 62
Insert mode (Word), 8
Insert Name command (Excel), 188
Insert New Slide command (PowerPoint), 222, 259
Insert Notes command (Excel), 189
Insert Object command, 234, 307, 324
Insert Page Break command (Excel), 192
Insert Page Numbers command (Word), 80
Insert Picture command (Word), 58
Insert Remove Page Break command (Excel), 192
Insert Symbol command (Word), 104-105

Insert Worksheet command (Excel), 183
inserting
annotations (Word), 9-10
AutoText entries (Word), 17
borders
PowerPoint, 230
Word, 18-19
bullets (Word), 20
captions (Word), 21
cell names (Excel), 188
cells (Excel), 183
chart data (Excel), 143
chart elements (MS Graph), 338
charts in slides (PP), 235
columns (Excel), 182
columns in tables (Word), 119
database records (Excel), 157
date/time (Word), 28
files (Word), 64-65
frames (Word), 51
graphics (Word), 58
mail merge records (Word), 69
notes (Excel), 189
numbers in lists (Word), 77-78
objects, 307, 362
page breaks
Excel, 192
Word, 84-85
page numbers (Word), 80-81
pictures, 340-341
range names (Excel), 188
ranges (Excel), 183
rows (Excel), 182
rows in tables (Word), 119-121
section breaks (Word), 99-100
shading (Word), 19
slides (PowerPoint), 222, 259
special characters (Word), 105
symbols (Word), 104-105
text
PowerPoint, 222-223
Word, 8-9
text boxes (PowerPoint), 223
worksheets (Excel), 183
installation, 341-343
italic text
Excel, 171
PowerPoint, 254
Word, 45

K

keyboard
navigating documents
PowerPoint, 260-261
Word, 77
navigating Excel worksheets, 185
text selection
Excel , 210
Word, 103
keyboard shortcuts, 303-304

L

labels (Word), 65-67, 72
landscape orientation (Excel), 193
Laptop installation, 342
layouts (PowerPoint), 258-259
Left Alignment button (Formatting toolbar), 226
legends (MS Graph charts), 337
line color (PowerPoint), 240-241
Line Color tool button (Drawing toolbar), 231
line spacing
PowerPoint, 259-260
Word, 49-51
Line Style tool button (Drawing toolbar), 231
lines
drawing, 334
moving (PowerPoint), 248
numbering (Word), 78-80
linking
dynamically, 343-344
OLE, 355
Word, 67
listing
file types, 309
files (Word), 65
lists
filtering (Excel), 158-159
numbered lists (Word), 77-78
sorting (Word), 103
locking cells (Excel), 203
Lotus 1-2-3 Graphics (PiC) files (Word), 58
lowercase text (Word), 21-22
luminance (color), 239

M

macros, 68, 344
recording, 345
running, 346
magnifying views (Word), 128-129
Mail Compose Note command (Mail), 347
Mail Merge (Word), 68-74
mail, *see* MS Mail
mailing labels (Word), 65-72
manual linking (OLE), 356
margins
Excel, 184
Word, 74
editing, 98
ruler, 75-76
markers (Excel charts), 144
marking Word items
index entries, 62
Table of Authorities citations, 111-112
Table of Contents entries, 114-115
masters (PowerPoint slides), 279-280
measurements (Word margins), 76
menus, 304-306
Office, 328-329
shortcut, 312-313
merges (Word), 68-74
Micrografx Designer 3.0 (DRW) files (Word), 58
mirrored margins (Word), 75
modes (Word), 8
modifying
chart data (Excel), 144
margins (Word), 98
see also editing
mouse
navigating documents
PowerPoint, 260
Word, 76
navigating worksheets (Excel), 185
selecting Excel items, 209-210
text selection (Word), 102
moving
clip art (PowerPoint), 237
drag-and-drop (Word), 31
frames (Word), 52
lines (PowerPoint), 248
objects (PowerPoint), 257, 266
outline text (Word), 84
sheets (Excel), 187
slides (PowerPoint), 281
text (Word), 76
windows, 319
worksheet elements (Excel), 186-188
MS Graph, 336-338
MS Mail, 346-354

N

naming cells/ranges (Excel), 188
navigating
dialog boxes, 293
documents
PowerPoint, 260-261
Word, 76-77
worksheets (Excel), 185-186
Note Indicator (Excel), 218
notes
Excel, 189-190
Word, 9
notes pages (PowerPoint), 282
numbered lists (Word), 77-78
numbering (Word)
lines, 78-80
pages, 80-81
numbers (Excel)
charts, 148
rounding, 162, 208
styles, 172

O

Object Linking and Embedding (OLE), 355-358
objects, 306-308
aligning (PowerPoint), 223-225
editing, 308
linking (OLE), 355
PowerPoint, 264-268
WordArt, 362
Office
customizing, 327-330
installation, 341-343
starting, 361

Office Manager, 313, 327, 354-355
Office menu, 328-329
Office toolbar, 327-328
OLE (Object Linking and Embedding), 306, 355-358
opening
- Clip Art Gallery
  - integrated, 324
  - PowerPoint, 237
- files, 308-309
- Find File, 294
- mailing lists (Word), 68
- password-protected documents (Word), 88
- Wizards (Word), 127-128

orientation (printing)
- Excel, 193
- Word, 91

Outline toolbar
- PowerPoint, 269
- Word, 82-83

outlines
- Excel, 191-192
- PowerPoint, 268-270
- Word, 82-84

Overtype mode (Word), 8

P-Q

page breaks
- Excel, 192
- Word, 84-86

page numbering (Word), 80-81
page setup
- Excel, 192-195
- Word, 91

panes (windows), 175
paper size (printing) (Word), 91
paper source (printing) (Word), 92
paragraph formatting (Word), 46-51
passwords (Word), 86-88
pasting
- PowerPoint, 244
- Word, 89

patterns (PowerPoint), 250-252
PC Paintbrush (PCX) files (Word), 58
percentages (Excel), 195-196
PIC files (Word), 58
Pick A Look Wizard (PowerPoint), 262-263
pictures, inserting, 340-341
pivot tables (Excel), 196-199
portrait orientation (Excel), 193
presentations (PowerPoint), 261-264
previewing printing
- Excel, 199-200
- Word, 92-93

print area (Excel), 200
Print Preview
- Excel, 199-200
- Word, 92-93

Print Preview button (Standard toolbar), 202
Print Preview toolbar (Word), 93
printing, 309-310
- Excel, 199-202
  - gridlines, 178
  - previewing, 199-200
  - reports, 207
- PowerPoint, 271-272
  - handouts, 258
  - notes pages, 283
- Word, 89-93
  - annotations, 11

protecting Excel files, 203-206

R

ranges (Excel)
- filling, 165-166
- inserting, 183
- naming, 188

reading
- mail (Mail), 351-352
- notes (Excel), 189

receiving mail (Mail), 351-353
recording macros
- Excel, 345
- Word, 345

records (Excel databases)
- deleting, 160
- inserting, 157

reducing windows, 318
reference marks (Word annotations), 10
rehearsing presentations (PowerPoint), 272-273

removing revision marks (Word), 25
 see deleting
Repeat command (Word), 93-94
replacing
 Excel, 166-169
 PowerPoint, 237
 Word, 40-41
replying to mail (Mail), 353-354
reports (Excel), 206-207
resetting columns (Excel), 153
resizing PowerPoint elements, 237, 266
revision marks (Word), 25, 94-97
rotating objects (PowerPoint), 268
rounding numbers (Excel), 162, 208
routing slips (Mail), 349
rows
 Excel
  deleting, 163
  deleting contents, 163
  height, 208-209
  hiding, 181
  inserting, 182
  printing headings, 201
  viewing, 181
 Word tables, 119-121
rulers
 PowerPoint, 224, 273-274
 Word, 75-76, 97-99
running macros, 346
running slide shows (PowerPoint), 274-275

S

saturation (color), 239
saving files, 310-312
scale (Excel charts), 148-220
searching
 databases (Excel), 159
 for files, 294
section breaks (Word), 99
section layout (Word), 100-102
selecting
 files (Find File), 298
 frames (Word), 52
 objects
  Excel, 209-210
  PowerPoint, 265
 text (Word), 102-103
selection handles
 frames (Word), 52
 lines (PowerPoint), 248
sending mail (MS Mail), 347-351
setting
 decimal places (Excel), 161
 indents (Word), 98
 tabs (Word), 97, 120-122
setting up
 databases (Excel), 157
 slides (PowerPoint), 275-276
shaded fills (PowerPoint), 251
shading
 PowerPoint, 276-279
 Word, 18-19
shadows, 277
shapes (drawing), 333
sheets (Excel)
 hiding, 180
 moving, 187
 viewing, 180
shortcut menus, 312-313
Show Auditing toolbar (Excel), 137
sizing
 fonts (PowerPoint), 253
 frames (Word), 52
 windows, 318
skipping
 bullets (Word), 20
 numbers in lists (Word), 78
slide shows (PowerPoint)
 annotations, 227-228
 running, 274-275
Slide Sorter (PowerPoint, 280-281
Slide Sorter toolbar (PowerPoint), 232
slides (PowerPoint)
 building, 231
 chart insertion, 235
 deleting, 244
 editing, 249-250
 inserting, 222
 inserting in layout, 259
 masters, 279-280
 setup, 275-276
 timing, 284
 transitions, 232

Sort Ascending button (Standard toolbar), 211
Sort Descending button (Standard toolbar), 211
sorting
Excel, 211
lists (Word), 103
slides (PowerPoint), 280-281
text (Word), 103-104
spacing
line spacing
PowerPoint, 259-260
Word, 49-51
paragraph spacing (Word), 50-51
speaker's notes (PowerPoint), 282
special characters (Word), 104-105
spell checker
integrated, 359-361
Word, 105-107
splitting windows (Excel), 212
stacking objects (PowerPoint), 267
Standard toolbar, 314
Excel
AutoSum button, 215
ChartWizard button, 150
Function Wizard, 174
Print Preview button, 202
Sort Ascending button, 211
Sort Descending button, 211
Text Box button, 216
PowerPoint
Format Painter button, 255
Insert Clip Art button, 238
Word
Columns button, 24
Paste button, 89
Redo button, 94
starting
applications, 313-314
Office, 361
Status bar (Excel), 218
styles
Excel, 212-213
assigning, 172
numbers, 172
PowerPoint, 254-255
Word, 108-111
subtotals (Excel), 213-214
Summary Info (Word), 29-31
summing (Excel), 215
switching between
applications, 314, 361-362
windows, 320
symbols (Word), 104-105

T

Table Delete Rows/Columns command (Word), 119
Table Insert Table command (Word), 118
Table of Authorities (Word), 111-113
Table of Contents (Word), 113-116
Table of Figures (Word), 116-118
Table Sort Text command (Word), 103
tables
pivot tables (Excel), 196-199
Word, 118-120
tabs
PowerPoint rulers, 274
Word, 120-121
indents, 48-49, 98
setting, 97
Tagged Image Format (TIF) files (Word), 57
templates
Excel, 215-216
PowerPoint, 262-263, 283
Word, 110, 121-123
text
Excel
cells, 133
styles, 172
dragging and dropping, 330-331
PowerPoint
alignment, 225-226
anchoring, 226-227
bold, 254
bulleted, 233-234
color, 238-239
copying, 242-243
deleting, 244-245
inserting, 222-223
italic, 254

pasting, 242-286
shadows, 278
underlined, 254
Word
alignment, 46
bold, 45
copying, 25
deleting, 29
finding, 37-38
formatting, 14-15
inserting, 8-9
italic, 45
moving in outlines, 84
numbering lines, 79
pasting, 89
replacing, 40-41
sorting, 103-104
selecting, 102-103
underlined, 45
WordArt, 363
Text Box button (Standard toolbar), 216
text boxes
Excel, 216-217
PowerPoint, 223
Text Tool (Drawing toolbar), 223
thesaurus (Word), 123-125
TIF files (Word), 57
timing (PowerPoint slides), 284
titles
charts (MS Graph), 338
organization charts (PowerPoint), 234
toolbars, 314-317
Excel
Auditing, 137
Calculate Now button, 139
Chart, 144
Chart toolbar, 142
Formatting toolbar, 134, 138
Show Auditing toolbar, 137
Office, 327-328
PowerPoint
Drawing, 223, 245-246
Drawing+, 246
Formatting, 226
Outline toolbar, 269
Slide Sorter, 232
Word
Borders, 19
Formatting, 20, 43, 45
Header and Footer, 59
Mail Merge, 70
Outline, 82
Outlining, 83
Print Preview, 93
Standard, 24
tools (drawing tools), 332
Tools Auditing command (Excel), 134
Tools AutoCorrect command (Word), 12
Tools Build command (PowerPoint), 231
Tools Envelopes and Labels command (Word), 35
Tools Grammar command (Word), 56
Tools Hyphenation command (Word), 61
Tools Macro command (Word), 345
Tools Mail Merge command (Word), 68
Tools Protect Document command (Word), 87
Tools Record Macro command (Excel), 345
Tools Revisions command (Word), 24, 95
Tools Spelling command (Word), 106
Tools Thesaurus command (Word), 124
Tools Transition command (PowerPoint), 232
Tools Word Count command, 128
ToolTips, 317
tracer arrows (Excel), 136-137
tracing dependents (Excel), 134-135
Transition Effects drop-down list (Slide Sorter toolbar), 232
transitions (PowerPoint slides), 232
turning on/off grids (PowerPoint), 256
Typical installation, 342

U

underlined text
- Excel, 171
- PowerPoint, 254
- Word, 45

undoing, 318
updating
- cross-references (Word), 27
- links (DDE), 344
- Table of Contents (Word), 116

uppercase text (Word), 21-22

vertical alignment (Excel), 133
View Annotations command (Word), 10
View Header and Footer command (Word), 59
View Outline command (Word), 82
View Ruler command
- PowerPoint, 224
- Word, 97

View Slide Show command (PowerPoint), 227
View Toolbars command, 314
View Zoom command (Word), 128-129
viewing
- annotations (Word), 10-11
- attached files (Mail), 352-353
- bookmarks (Word), 18
- Clip Art Gallery, 324
- Clipboard, 326
- columns (Excel), 181
- graphics before placing (Word), 58
- outlines (PowerPoint), 269
- Print Preview documents (Word), 92
- revisions marks (Word), 96-97
- rows (Excel), 181
- sheets (Excel), 180
- Summary Info (Word), 30
- ToolTips, 317
- worksheets (Excel), 218-220

views
- customizing, 329-330
- Find File, 297
- PowerPoint, 285-286
- Word, 125-126

W

Window Arrange All command, 320
Window Freeze Panes command (Excel), 175
Window Split command (Excel), 212
windows, 318-320
- Excel, 175, 212

Windows Bitmaps (BMP) files (Word), 58
Wizards, 320
- PowerPoint
  - AutoContent, 228-229, 262
  - Pick A Look, 262-263
- Word, 126-128

WMF (Windows Metafile) files (Word), 58
Word Count (Word), 128
WordArt, 362-365
worksheets (Excel)
- auditing, 134-137
- calculating, 138-139
- editing groups, 164
- grouping, 164
- inserting, 183
- moving elements, 186-188
- navigating, 185-186
- notes, 189-190
- protecting, 204
- viewing, 218-120

WPG files (Word), 58

X–Y–Z

zooming, 219
- PowerPoint, 286
- Word, 128-129